A Catalyst for Change

How Alignment and Relationships Accelerate Change

By John R. Bost
And Patty Jo Sawvel

Bailey Press

A CATALYST FOR CHANGE
By John R. Bost
Clemmons, North Carolina
mastercounsel@gmail.com
www.JohntheCatalyst.com

Co-Authored by Patty Jo Sawvel
Classic Writing and Public Relations
Kernersville, North Carolina
1.336.906.7238 pjsawvel@gmail.com
www.ClassicWritingPR.com

Published by Bailey Press, a division of
Classic Writing and Public Relations
Kernersville, North Carolina

No part of this book may be used or reproduced in any form, stored in a retrieval system, or transmitted in any form by any means, electronic, photocopy, mechanical, recording or otherwise without written permission from the author. The only exception is for critical articles or reviews, in which brief excerpts may be used.

ISBN: 979-8-6406687-8-0
Copyright © 2020 by John R. Bost
All Rights Reserved First Edition
Printed in the United States

Cover Designer: Nimesh Weeranga
www.fiverr.com/art_infinity

For more information contact the Author:
John R. Bost Email: **mastercounsel@gmail.com**.
www.JohntheCatalyst.com

1. Social Activism.   2. Community Development   3. Biography
   Bost, John R.

Printed in the United States of America

Endorsements

John Bost has lived a life of "what ifs" and "why nots?" What if felled trees from a hurricane in Nicaragua could be sold to benefit the local village? What if ex-offenders could staff an enterprise that protects the environment? What if a 100-year old congregation could create a new vibrant downtown? Through a series of personal stories and practical tools, Bost shows the reader how a "what if" – "why not?" lifestyle makes a world jarring impact.

Dr. Michael Comer, President
The Hayes Group International, Inc.

I enthusiastically recommend A Catalyst for Change, *proof that collaboration is key to bridging gaps of cultural perspectives—both common and uncommon. It's a story of mutual respect, self-determination, historical pride, old lessons relearned, and friendship—all imperative for mutual success.*

Lafayette Jones, CEO
SMSi-Urban Call Marketing, Inc.

John has had a major impact in a number of areas in our community, across all socio-economic sectors. In doing so, he has embodied his strong beliefs as a Christ follower and always demonstrates amazing character and competency.

Allen Joines
Mayor of Winston-Salem, NC

As our world enters a new era, steeped in the unknown, this book provides a remarkably relevant leadership example in how to face the future and lead our diverse and fragmented communities to a new place of equity and opportunity for all. John's stealth leadership is a constant throughout the story.

Sandi Scannelli, CEO
Clemmons Community Foundation

John Bost—a life coach and father figure whose tutelage has been an ongoing journey over multiple decades. Our relationship has seen the gravel road—sometimes walking barefoot—several times over the years. From the beginning to the end, A Catalyst for Change *offers insight and inspiration on how life should be lived with personal growth and joy.*

Brad Hunter
Hunter Realty and Property Management, LLC.

I have had the privilege of knowing John Bost for over twenty years in my professional and community life. John's insight into the five sectors which impact societal and cultural change is priceless. John identifies vision, relational capital, an understanding of history, effective communication, and servant leadership combined with a willingness to take risk and pace change as the building blocks for better communities.

Jay Helvey
Cassia Capital Partners LLC, Managing Partner
New Canaan Society Board Chairman

A Catalyst for Change *provides blueprints for transformation in every arena of life. Scholarly change theory is matched with real life practical examples of the relationship model in action which leads to meaningful and lasting community partnerships! Some may call it serendipity; I call it spiritual led passion and back breaking effort!*

John Holleman Jr.
Former WS/FC School Board
Former Forsyth County Commissioner

John Bost's book provides fascinating proof that change doesn't just happen. It requires rolling up one's sleeves, seeing through others' eyes, having the courage to fail and the stamina to persevere. Today, those of us who are benefiting from his efforts—to leave the world in a better place—are called upon to dream new dreams, cast vision, and serve as catalysts for change.

Audrey Davis
Child Care Consultant
NCDHHS- Division of Child Development & Early Education

For decades, John Bost has been telling us that we are moving from a model of traditional organizing into new and uncharted waters. Now, we are seeing it for ourselves—in multiple sectors—including the church. This book is not just a story of the past, but gives real hope for the future.

Dr. Mike Rakes
WSF Pastor
Founder of 24sixchurch

John Bost's book provides wise counsel to those searching for sensible solutions to complex issues. He understands the connection between education, economic development, and the success of local communities, states, and our nation. I highly recommend it for your consideration.

Dr. Richard L. Thompson
Former Superintendent, Lexington City Schools
Former Superintendent State of Mississippi

I am excited that John Bost has put his story into print. The principles he gives not only made an impact on his community, but inspired me to lead better. Thanks, my friend, for sharing your life lessons with us.

Randall Ross, Sr. Pastor
Retired, Calvary Assembly, Naperville, IL.
Former Pastor, Winston Salem First

A Catalyst for Change is a must read for anyone interested in leadership and change. John's leadership, so thoughtfully expressed in this book, is in its purest and simplest form. A truly purpose built life. I'm so proud to call him friend!

Paula McCoy, Director
Partnership for Prosperity

John Bost is an out of the box thinker; a serial entrepreneur; a lifelong community organizer; and a joyful servant of Jesus Christ. I heartily recommend that you read his story. It will inspire you to become a person of influence and impact.

Walker Armstrong
Executive Director Pilot Mountain Baptist Association

I read Bost's book from cover to cover in one sitting. It's not only packed with practical principles—it raises excellent questions that my generation wants to answer. How can we make the world better for everyone? How can we create our preferred future? This book has something for everyone, but is especially enlightening for people just gaining traction in life.

William Comer, Student
The King's College, New York, NY
Class of 2022

Dedication

To those who will inherit this world,

my grandchildren John Luther and Caroline Jackson,

and yours.

*"Leadership is the **catalytic process**
whereby a person or persons
influence others and impact organizations
to move together
toward accomplishing an aspirational objective."*
—Walker Armstrong
2020

Contents

Sector I—Public Education

1. Early Choices 1
2. Building More Capacity 7
3. A Perfect Match 15
4. Building Momentum 21
5. Making a Change 27
6. Call in the Dogs 31
7. Full Speed Ahead 37
8. Best Year Ever 43
9. Starting Over 47

Sector II—Religion

10. A Deeper Calling Yet 55
11. Different Hats 61
12. Vision 2000 65
13. Be Careful What You Ask For 73
14. Reaching Back to Move Forward 77
15. Others-oriented Put to the Test 81
16. Thank You Carl Conner 85
17. The Children—Our Future 87
18. Time to Make a Change 93

Sector III—Business

19. A Call for Courage 103
20. A Quick History Lesson 107
21. Sharpening My Saw 115
22. Networking 121
23. Defining My Quest 127
24. One Man's Trash 133
25. Two Birds with One Stone 139
26. Making Dirt 145

27. Others-oriented Habits 149
28. Nicaragua 153
29. Deacon Place 165

Sector IV—Politics

30. What? Run for Mayor 175
31. We Need a Compass 179
32. Clemmons Community Day 183
33. Village Point 185
34. Bond Referendum 191
35. Churning Concrete 197

Sector V—Social Activism

36. Jumping on the Truck 203
37. What's Your Story 205
38. What It's Like to Live in Winston-Salem 209
39. Gain Trust 215
40. Build a Machine 221
41. Money Will Find You 227
42. Love Out Loud 233
43. Clemmons Community Foundation 239
44. Salt Box 245

Section VI—A Call to Action

45. Rewriting Our Script 257
46. One Step at a Time 265
47. Possibility Thinking—5 Sectors Strong 271

Epilogue—Landing the Plane 275
About the Author 279
About the Co-Author 281
Appendix 283

Foreword

*"The way you get meaning into your life
is to devote yourself to loving others,
devote yourself to your community around you,
and devote yourself to creating something
that gives you purpose and meaning.*
- Morrie Schwartz

    The genesis of my relationship with John started with the Forsyth County Early Childhood Partnership (Smart Start). We both had the privilege of serving on the board of the partnership as it started and gained traction in the community.

    I've had the opportunity to sit across a table for breakfast as we discussed many issues and the well-being of the community. While those fierce conversations didn't always produce solutions, they did deepen a relationship that works together across many of the sectors that John identifies in this book.

    A fierce conversation, as author, Susan Scott, describes is "One in which we come out from behind ourselves, into the conversation and make it real."

    As I read through this draft, perhaps those conversations reignited what a life in the spirit had already sparked and framed. His objective is to capture and communicate 72 years of learning through deep and, at times, fierce relationships within at least five core community institutions.

    My role perhaps was to encourage accountability and transparency as a black male, professional peer, and Brother in Christ. This book is a journey about a higher calling (purpose), the transitions that evolve over time that align with community and, the value of relationships that facilitate proactive engagement.

Prepare yourself to learn who John is (the foundation of his being); how each transition is influenced by his purpose; his ongoing preparation (lifelong learning and application); and, most importantly, the relationships developed along the way.

Enjoy the journey as each chapter unfolds, and prepare to be challenged to do better, because that is the right thing to do.

Nigel D. Alston
Community Advocate
Columnist
Trainer
Motivational Speaker

Acknowledgements

This book, in part, honors those who have engaged with me for the betterment of humanity. Be they individuals, my family or entities—for profit or non-profit— they stayed with me, dreamed with me, came along side of me, and believed in me. Their admonitions and insights proved to be their gift to me, now bundled within these hindsights, as my gift to you.

You will hear repeatedly a sense of calling and covering —Divine grace— all in the context of support and tolerance by a spouse who has perhaps sacrificed her dreams to my drive? Yes, beside every good man, there is a good woman, in this case, LaDonna Setzer Bost. I owe her in ways that only God knows and for that, I trust there are "treasures laid up in heaven for her."

My daughter, Summer Bost Jackson, experienced a limited childhood due to my many engagements with others outside of our home. Nonetheless, it's obvious by her present leadership and personal development, she was watching. She's now a public school principal and far ahead of where I was at her age.

And, yes, thanks to my mom, Peggy Earnhardt Bost, now deceased and my dad, Ben Ray whose spiritual mantle I have felt all my days.

Lastly, to all the people—named and unnamed in this manuscript—who let me stand on their shoulders and drink water from wells that I did not dig. Together we changed our world.

Introduction

Catalysts don't remove barriers. They lower barriers just enough to create an alternate path. It's that unconventional path that spawns unprecedented and significant change.

Bost's life journey provides evidence that regardless of which sector he is in—education, religion, business, politics, or social activism— the remaining four sectors often unknowingly present barriers to progress. It is up to him—the catalyst—to embrace the limiting sectors, forge new alliances, and accelerate a change that excites everyone.

In sharing his learnings, Bost has two choices. He can produce a book of pithy factoid truths, duplicitous quotes, and sterile stories—so sanitized to protect the people, that the lesson is lost. Or, he can choose transparency—sometimes revealing his flaws and even respectfully those of others—in honor of truth and in order to demonstrate the nature of growth and maturity. Bost chooses the latter.

When you've finished reading this book—if you are content—then Bost has failed. His greatest dream is that you, too, will become a "hungry hound"—always searching for a way to create a better world.

Sector I

Public Education

Beginning his professional life as a high school science teacher, Bost soon discovers that he can impact more lives by moving into a leadership role within the schools. Next, he invites other sectors of the city to help the schools make public education better for all the students (haves & have-nots). Thus, Bost—a young catalyst for multi-sector collaboration—learns some of the upper and lower limits of community change.

Chapter 1

Early Choices

The year is 1970. I'm fresh out of college—almost 22 years old—with my biology degree in hand. My friend, Joe, has arranged for me to interview with his new boss. If I land this job, I'll be making $8500 annually, selling pharmaceuticals out of Greensboro, North Carolina.

The interview goes well. I'm comfortable with people and of course, I love science. The man across the desk schedules a second appointment.

However, just before I open the door to exit, he says, "Mr. Bost."

"Yes, sir?" I reply

"Do you own a suit?"

Instinctively, I look down to confirm that I'm still wearing my new cream-colored double-breasted sport coat with matching slacks. I'd invested over $100 in this best ever owned outfit from the upscale Norman Stockton Clothier! An average suit could be had for around $40.

With puzzlement in my voice, I respond, "Yes, sir."

Sharply, he demands, "Make sure you have it on next time you come in."

I remember walking out the door with a courteous, "For sure!"

In my inner thoughts, "I am never going to work for you, nor anyone who treats people like that."

Instead, I head right back to Davidson County Schools—where I'd done my student teaching—and low and behold a Chemistry teacher has resigned. Not only am I in my field, but I get to follow my much loved first class of ninth graders to the high school. Easy adjustment, so I accept a position teaching the sciences.

This is certainly not a dollar decision—my starting pay is only $4500 per year. Interestingly enough, my part time job hustling freight at a local freight line, actually paid more per hour than the classroom. But, my heart comes alive and my creative energy explodes when I'm in front of students putting on a show with science gadgets. Work should be fun, right?

In fact, every year, I tell my students there are only three requirements to stay in my class. One, show up and don't disrupt others. Two, we *will* win the end-of-year tug-of-war—of course, using the laws of physics! Three, our class *will* sell the most chocolate.

Chocolate provides the money for all our gadgets, science equipment, and lab experiments each year. Once I have my toys, I never have a problem controlling my class or getting students to pay attention. So, here is the secret to winning the chocolate sales.

First, I let students eat chocolate in my classes, but only if they buy it through my homeroom. It's true! In fact, after roll call, I begin to auction off chocolate. Second, I know that most of my homeroom students couldn't sell chocolate if their life depended on it. So, I help them see new possibilities.

"Mary," I ask, "where does your mother work? Doesn't she own a beauty salon?"

"Yes."

"Here, take this box of candy and ask your mom to set it out at work."

Soon, I know all my students and where their parents work. We build relationships. The students and parents are supportive because they know that I care about them. I respect that they have different experiences, abilities, and learning styles—and I make allowance for that.

For example, we all know that some students don't test well. That's okay. Each quarter, I assign a hands-on project. Students can build a model, draw a prototype, create a display board—or propose any idea, as long as it ties to our topic—and if they do a half way decent job articulating it, they can earn an easy "A" to average into their quarterly grade.

This seconds as a way to build relationships—between the students and me, between the students and their helping parents, and between the parents and me. For the few students who have zero parental support, I offer extra assistance.

EARLY CHOICES

Between chocolate sales and quarterly projects, I demand quite a bit of engagement from my families. Indeed, I have to laugh when one mother of five says to me, "Mr. Bost, I was never so happy in my life as when my last child left your classroom. No more chocolate sales and no more science projects."

She says that half in jest because her children loved my class. Even though four of her five went through middle school under my watch—none of her children learned the same things. I am always changing it up, believing that if teachers teach the same lesson plan year after year, they are not teaching children, they are simply teaching material. Students and parents can readily sense that.

Instead, my lessons are quite unconventional. I remember year one when I taught high school chemistry, I explained that elements found near the top and on the sides of the periodic table tend to be less stable.

John Bost, age 22
Chemistry Teacher

To demonstrate, I remove a marble-sized chunk of phosphorus, always submerged in oil and throw it out the window. A few seconds later, we witness spontaneous combustion as the oil drains from around the small piece. As we watch from the inside, I ask one student, who I had noticed his preoccupation that day, to please step outside and with his shoe, smother out the flame. Every time he mashes it with his heel, the flame goes out—no oxygen. But when he lifts his heel up, the flame ignites again—spontaneously feeding on oxygen.

The class and especially this student, never forgets that phosphorus is reactive with oxygen, that the earth—even the dirt—is filled with free oxygen, and that this nonmetallic element "P" requires being submerged in a substance like oil to keep it from reacting.

We do a similar experiment with sodium— a metal—which reacts with water. In this case, we watch fire dance on water. Now typically, this is a pretty safe experiment. But I remember one time, chiseling away the sodium oxide that has formed a crust on the top of the sodium.

Because the oxidized sodium is essentially inert—I toss this useless material down the lead sink. Little do I know, but some of the pure sodium is clinging to the crusted material.

Suddenly, there is a BANG like a gunshot. Apparently, all the material that has built up in the sink trap is propelled by the ignition of hydrogen gas, blasting pieces of spent match sticks and other debris onto the ceiling! I don't do that again and today, I would be lucky to keep my job!

And then, there is the time that Darrell, a big football player, decides to grab ahold of the wires coming out of a hand crank generator. I am demonstrating the difference between voltage and amperage and have actually attached a coil to the generator. He thinks he's man enough to take the jolt.

Well, he takes it, but the force thrusts him up against the concrete wall and knocks the wind out of him. The students talk about that "lesson" for weeks. I am soon instructed by my principal to better mitigate risk as I mature as a young teacher.

My growing passion is to motivate students to be aware of the physical forces around them and to pursue the higher sciences. Of course, this will better enable their vocational and life choices, and for those who so choose, best qualify them for college. Through trial and error, I find that they are most motivated when the lessons apply to real life. So when I "teach" Newton's Laws of Motion—particularly acceleration and deceleration—most students would normally hear, "Blah, blah, blah, blah."

But when I give them boxes of toothpicks and challenge them to individually construct an apparatus that will protect "Humpty Dumpty"—a raw egg—through a 50-foot fall, suddenly they are on a mission. One year, we go really big with this.

On the given day, I take the 30 boxes to the gymnasium rooftop and drop them one by one. Yes, I was careful not to damage the roof—concerns from Maintenance with folk like me!

As each uniquely designed and often bizarre apparatus hits the ground, the students rally to see results.

EARLY CHOICES

"Wow! Your egg survived," a student shouts in amazement.

"Of course it did," the budding physicist says. "I know what I'm doing!"

And then, there is the "ooohhhh" and "yuck" when a less fortunate egg spills its yolk! As the youthful banter escalates, one of my young scientists brags that he built his apparatus so well that it could probably stand a drop of 100 feet. Another student raises the ante to 500 feet.

Instantly, my mind jumps in. I suggest to the class, "Let's put this to the test. Let's take our winners and do an even higher drop."

"How are we going to do that?" a student asks.

"I'll figure something out," I assure them.

I thought it would be easy. I'd just rent a hot-air balloon. But in doing the research, that one event would eat up more than half our chocolate budget.

Then, one day, while watching the evening news, I see the Channel 2 helicopter. I call the station, ask for help, and they agree. So, I go up with the pilot to an elevation of about 500 feet and one by one drop the egg containers!

Each device has a streamer attached, so the students on the ground can see it coming. When the egg container hits, the students run up to see if the egg survived. Amazingly, some eggs actually survived. They are now better understanding geometric structures and stopping distance!

All of this live action is caught on film and aired on the evening news. Our students, of course, feel like heroes. Our science program becomes the talk of the town. And our school—North Davidson Junior High School—is elevated in the eyes of the community.

This serendipitous success gives me a taste of how powerful community—common unity—is for a healthy educational system. This epiphany inspires me to do more to bring the outside community in.

When my students start questioning the relevancy of Bernoulli's law, Boyles law, or Archimedes' principle, as in, "When will I ever use this in my real life?"—I go to the community for the answer. Among others, I bring in Harvey Davis from Davis Garage in Winston-Salem.

A CATALYST FOR CHANGE

Harvey is a second-generation master mechanic. He not only understands the science and physics of automotive technology—his eyes light up when he has an audience.

I remember the first time he comes to my class. He brings a cut-away engine and talks with such awe and authority that—from the looks on the students' faces—you would think that he was showing us some prehistoric dragon's heart.

He disassembles a carburetor and then puts it back together with the flare of a magician—all the while explaining the wonders of science. He is just as passionate when he demonstrates hydraulics and automotive electrical systems.

Suddenly, everyone in class—including the girls—better understands the laws of physics. Additionally, they can see how someone can make a living by applying scientific laws in the real world. I say even the girls, because times were different in the 1970s. Likely, due to cultural conditioning, not too many girls were inclined toward science or engineering.

It was at times like this that students like Rodger—who self-claimed the back row—would be drawn like a magnet to the front row to get a better view. After a while, Rodger made the front row—in science class only—his new home. In fact, forty-some years after graduating high school, Rodger sent me a Facebook message.

He said, "You and Dr. Beimisderfer (an amazing science teacher) were the only two teachers in my entire career of schooling that motivated me to move to the front row."

Rodger—though he declined college—was one of the brightest students that I ever taught. Like Harvey Davis, he became a very successful entrepreneur. Rodger, along with dozens of other students still occupy a front row seat in my life. It is with this long leash of instructional freedom that I revel in the classroom—knowing that I am touching lives and changing futures.

Before I know it, I've married the English teacher across the hall—LaDonna Setzer—we've bought our first house, and 13 years have passed. Then, something happens that changes the trajectory of our lives.

Chapter 2

Building More Capacity

"John," a fellow teacher calls out as I walk past his classroom. "I just got my master's degree."

"Really? I didn't even know you were working on that," I say.

"Yes. And you know what that means? I can be a principal," he says excitedly.

"Congratulations!" I was truly excited for him.

The thought then occurs to me, if he can be a principal, he can be *my* principal. Now I'm not so sure of my excitement. It's all good, but our approach to the classroom and priorities are quite different. He is more interested in athletics; however, I tend to lean heavily toward academics.

That very day, I make it a point to talk to Ed Hill. He works at the community college in adult education. Ed knows my goals, and he understands the ropes of higher education. When he arrives to pick up his wife, Mildred, I ask to have a word with him.

"Ed, I've been thinking about getting my master's degree," I explain. "You know how much I love teaching. And, you know how much I love volunteering in the community and especially at church. So, I'm torn after 15 years in the classroom. I'm thinking that I can have a broader impact, but it will require more education."

I pause for a minute and then add, "And just today, one of my fellow teachers shared that he had recently received his master's, which means that he could be *my* principal."

Ed smiled and said, "That's right, John."

"Well, what sort of programs are out there, Ed? I'm going to be 35 next month. So, if I'm going to do this, I need to do it soon."

"You're not going to believe it, but Appalachian State University—your alma mater," he says slowly with a grin, "is offering a field-based program at Winston-Salem State University. It's going to focus on adult and community education. Plus, it covers community engagement, foundations, and fundraising."

"You've got to be kidding! That's everything I want in one package. And it's only 30 minutes from my house. How do I sign up?"

"You better just show up," Ed advises, "given that the first class begins tonight!"

As I often share with folks, the main move is often simply that, showing up!

So, I show up. It proves to be an easy decision. I run the option through all three brains. First, my *gut*—which early on, and intuitively tells me that this is a good match. Next, I run it through my *heart*—my values station—and it matches my sense of calling, so that I can be of the highest possible service to God and to man. Lastly, I process this cerebrally (*head*)—the most negative of my three brains—to see if I can manage the risk. Again, a green light.

Oh, and I have to check with my fourth brain—LaDonna. She's teaching full-time and caring for our beautiful daughter, Summer, who is in the midst of her terrific twos. Thankfully, LaDonna fully supports my decision to move forward.

One of my first classes—Leadership Theory—affords me benefit in almost every aspect of my life. For instance, one of our required reads, *Situational Leadership,* by Kenneth Blanchard, differentiates *task behavior* and *relationship behavior.*

I'd never really connected appropriately with the two. However, by examining relationships with students and church members, I am affirmed that if I continue to invest in my one-on-one *relationships*— especially in understanding each one's technical skill sets— then I can offer appropriate leadership strategies to match any given *person* and *task*. Just this one idea alone, makes me a better teacher, husband, assistant pastor, board member, and daddy.

Once I understand the science behind situational leadership, this becomes my go to strategy for any decisions involving people.

A subsequent class digs deep into relationships with an emphasis on the fact that you can't fake relationships.

BUILDING MORE CAPACITY

Relationships are built on trust and over time, it's a bit like compound interest. The intention is to "deposit" within the other person more "relational capital" each time you meet. Repeated "investments" in that person creates a strong emotional bond which accrues interest over time, in the form of trust, transparency, and collaboration.

Again—it's all about being others-oriented—doing what is best for the other person. This goes a bit contrary to my blue collar upbringing. Leadership had been more about selling one's own ideas in order to make a buck and "get the job done."

What I'm now hearing doesn't sound as much like rank American capitalism—you know, show me the money. We are exploring the nuances of intention. Two people can do the same thing—one with a motive to enrich himself and the other with the motive to enrich the other person. The recipient can easily sniff out the difference.

It's like theologian Carl W. Buehner, born in 1898, said, "They may forget what you said, but they will never forget how you made them feel."

People can sense when we are putting their interests ahead of our own. Suddenly, I find myself on a new path of discovery— perhaps the fine art of leadership rather than simply the math and science approach used in the 15 years before.

Here are my Cliff Notes on relationship building: make yourself available, be present 100%, actively listen, and if need be, ask clarifying questions, maintain eye contact and notice shifts in body language, always intending to add value to that person.

At first glance, this all seems rudimentary. But when I examine my behavior honestly, it's apparent that I'm often so busy, that I'm not easily available. My new goal—when someone calls—is to quickly extract myself from my current focus, if at all possible, in order to make myself available.

In short order, I find that being available is a powerful way of saying, "I value you." Being available builds trust. Trust is like gold in relationships.

A CATALYST FOR CHANGE

The same principle applies to being 100% present. I always thought I gave people my full attention. After all, people fascinate me because no two are alike. However, during this degree program, I begin to check myself.

What I find is that when someone brings up an idea that triggers a memory or a new thought, my mind takes off like a beagle down a rabbit trail. In other words, I mentally abandon the person—if even for a few seconds. In time, I learn to keep the "dogs" on a tighter leash so that I can stay fully focused—100% present. Even at 71, it's a work in progress—according to my wife.

Later in class, we circle back to a key concept—cultivation. The professor convinces us that it is not enough to *start* relationships—not if we want to significantly impact a community. Like plants in a garden, relationships need regular attention—for weeks, years, and even decades—to become mutually fruitful.

Again, I make a personal adjustment and begin a journey that is even easier today via social media, often calling attention to pertinent and congratulatory posts. I'll even buy breakfast to *cultivate* better relationships, a little more costly than handwritten notes, but when your cursive resembles scribble, well! In fact, breakfast is one of the best investments I make in the lives of others. Trust me; there has been quite an ROI over time.

Another professor changes it up. After a few weeks of traditional classwork pertaining to Community Development, the professor suggests a "learn by doing" practical approach.

He says, "I wish I could find a local fair or festival so that we could truly experience community."

"My town—Lexington— is launching its first annual Barbecue Festival tomorrow. It's only a 25-minute drive from here."

Excitedly, he says, "Okay. Class is canceled tomorrow. We'll all go to the Lexington Barbecue Festival."

The next day—October 27, 1984—before turning us loose at the festival, he reminds us, "Without relationships, there is no community (common unity). Your task is to understand the networks and transactions that make this festival possible and to identify how events like this strengthen a community."

Amazingly, 30,000 people (twice the population) show up to consume about 3,000 pounds of Lexington's world-class pork barbecue. Energy is high as people hug and linger in conversation, children squeal with delight at the sight of live pigs and piglets, and business leaders—who have exchanged their suits for "Pig Out" T-shirts—volunteer and beam with community pride! (See appendix.)

What I witness is an all-inclusive—something for everyone—culturally diverse celebration. People are giving and taking, buying and selling, and yet there is something greater taking place than the sum total of the individual transactions.

In a sense, it's like a hologram. At first glance, it's an interesting 2-dimensional pattern. But, when you change your focus, an amazing 3-D image appears. True community—when it is occurring—is felt at a deep soul level! Lesson learned, and in fact, the beauty of my field based masters program.

However, when I take the time to trace the networks—how this is a true collaborative between the city, the county, and the business owners—all orchestrated by Kay Saintsing, who is hired to create this landmark event—I discover incredible planning, buy-in, participation, engagement, and execution. I'm taking notes!

More than that—everyone has set aside their personal agenda in favor of what is good for the group—causing a collective community identity to emerge right before our eyes! This identity—of serving and being served, of honoring the legacy of local barbecue which can be traced to 1919, and actually putting Lexington on the map as "Barbecue Capital" of the world—gives residents a sense of pride, unity, and ownership.

It's a beautiful thing to witness, when—collectively— the "me" becomes a "we."

Suddenly, my mind begins to wonder, "Why can't it be like this all the time? Not that life has to be a party. But, why can't we put the interest of the greater good, ahead of our own personal interests?"

A CATALYST FOR CHANGE

That question spawns another: "If we can do this for a hometown festival, why can't we do this for the things that really matter—such as education, housing, healthcare, and employment?"

Like wind in a sail, I can feel these questions driving my life in a new direction with new possibilities.

One component of my degree—Resource Development (Fundraising Theory)—proves to be a keystone for me. I've always had a heart for nonprofits, such as schools and churches—which always seem to be underfunded. At the same time, nonprofits really do benefit the whole community. So, how do we get the for-profit sector, the core of philanthropy, to be more supportive of the non-profits?

Now whereas others may have found the classwork on grant proposals, 501(c)(3)s, and fund development strategies to be excessive or tedious—I'm as drawn to it as a barbecue sandwich with red slaw!

Bottom line, here's my take away from two years! Once again—it's all about relationships! People give to people—not to programs.

Being others oriented is of foremost importance. Then, as outlined so nicely in Kouzes and Posner's book *Credibility*—first build your personal competency. That will lead to increased personal confidence. Then, cap it off with a predictable consistency in how you treat and speak to others—otherwise known as credo. Those three C's take work. But relational capital—credibility— trumps financial capital every day of the week.

Circling back to other people, when we genuinely come to know other people's dreams, goals, and desires—something called *Appreciative Inquiry*—we add value to their lives and to their calling. Only then, can we best connect the person that has more money than time, to the person of passion—who often needs more funding,—such that both benefit. When that happens, the whole community wins!

All of this newfound knowledge feeds my soul in a way that surprises me. As a first generation college student, I had no idea of the personal joy that comes from personal growth. Who would know that so much knowledge was available—all related to my passion to impact a community!

So, though I continue to teach eight hours a day, attend evening and weekend classes, as well as tend to my community volunteer work—I feel energized. My mind is exploding with new possibilities on how to make best use of this degree.

However, I need to be honest here. Early on, I almost blew it. Thankfully, my first professor set me straight in a hurry. In my whirlwind of work and family life, I'd procrastinated on a couple of papers. I knew very well that the solitary grades per each paper would be my grade in the class—but I have been used to pulling a rabbit out of the hat when needed. So, I wrote the papers in a rush, took them to a typist (before home computers), and then carried them to class.

On the night that he returned them, Dr. Kussrow did not place the papers on our desk per usual. Instead, he waited at the back of the room, oddly akin to how a small town pastor might do at the end of a service (he understood the culture wherein I was raised). As each student approached the exit door, he shook the student's hand and returned the graded paper.

When I approached the door, he grasped my hand and said tersely, "Consider this a gift."

I looked down and saw a bright red B- on the top of my paper. Had he given me a C, I would have been required to repeat the class.

Then he added, "I don't know what you are used to getting by with, Mr. Bost, but this ain't church."

"Enough said," I reply graciously. He apparently saw something in me worth developing.

I somehow thought of my eighth grade teacher, Mrs. Charles Hill! While working in small groups I was goofing off, when I overheard her say, "Why don't you ask Johnny Bost. He always has good ideas." Her affirmation and validation stayed with me for the rest of my life.

On the drive home, I thought about what Dr. Kussrow said. It was true. Either I was acting like an irresponsible 9th grader—teachers tend to take on the persona of the grade level they teach—or I was acting like a volunteer pastor, always easily forgiven by a gracious church membership.

A CATALYST FOR CHANGE

Either way, I made a decision that evening, that possibly changed my trajectory! That's the last B that I would ever make in the program. I give my classes the attention they deserve because I'm not earning a master's degree to hang on my brag wall or to increase my income. I'm learning a new way of thinking so that I can make a significant impact on a community.

As the program winds down—even as I am taking my comprehensive exams and saying goodbye to a 15-year career in teaching—I'm uncertain as to my next move. I'm leaning toward fund development—likely with a faith-based college.

However, when I walk in our back door after a long weekend of testing, my eye catches the local newspaper. LaDonna has left it on top of the washer. After reading a front-page story, a voice in my heart says, "That's your job."

Chapter 3

A Perfect Match

The Dispatch—Lexington's hometown newspaper—announces that Dee Dee Philpott resigned as Director of the Community Schools to accept a public relations position with a local firm.

I know of Dee Dee. She married into the Philpott family—giants in the local furniture industry. In 1985, furniture and textiles are the mainstays of this North Carolina town, along with agriculture.

Her directorship was with our sister school district—Lexington City Schools—whereas I work for the Davidson County Schools. Because I don't know Dee Dee well enough to contact personally, I call a lady at our church, who works in accounting at the city schools.

After hearing a brief job description—growing the volunteer base, renting facilities, and nurturing business partnerships— I respond, "Sounds like community development, exactly the focus of my degree."

Apparently, the position is fairly new and quite pliable. First thing Monday morning, I contact the office of Superintendent Dr. Richard L. Thompson. Having my master's degree in community development and residing within the city limits boost me over the first two job requirements.

On the day of the interviews, a fellow candidate verbally outlines her pedigree, connecting herself by blood and by marriage to many of the movers and shakers—the power brokers—in Lexington.

As intended, this proves to be a bit unnerving. I have few connections with local city folks and know even less about the small town politics. I also know that last time they awarded the position, it went to a person with name recognition—Philpott. The final strike against me is the entire crux of my degree—relationship, relationship, relationship. It seems that I have few.

Thinking that she is pounding the final nail in my coffin, she says smugly, "You'll never get the job. No need to apply."

A CATALYST FOR CHANGE

Instantly—as always happens when I hear those words—my doubt vanishes. By the time the panel calls my name, my three brains are fully aligned and engaged. Let the fun begin.

After necessary introductions by an austere panel of 10 interviewers, Dr. Thompson says almost exactly the same words that I would later read on the superintendent's page of the school's annual report.

"Mr. Bost, there has been much discussion recently in this country comparing education and business and the demand for accountability of the highest degree from those of us who are privileged to serve the children of our nation. Our primary purpose for existing is to meet the needs for *all* children who attend Lexington City Schools. How would you propose to do that, if you were hired as Director of Community Schools?"

Instantly, my heart and mind click into gear. In fact, because I completed my written master's degree exams just days ago—this seems like nothing more than an oral exam.

"It's all about relationships. In fact, during my 15 years in the classroom, I found that the best way to motivate under-performing students is to bring in resource people—like Harvey Davis or the engineers from AT&T—so students can see for themselves how school relates to real life," I say enthusiastically.

After relating some actual stories, I continue, "Of course, teachers don't have time to dig around for contacts and resources. As Director, I'll construct a guide that matches curriculum with available professionals and materials."

"What about the wealth gap?" another panelist asks. "If you were Director, how would you propose to bring more equity to our minority students?"

A dozen practical ideas popped into my mind as I stirred 15 years of classroom experience into the catalyst of leadership training—while sitting on this hot seat.

Thoughtfully, I say, "Research says that just throwing more money at the problem is not the answer. So, I have to agree with Dr.

Thompson's earlier words that schools need to be held accountable just like any other business.

First, I'd look at the *relational capital* in the schools. How can we strengthen the relationship between students and their parents? How can we engage more parents in the classroom and school at large? Maybe we can host evening adult education programs. Findings show that inter-generational learning reinforces the belief that the schools belong to the neighborhoods.

Then, we have the teachers. We know that having a positive relationship with each student is critical. One tremendous help for me was learning the principles of situational leadership. This one tool freed up time and energy so that I could focus on my passion—which was teaching.

As far as *financial capital*—I'd look to the business partners for that. I know that right now they don't do much more than provide free putt-putt passes, or pencils, or factory tours for the schools. But I firmly believe that if we nurture our relationships—grow "real" partnerships with them—that they will step up to the plate. After all, we are training their future employees, so they have a vested interest in the outcome. As Director, I'd actively seek out and grow those relationships."

I can feel the heightened temperature of the "soup in the room." Clearly, the panel likes what it is hearing.

"Mr. Bost, how many business leaders in the city of Lexington do you actually know?"

Immediately, I think of "the name"—the next contestant—sitting in the waiting room. But, just as quickly, an appropriate response surfaces.

"Just this year, I worked with the Lexington Chamber of Commerce. I was doing a needs and feasibility study for a new foundation, as part of my master's degree. And I was amazed at how welcoming and helpful the business leaders are here in the city. I'm convinced that if we offer them a bigger slice of the pie—in terms of financial responsibility and decision making to make our schools better—they will welcome the opportunity."

A CATALYST FOR CHANGE

After a few clarifying questions, an intrigued panelist asks, "Mr. Bost, managing a classroom of 30 students, and even your latest achievement of learning the concepts of community development in your degree program are both commendable. But what *experience* do you bring to the table around actual community development?"

"You're right," I say with a smile. "I can't point to the classroom or to my degree program for this experience. I actually learned community development through my volunteer work at church. Here in Lexington—as volunteer associate pastor for nearly 10 years—I've been privileged to organize about 100 members for community outreach.

But my real growth has come from working with the Assemblies of God on the State and National level. In 1980, the church appointed me as Men's Director for the District—which put me in charge of creating men's retreats and organizing the Royal Rangers. They are the church equivalent of Boy Scouts.

Of course, I had excellent mentors—and I jumped right in with both feet. Then, just last year, I was one of four who served on the National Men's Committee. In fact, just this year, I declined an offer to serve as the National Men's Director—because I'm looking for a more local opportunity just like this.

What I see here is a chance to reform a small school district—to truly serve *all* the students. We are small enough—here at Lexington City Schools—to implement real change. I believe we could become a model to the nation."

The panelists glance at each other in pleasant surprise—as if to say, "Where did this guy come from!" After asking a few more questions, they advise me that I will be notified of the outcome after all three candidates are interviewed. I leave with a good feeling in my heart.

One Saturday, my neighbor and school board member—Harold Bowen—stops by as I am tending to my 100 rose bushes. Harold was one of the 10 panelists during my interview.

With a subdued grin, he says, "This conversation never happened, but you got the job. The superintendent will call you next week."

A PERFECT MATCH

"Really! Thanks, Harold. I felt really good about the interview. I won't say a word," I promise.

A sense of excitement wells up inside me, but I know that it isn't "official" until the superintendent speaks the words. Until then, anything can happen.

The next week, a telephone call comes to our home while I am out doing my summer job—painting houses. LaDonna and Summer drive to the job site—all smiles—and tell me that the superintendent will call back at about 6 o'clock.

Immediately, I rush home—leaving the clean up to my more than capable partner. At 6:00, the call comes in.

"Mr. Bost, this is Dr. Thompson. I want to congratulate you. You've been selected to serve as our new Director of Community Schools. You can come in on Monday to meet the staff."

"Thank you, Sir," I say with genuine gratitude.

Then, on the heels of excitement, comes the racehorse of reality.

To quote from my all-time favorite movie, "Toto, I have a feeling we're not in Kansas anymore!"

A CATALYST FOR CHANGE

Chapter 4

Building Momentum

After meeting the staff, I'm handed a 35mm camera—which I know little of how to operate— a calendar of the facility rentals, a list of volunteers, and the previous year's annual report. These are the new tools of my trade.

They seem so mundane to my somewhat idealistic and personal mission—which is to assure an equal educational opportunity for all children. Oh, and did I mention that my office is in the basement? Talk about starting at the bottom!

So, at the onset, I devise a conscious strategy to find my way out of the basement, because I know that real change is happening with the leadership team upstairs. To earn my place at the table, I'll have to get the ear of the superintendent and the school board.

To do that, I'll have to bring enough value to the principals—who report to Dr. Thompson and the board. But how can I build solid relationships with the principals? They don't usually like people from central office poking around their schools. How can I get invited and welcomed with open arms?

As I fidget with the camera and flip through the annual report—the answer hits me like Newton's apple. Give the principals what they want—which is recognition for a job well done.

So, I call the principals—one by one—and ask for tours of their school, mentioning that I'm collecting photos and stories for the next annual report. Soon, they are inviting me to special events, and before long, I'm a regular guest. All of that spells—relationship.

While on campus, principals are keen to introduce me to their favorite teachers. And it is here that I can make a real impact—for everyone.

For instance, after meeting with a biology teacher, I ask, "What is it that you really need so that you can do your job better?"

He said, "I could really use a refrigerator for specimens for the class."

A CATALYST FOR CHANGE

I said, "Let me check with the business community to see what we can do."

Initially, he may have believed these to be idle words, because from the look on his face when we wheeled in a new refrigerator—you would have thought that we'd just given him a collection of recently discovered insects from the Brazilian Rain Forest.

In another school, a top-notch history teacher excitedly relates how she uses 35mm films, artifacts, and photos to capture the attention of her students.

As she's explaining a particular project—my "dogs" jump off the leash and I can suddenly envision Ben Franklin standing in her classroom talking to her students.

I ask, "What if we could partner with the North Carolina School of the Arts and have professional actors visit the classroom. They could be in period dress and share a message that dovetails your curriculum."

"That would be great," she says wholeheartedly. Then she adds, "Do you know someone at the School of the Arts?"

"No," I admit. "But I know they exist and I'll make an appointment with the Dean." Actually, by way of my district engagement, I know someone who has relationships with the school due to an annual Easter drama.

She says, "Well, I know the students would love it, if you could make that happen."

A few days later, I meet with the head of the Department of Drama—Dr. Leslie Drum—and a few weeks after that, Eleanor Roosevelt spends the day on our campus. I have the picture to prove it!

Word spreads and before long, the high school football coach calls me. When we meet he says, "We could really use some more sponsors for our ads."

"Let me take care of that for you," I say with a smile. "It will give me a good excuse to go out and meet more business leaders."

In this manner, I slowly start the train of change, getting more and more people—principals, teachers, and business leaders—to jump on board and throw a little coal in the firebox to build more steam.

BUILDING MOMENTUM

At the same time, I'm learning more about the staff at central office. In an early, rare conversation, I find out that Superintendent Thompson is making changes in the schools for all the right reasons.

He grew up in poverty in rural Warren County, NC. This sparsely populated agriculturally based community—mainly tobacco and cotton farms—has as many people sprinkled throughout the entire county—about 20,000 people—as are people living in the greater area of Lexington.

And whereas, Dr. Thompson is able to pull himself out of poverty and all the way up to the role as superintendent—he never forgets about the struggles of the other poor children. In Warren County, the population is about 50/50 African-American and white, and too many of them seem to be stuck in a pattern of poverty.

When he comes to Lexington City Schools in 1980, he sees a disparity in the educational opportunities between a few very wealthy white families, and everyone else. Incidentally, Lexington has a population of about 81% white and 10% African-American—with a handful of wealthy white families atop the pyramid, at least at that time.

In many cases, the wealthy minority are sending their children to private schools in neighboring Forsyth County for grades K-8. Then, the students return to Lexington City Schools for high school where they are enrolled in "gifted programs" and play competitive sports. In fact, Lexington has always had a very rigorous sports program—often winning two or three championships in a year.

However, Dr. Thompson wants to "meet the needs of *all* children who attend public school,"—black or white, rich or poor. His goal is have *every child* college ready by graduation or prepared for a trade of their choice. If he accomplishes this, he will truly have a model school district.

Dr. Thompson believes this is possible, because Lexington has enough resources to fix the problem—if he can get everyone on board. Namely, if he can convince those he affectionately refers to as the "silk stocking" crowd –old money folks, who are the small town power brokers—to back this. Again, he alludes to their third generation wealth, but it is these same folk that we can go to when capital is critical.

A CATALYST FOR CHANGE

Amazingly, though he comes from humble beginnings, he is accepted and respected among the local top 1%.

He test markets ideas by purposely leaking information—long before WikiLeaks—to certain individuals who he knows will share the information with the power brokers. Based on the rumblings, he will then decide to move forward with a formal announcement or to try another path.

Often, that information is processed with principals and lead staff by way of a road trip around town in a nine-passenger station wagon until all is resolved! I kid you not, a true out of the box mentor for me!

The year before I begin working with the city schools, he's garnered considerable support and has accomplished great strides in helping the younger students. For instance, by 1985, every kindergarten through third grade teacher has a full-time aide. Tuition-free summer school is already in place. Several homework centers—with teachers on duty to help—are operating throughout the community.

Additionally, thanks to donations by Apple—the middle and high schools have computer labs and the elementary schools' classrooms each have their own computer. This brings the computer to student ratio to 1:16 in 1985. This District is progressive.

As I look for new opportunities to network, it sometimes feels like I'm an octopus—reaching out in eight different directions—and yet, like an octopus, each arm seems to support the other.

Still, no matter how busy I stay with my new aspirations, my heart tugs me toward the classroom—especially science class. So, I have a conversation with the Assistant Superintendent and Director of Curriculum, Dr. Sandra Gupton.

"This school system is doing so many things right," I say sincerely. "I wonder what we could do to give our students a more competitive edge in science and technology."

"What do you have in mind? We're already on track to bring in more computers."

"Well, I'm just brainstorming, but I wish you could have seen the students light up when engineers from AT&T brought in fiber optics. The scientist told our students that just one year earlier, AT&T set a world record by making telephone calls between New York and Washington, DC,—which are 372 miles apart—using fiber optics. And, he said that it's going to be light pulses and not copper wires that will drive the new information age."

"That's amazing," she said. Then, she added, "Of course, it will probably be years before that shows up in the new text books."

"That's what I was thinking. This information lag always keeps our students behind. They don't even know that they are the ones who will be fixing these new computers in the classrooms. Or, that they'll be inventing new uses for fiber optics. Or, they might even discover something we haven't even imagined yet. So the question is: How can we give our students the edge—by giving them up to the minute information—when it comes to science?"

"Well," Dr. Gupton replies, "we can't be buying new science books every year. Maybe we could invite experts—like you did when you were a teacher—to visit our classes. After all, these experts were once high school students, so they should have a pretty good idea of what motivated them."

"That's a great idea, Dr. Gupton," I say graciously. "I'm on it."

Later, I would have the privilege of working with Dr. Athelene Carter as she introduced our system to an established national program entitled, Odyssey of the Mind.

One of my other mandated responsibilities includes facility rentals. The State wants to extract the most value out of the existing brick and mortar—and rightly so. The idea is to rent the schools in a sustainable way during non-instruction hours.

Additionally, community use of facilities builds a sense of ownership that eventually diminishes vandalism. When I look at the calendar of rentals, it is clear that Dee Dee Philpott has done an excellent job securing rentals.

Churches rent the school gyms for youth sports instead of constructing their own facility. A dance studio—with a talented teacher, but no space—turns to the school for the solution. Local clubs, Boy Scouts, parent groups and more, consider their neighborhood school to be their meeting place.

A CATALYST FOR CHANGE

The calendar is so well-organized and so complete that I simply turn this task over to my administrative assistant, Modestine Charles. She understands the costs and constraints and does a fine job managing this.

My final frontier is to beef up the volunteers. I have to laugh when I think of this, because my first thought is to always go to an existing relationship first.

So, I call my friend, Ronnie Robbins—the assistant principal at Lexington Middle School—who is highly involved in a large local church.

"Ronnie," I say, "you've got about 300 people at your church. I want to provide an opportunity for some of those folks to volunteer at the schools."

"What exactly are you looking for, John?" he asks.

"You know, people who love kids, are good role models, and who could come in about an hour a week. You know, people in your church that *you would want in your school*. How many can you think of?"

He hesitates and then cautiously says, "One."

"One!"

"Well, principals don't want just anyone walking around in the schools," he explains. "Some 'volunteers' can cause more problems than they solve. We have to be selective."

This is good insight. I'd bypassed the principal's position in my personal career—so he is helping me to see the bigger picture. However, I also realize that he knows the idiosyncrasies of the people in his church too well to be objective.

I'm not deterred. But as I think on this, I realize that he's created another opportunity for me meet with the principals. Together, we can answer the question: What does a viable volunteer look like? When that question is answered, I create a guidebook.

In time, I meet the goal of growing our volunteer base in a big way—garnering statewide recognition for our school.

However, before I have time to complete my first annual report—the silk stocking crowd calls Dr. Thompson to task.

Chapter 5

Making a Change

Dr. Thompson calls me into his office late one afternoon.

Clearly frustrated, he says, "I need you to get me something by 6 o'clock."

"Why?" I ask. "What's going on?"

"I have an unsolicited meeting at Town Hall. I need you to find the language that will convey my vision for transforming our schools."

He pauses and then clarifies, "I need something to help people understand that we are taking a bold and different route."

"Okay," I say.

He leaves and immediately all my senses heighten. I actually thrive in a crisis. But I'm not going through this one alone.

On the way downstairs to my office, I actually say out loud, "Dear God, I need your help!"

I'm scanning my desktop, when a piece of junk mail jumps out at me. It's something about a Boston concept called Schools of Choice, or Magnet Schools. I haven't even read it, but I'm a quick learner, albeit auditory. So, I dial the number on the brochure, though there is a fat chance for an answer, because it is now after 5 o'clock.

Unbelievably, the gentleman who had sent the mailing answers.

Shocked, but as calmly as I can, I say, "This is John Bost with the Lexington City Schools. I just opened your flyer. What can you tell me about Schools of Choice?"

He says, "Well, each school, like a magnet, has a theme—such as math, the arts, or science—and the idea is to *attract* students with similar interests to the school of their (parent's) choice."

"What's the advantage of that?" I ask.

"For one thing, students of similar interests tend to have similar learning styles, so it's much easier to tailor the teaching to the students. Also, this is one of the easiest ways to fully engage parents and improve diversity—because people are making a choice. And, early studies show that these factors combined can reduce the achievement gap," he says.

"What's the downside?" I ask, knowing that my formal preparation is more about community relationships than pedagogy. His answer is more practical.

"The only real cost is that the school district has to provide busing for everyone. But we have found it well worth the investment here in Boston."

Like always, the downside is not research and application—it's money!

We talk for a few more minutes, and then I extract a commitment. If we decide to pursue this, either we can send a team to Boston, or he will come to Lexington City Schools on our nickel to show us the ropes.

By the time we're done, and I walk to Dr. Thompson's office, it is almost 6 o'clock.

"Dr. Thompson," I say, as I hold up the flyer, "I think this might be what we are looking for."

"Come with me," he says. "You can drive and tell me about it on the way."

I'm not sure why the wealthy few have stirred up this commotion. I do know that they didn't give Dr. Thompson much notice.

Maybe it has something to do with President Reagan's new appointment of William J. Bennett as Education Secretary in 1985. Nationally, the public is demanding reform within its schools.

In his report, *A Nation at Risk*, Secretary Bennett boldly asserts: "If an unfriendly foreign power had attempted to impose on America the mediocre educational performance that exists, we might have used it as an act of war."

This ignites a firestorm of accountability. He then fans the flames by stating in a *New York Times* story, "The American people, equipped with the right answers, equipped with what's true, equipped with the facts, can in my view go about the business of fixing their schools."

This is pretty much what the Lexington folks are demanding of Dr. Thompson. They want answers—now—and they want to see that their superintendent has a game plan.

MAKING A CHANGE

So, off we go—to Town Hall—with our new game plan. I don't know how he does it, but he goes into a large audience—that seems ready to string him up—and comes out an hour later wearing their good graces like bling on Mr. "T." (From the popular television series The A-Team.) In fact, that's what we call Dr. Thompson, "Dr. T!"

Later, in his off-handed way of complimenting me, he says, "Bost, I don't know why the hell I hired you."

I say, in all seriousness, "The Lord sent me to help you." Perhaps this is a little bold in my faith, but I had just witnessed a miracle!

He just looks at me like I'm crazy, but I did notice as he caught a tear in the side of his eye! I think he partially believes it, because not too long after that, he sends me on a nearly impossible mission.

He wants a principal—who is a mediocre manager and definitely not an educational leader—removed so that he can fill the spot with someone passionate for progress. The problem is this: Once a teacher or principal reaches tenure, it is nearly impossible to remove them without a very compelling reason. Mediocre job performance isn't usually justifiable cause for removal in the public school sector. Go figure!

Having walked the halls of this particular school for over a year—and being passionate about the District's new direction—I agree with the superintendent. Someone needs to do something. But what am *I* supposed to do?

And then it dawns on me—practice what you learned for two years in your master's degree program. So I meet with him, with the sole intention of building an others-oriented relationship—looking out for his best interest.

I listen with patience and curiosity as he relates his path to becoming a principal—Appreciative Inquiry.

Then, I ask, "What did you do before that?"

Surprisingly, he says, "I was a missionary."

As he relates this part of his life, the principal lights up with a new energy and pride. That provides a breakthrough moment for both of us! We compare stories—as I've done some mission work too. We laugh and at times, nearly cry.

A CATALYST FOR CHANGE

When we are done, I ask in all sincerity, "What are you doing here—stuck in this office? Do what you love. Go with your calling!"

And he does. What makes this so inspiring is that we each do the right thing. He resigns from a position that feels like a weight, so that he can give wings to a calling that lifts his spirits.

Likewise, in my putting his interests first—always the right thing—I can be a true mirror for his feelings, making it easy for him to see the benefits of changing his profession.

Chapter 6

Call in the Dogs

Before I know it, the calendar has spun around and we are back to the first day of school, except this time it's the 1986-1987 school year.

I bring in Rick Smyre—a Futurist, Entrepreneur, and School Board Member from nearby Gaston County to keynote our Back to School Celebration.

Rick sets our imaginations ablaze when he tells us, "You are training students right now for jobs that don't even exist."

Before he's finished, everyone in the room is convinced that true partnerships with our business community is the only way to keep our students competitive in this rapidly expanding age of information and technology.

As a finale to the event, I hand out the 1985-86 Annual Report. This feels a bit like handing out birth announcements. It's a time of new beginnings. For the District, we truly are transforming, redefining, and breathing new life into the Lexington City Schools.

For me, personally, this is the first annual report I've ever produced. I've changed it and nurtured it like a child. Today, it will meet the public.

The cover of this 24-page beauty features a hand-drawn sketch of the stately Grimes School by local 10th grader, David Inabinett. Inside, dozens of the very best of my hundreds of pictures—thanks to that 35mm camera —bring to life the words on the page. And, right in line with the national push for Effective Schools—"effective" is the key word in my various headings.

Incidentally, Effective Schools promote the concept that all children can learn and that the schools control the factors necessary to assure that.

Back to the brochure, on page four, Chairman of the Board of Education Miss "Bill" Wright says boldly, "*All* students have the right

A CATALYST FOR CHANGE

to expect the availability of education…that will assure…the ultimate development of their fullest potential."

On the brag sheet:

- We've established a Magnet Schools Committee
- Our athletic teams won three championships
- The Computer Team finished eighth in the nation
- 50% of our classrooms have ITV (Instructional TV)
- We are caring for 402 children with handicaps and 239 academically gifted children (3353 student population)
- Our Pre-Kindergarten is well attended
- Our high school drop-out rate is only 2.8%
- School volunteers are up by 14%
- We now have several Adult Education programs in the neighborhood schools.

Thinking back—just 15 months earlier—I'd interviewed for this job and had seen the *need* for genuine school reform and the *possibility* of becoming a national model. Now, I am witnessing the unfolding reality.

In just one year's time—starting from the top down— the school board, the superintendent, the principals, the teachers, the parents, and even the business community all align for a singular purpose. This community really wants effective schools—effective for *all* children.

So it is with great enthusiasm that I dive into my second year as Director of Community Schools. In fact, each day as I drive past our giant commercial billboard—near the highway—I'm confident that the 8-foot child on the sign is reminding everyone of our new goal.

At first glance—this caricature looks like any kindergartner's self-portrait with big hands, straight legs, colorful clothing, and a big round head with a smile. But on closer examination—as in driving past this daily—viewers see that the arms on the child are brown, the face is white, and the hair could very well be a modest "afro".

In other words—this one, happy, open-armed child—represents *all* our children in Lexington. This portrait—drawn by an elementary student with insight before his time—was part of our system-wide art contest.

Welcoming in the new year, the billboard says, "Thank you (in advance), citizens, for your support of the children and programs of the Lexington City Schools."

However, as the year progresses, the Magnet School Committee—comprised of principals, parents, and business leaders, including the silk stocking crowd—begins to see that this solution will involve some real sacrifices if *every* child is to benefit.

For instance, wealthy whites living in one sector of the community were accustomed to their children attending a few select private schools, in the adjoining county. Therefore, they would pour financial and relational capital into those schools.

With the Magnet School model, special programs can be placed in lower performing schools, attracting the wealth-based students —along with all the support that comes with them—to the schools that could really use a helping hand. In other words, instead of carting privileged children and assets off to another county, why not invest in special programs and attend the local, public schools?

As people continue to drive by the billboard they now have to answer a question: Do I want what is best for *all* children? Or, do I want what is best for *my* child—especially if my child is privileged.

If you live in the Southeast sector—predominately working class—you yearn for the influx of better books, more highly educated teachers, and a stronger volunteer base. Sheer hope that every child—*my* child—could reach his or her full potential—would bolster school pride like no other antidote.

However, if you live in the Northeast sector—predominately wealthy whites—you might opt for status quo. You want the best for *your* child—and you're already doing a pretty good job of making that happen. In fact, changing things—diverting assets and resources to these lower performing schools—will not benefit *your* child at all.

At present, most of these children attend private schools until they approach middle and high school age. So, if parents are going to make a change, they need some assurance that it will be worth it. Until this is resolved to their satisfaction, some folk seem to be riding the brakes on this new Magnet schools initiative.

This time, they employ a tactic—that in hindsight—now surprises even me. They approach the African-American pastors—who have tremendous influence over their members—and in so many words say, "Dr. Thompson is fixing to change the schools—to where you will have to make decisions about your children's futures that you are not prepared to make. You don't want this to happen."

In an effort to maintain control—even as the Magnet schools unfold—they manage to convince most African-Americans that whereas they are not prepared to look out for their own best interests—the factory owners will look out for them like they always have.

Once that is in place, the power brokers "invite" Dr. Thompson to an informal meeting to sort out who will control the purse strings. Meeting location: one of the homes near the Lexington Country Club.

Amazingly, Dr. Thompson—again I admire the man for his ability to think on his feet—is able to offer the crowd an option that appeals to everyone. He proposes the creation of the Lexington Education Association (LEA)—a foundation—to collect donations and decide how that money will be invested in the various schools.

CALL IN THE DOGS

This foundation will be arms-length from the school board. The LEA board will be comprised of business leaders, including African-American representation. In other words, the purse is back in the lap of the power brokers.

It appears that disaster has been averted again. However, a few days later, Dr. Thompson calls me to his office.

When I arrive, he says, "Shut the door and sit down."

After I comply, he continues, "Call in the dogs and piss on the fire. The hunt is over."

"Excuse me?" I say in confusion.

"I'm going to Tupelo, Mississippi. I've accepted a job as Superintendent," he says matter of factly.

My head is spinning, but I manage to utter, "Congratulations."

However, I'm wondering, "Now, what am I supposed to do?

Because he doesn't offer me any explanation, I figure that reforming the schools is proving to be much too much for Dr. Thompson. After all, he's a single dad with a daughter battling serious health issues. He may be opting for a fresh start.

Years later, I'd find out that due to the extraordinary success of the business partnerships in our system, Dr. Thompson's name came up in a national search for Tupelo, Mississippi. When they offered him the job, he accepted the challenge.

He also told me why he hired me.

Dr. T. said, "Number one, you had conceptual skills—you could see the big picture. Secondly, you had technical skills—you knew how to deliver or how to figure it out. And lastly, you had human skills—you knew how to bring people around an idea. I saw that in you during our first interview." (See Appendix)

Back to the story, I still believe that we are on our way to becoming a national model for schools. This is further confirmed when I review the past year, while preparing the 1986-87 annual report.

We've laid the groundwork for school Leadership Teams—made up of faculty, parents, students, and business partners. We've obtained a promise from the school board that we will develop a Quality Assurance program. The Business and Education Committee—part of

A CATALYST FOR CHANGE

the Chamber of Commerce—is providing speakers and dollars in our schools.

Test scores are up—the students showed an average of 1.1 year gain of their achievement scores. The computer to student ratio is now 1:10. And pride is running high with Lexington City Schools winning six championships.

Chapter 7

Full Speed Ahead

Over the summer, LaDonna and I repeatedly discuss the plight of our schools with our close friends, Ronnie Robbins, and his wife, Carla. Ronnie is an assistant principal and Carla teaches in the gifted classes. All of us are concerned that with no permanent Superintendent named, the engine of change might grind to a halt.

As weeks pass, an odd sense of déjà vu grabs hold of me. I've been at this junction before. Last time, it was a principal who had the potential to alter my course. The problem was solved by earning my master's degree. Now, it is a Superintendent.

Serendipitously—even as the thought is making its way to the front of my mind—Carla says, "I've decided to get my Ed.S. (Educational Specialist degree) and I need someone to ride up the mountain with me."

Instantly, I check with my three brains—and LaDonna. At first, LaDonna is opposed. My life is already so busy. But then, she is persuaded—and I tell Carla, "Let's do it."

We enlist—for the next two years—in the evening and weekend EdS program at Appalachian State University. Several times a week, we drive two-hours, one-way—literally up a mountain—to attend classes.

When my Ed.S. is completed, I'll have the credentials to become a superintendent in Lexington. This is a real possibility, because the school board and the business community are pleased with my progress in creating a true "community school"—district wide.

In fact, I'm so sure of retiring in the Lexington City Schools, that LaDonna and I purchase a beautifully wooded lot at 257 Oakmont Terrace—where I promise to build my wife's dream house.

With these plans in place, we await the arrival of the new superintendent. One day—before the 1987-1988 school starts—two men peek their heads into my office.

A CATALYST FOR CHANGE

"Hi, I'm Jim Simeon—the new superintendent—and this is our new Director of Finance, Gene Miller," he says pointing to Gene.

About an hour later, when the school board is preparing to introduce Mr. Simeon and his wife, Emilie, I notice their two young sons with them. So, I offer to take the boys—ages three and six—to my seat during the introduction. We do fine.

A few weeks later, my office is moved out of the basement and just down the hall from Superintendent Simeon. Not long after that—when the new administration wing is completed—Jim Simeon moves me into an office with enough room for my secretary, Modestine Charles.

Shortly after that, he adds me to the Leadership Team—comprised of Superintendent Simeon, Assistant Superintendent Sandra Gupton, HR Director Dr. Martha McCall, Director of Finance Gene Miller, and me. Every Friday, we review the district's progress and set our new agenda.

All of this happens because Jim Simeon and I see the same vision. His mentor—former Superintendent of the Winston-Salem Forsyth County Schools and current NC Superintendent of Education Dr. A. Craig Phillips (1968-1988)—believes that *all* children can learn and be successful.

Of course, Dr. Thompson believed that too. But whereas Dr. Thompson was more hierarchical in his leadership style, Jim Simeon and I speak the same language—others-oriented relationships.

Literally, Jim Simeon is constantly trying to leave me with more value than I bring to him. Likewise, I'm working hard to bring more value to him than he is bringing to me. In doing this we create a synergy—not only between ourselves, but in the community.

It's like the schools and the community always existed side by side, much like hydrogen and oxygen. But when we really bond—think H_2O—something wonderful happens. Instead of occasionally bumping into one another, we begin to flow. Like a river—our ideas and actions harmoniously head in the same direction.

In the coming months, the Chamber of Commerce adopts education as the #1 goal. Soon, businesses are putting notices in their newsletters and encouraging employees to volunteer in the schools. In addition to businesses, non-profit organizations such as the YMCA, Davidson County Community College, Women's Junior League, the Optimist Club and more are partnering with the schools.

Parents come out in droves. Many of them are highly committed—like our Volunteer of the Year, Jan Williams. Jan logs 500 loving hours at Southwest Elementary. Jan says, "My best home away from home is my child's school."

So, it's no surprise that by 1988 the accolades start coming in—from surrounding district superintendents, NC Department of Instruction, and even NC Governor James G. Martin. However, the greatest surprise—and affirmation—comes from the North Carolina School Volunteer Association. It names the Lexington City Schools as recipients of the prestigious North Carolina Volunteer Program Award for Excellence.

This is not just because we have 300 volunteers—roughly the equivalent of one volunteer per 10 students district wide. This award recognizes the diversity of our volunteers, as in, parents, businesses, and non-profits. It also applauds the types of resources provided—time, money, and materials.

In one of the newspaper stories about this, it's clear where my heart is. Even as we are being recognized as number one in the state for our volunteering, I believe we can be a "model system in the state" for everything—especially in helping *all* children to succeed.

At the same time, Superintendent Simeon is doing everything in his power to help *me* succeed. Even as I progress through my Ed.S. program, he is on the lookout for ways to help.

One day, he says, "Gene Miller tells me I can't give you a pay raise because you don't have your Principal's certificate."

Shocked, I say, "I never asked for a pay raise."

He said, "I know. But you are doing everything an associate superintendent does and more. I want you to be fairly compensated. So, I've made arrangements for you to start your principal's internship with Ronnie Robbins. You can start on Monday—working half-a-day at his school and then coming back here in the afternoons."

A CATALYST FOR CHANGE

Assistant Principal Robbins puts me through the rigors of leading a middle school. After he assigns me to student discipline, I see a teacher in the hall with a seventh grader. They are going at it verbally.

I ask, "What's the problem?"

The teacher says, "He has been acting up in the classroom and now refuses to even address me properly."

Both student and teacher are African-American, so it isn't racial. Apparently, all the teacher wants is reduced anger on the part of the student and a requested, 'Yes, sir.' When I speak to the student, his only response is a guttural grunt!

"I'll handle this," I say flatly.

Now, just a little background, in the 1980's—in a small town in the deep South—every student is expected to address all adults with the customary "Yes, sir" or "No, ma'am." To compound his problem—this particular student has a long history of discipline problems that follow him from grade to grade. So, it is with this knowledge that I take the following actions.

As soon as we get to the office, I ask the student—who has been nicknamed "Fat Cat" by his mother—to have a seat.

Then, I call his mom at her job and say, "You need to come pick up Fat Cat. He's being sent home for three days."

When she bursts into my office, she looks straight at me and practically screams, "I don't give a damn about Fat Cat. I'm just trying to keep my job so I can pay my bills and keep my house 'til my old man gets out of prison."

Ignoring her insults and anger, I calmly ask, "How long has Fat Cat been like this?"

She looks at Fat Cat like she doesn't know and doesn't care. It's heartbreaking for me.

I say to her sternly, "Let me tell you this. I'm going to suspend Fat Cat for up to three days."

Now, she pleads with me, "I *can't* miss work."

"I know. Take him home today and spend some time with him. You can bring him back *before* the three days. Here is what is required of you. All you have to do is hug him. Then, you can bring him back."

FULL SPEED AHEAD

I'll never forget the look on her face. Without saying the words, her expression says, "That's the dumbest thing I've ever heard!"

The next morning, I'm standing at the door as the students come in. A young, African-American boy comes up to me—all smiles with bright white teeth sparkling. As I peer into his eyes, I realize this is Fat Cat—completely transformed. I barely recognize him.

My response, "Your mom hugged you, right?"

He grins even bigger and says, "Yes, sir."

Witnessing that miracle—changing a child's life and academic potential by helping the parent—proves to be instrumental in rolling out our Intergenerational Parenting Project the following year. This program invites families to come to school in the evenings. Parents can bring all their children—even babies. While parents earn their diploma and attend parenting classes, all the children's needs are met—be it babysitting, games, or homework help. Best part: It's all free.

Additionally, for a small course fee—$15 to $20—parents can take classes in woodworking, small engine repair, or learn other skills to advance their employment opportunities. Again, the solution is all about relationship—see the need and then, care enough to meet the need.

When my principal's internship is completed—it's time to meet LaDonna's needs. We've been married for 15 years, living in the same modest starter house. Now it's time to build her dream house on the wooded lot.

However, because my father is a brick mason and I've worked on many building projects—I don't want to hire a contractor. I want to build it myself. Once again, Jim Simeon is unbelievably supportive.

He agrees that I can work on my house daily from six o'clock in the morning until early afternoon. Then, I'll shower and come to work for the school from 2 o'clock until about 10 at night.

He says, "Just let me know how to reach you. You get more done in the evenings than most people get done all day anyways!"

A CATALYST FOR CHANGE

Chapter 8

Best Year Ever

Jim Simeon and I—now showing up together at business meetings—begin to plant the seed of "quality teachers." In short, if we want to attract highly capable and motivated teachers to our schools, we need to give them income supplements that match our neighboring counties.

Lexington taxpayers and businesses are willing to step up, but insist on *Quality Assurance*. They want the school to operate like a business, with track-able, measurable outcomes.

So, I begin asking everyone: Who has the best model for Quality Assurance? Someone suggests Florida Power and Light.

Three of us, including Jim Simeon and Larry Freeman—the Quality Control manager and local business partner, Leggett & Platt—fly south to meet with the FPL executives. They are thrilled that a school system wants to employ this business tool and allow us to borrow their model.

In a nutshell, the Master Team (MT) devises the measuring sticks—by adapting industrial models, while retaining assessment tools from the State Department of Instruction. On site, each school's QAT sets priorities and secures strategies and resources—with help from MT. QIP assesses improvement and rewards individuals who supply the energy and ideas that drive the system. QIW encourages personal excellence—from the superintendent to the janitors—and rewards those who lead by example. Importantly, *all* teams include parents, business leaders, and school personnel.

While in Florida, we take a field trip to Disney World—much like my class trip to the Lexington BBQ Festival—to *experience* quality assurance in action. Perhaps, most telling is an interview with a man on litter patrol.

I ask him, "Does Disney provide your uniforms?"

A CATALYST FOR CHANGE

Quality Assurance Model
An Adaptive Change Approach

This model creates a climate where employees continuously improve to meet ever-changing needs. Additionally, it produces measurable outcomes. The MT is responsible for creating the vision or Big Picture. The QIP—those responsible for the process itself—uses the MT vision to build a strategic plan. The QAT provides specific site-based training, technology, and accountability.

Simultaneously, the QIP assures that the individuals (QIW) are receiving the support they need from the QAT. This process promotes ongoing adaptive change by allowing the QIP to serve as the communication and processing hub between MT, QAT, and QIW.

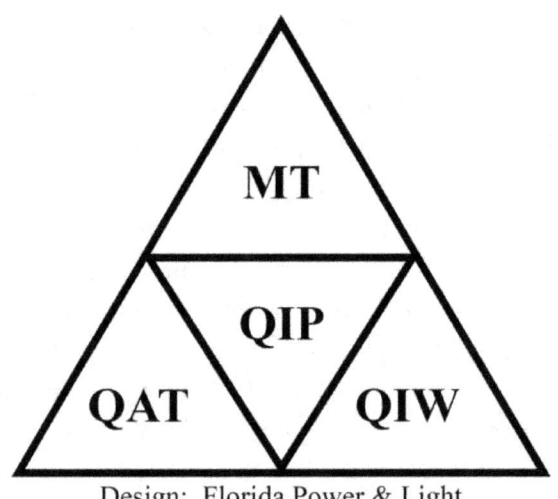

Design: Florida Power & Light

MT   =   Master Team → Vision

QIP   =   Quality Improvement Program → strategic planning

QAT   =   Quality Assurance Team → site specific training

QIW   =   Quality of Individual Work → personnel work plans

For more information visit www.JohntheCatalyst.com

He says, "No, this is my costume (versus uniform). When we come to work at Disney, we are *all* on stage. We are all busy making a positive memory with any child that sees us!"

When we return to North Carolina, the community—business, residential, and educators—fully embrace our new ideas for Quality Assurance and the Disney spirit.

I remark to Jim Simeon, "These changes are so refreshing, they almost feel illegal!"

By early 1989, we are already reaping the benefits of our new model. Though not perfected—and the FPL team told us it would take "courageous patience,"—we have now connected our parents, teachers, businesses, churches, and non-profits into nothing less than a relationship superhighway. Access between these various networks is as seamless as entry and exit ramps onto Interstate 52 or Interstate 85.

In fact, in a front page story in *The Dispatch*, dated February 11, 1989 and titled *Handling the Business of Education,* I explain that when there are problems, they are resolved through the *networks* of the people on our various teams.

"If the problem isn't being solved," I say frankly, "there is someone we haven't talked to."

It is just that easy. When we come up with an idea—because of our strong relationships—the money or other resources always follows. Trust me, there is no shortage of new ideas.

We even launch our first ever Kindergarten recruitment event. Amazingly, 225 parents and children show up. Why? Our networks beckon our parents to come see "one of the best kindergarten opportunities available" in America.

Then we circle back around to strengthen the network between the parents, their children, and the school by creating a Friday Folder. Superintendent Simeon's district motto: *Leading Children to Success* (LCS) is printed on a beautiful folder and sent home at the end of each week. Children share their work and parents provide a signature. Think accountability.

A CATALYST FOR CHANGE

Next, we reach down to pull up our 217 failing students. By the end of summer, we've mentored and motivated 91% of them to qualify for promotion.

Even with all of this success in the schools, I ask myself, "What can I give back to this community—beyond what I do for my career?"

So, I volunteer with Davidson County Parent Aide Board to change the way we work with neglected and abused children. The answer is not to remove them from their homes.

The answer is to help the families—by providing a trained volunteer available 24/7 and in the home 4-6 hours a week—so that abuse and neglect are the only things removed. Everybody wins when the cycle of abuse is broken.

In the summer of 1989—this goal becomes a reality. The Philpott Parent Aide Program comes alive when we join forces with Baptist Children's Homes of NC and secure funding from several sources. Who knows—now that we are embracing and healing our hurting families—what unimaginable blessings await us.

And lastly, during the 1988-1989 school year—after two years of driving up and down the mountain—Appalachian State University awards my third degree, an Ed.S. in Leadership and Administration. I've now learned the basics for the role of Superintendent— busses, books, butts (enrollment), and buildings! LaDonna and Summer—now eight years old—look forward to seeing more of me. And, our dream house is almost completed!

It is at this moment, when I am enjoying a mountain top experience—professionally and personally—that the whole world shifts under my feet.

Chapter 9

Starting Over

When the doors open for the 1989-1990 school year, it appears that this year will be even better than the last. Our quality assurance teams and community networks work so closely that we can now declare: "The schools are in the community and the community is in the schools." Community pride is at an all-time high.

By October, Lexington City Schools are back in the Governor's spotlight. This time, it's our own Coble Dairy Products, Inc.—one of 23 businesses in that State—that receives recognition for having "gone beyond the call of duty to make learning better for the children."

But a few weeks later, the first visible tremor occurs. The Superintendent fires the new band director, who happens to be African-American. The African-American community believes this is racially motivated. They demand to meet with Jim Simeon at Files Chapel—an African-American Baptist Church.

He asks me to go with him. Joining us are the two African-American school board members and Coach Charlie England and his wife. Charlie and Mrs. England—African-Americans—are highly respected in the schools and in the community, by blacks and whites alike.

The atmosphere is so volatile, that unbeknownst to Jim and me, one of the African-American board members has placed a plain clothes police officer near Jim.

Jim later tells me, "Standing in the front of the church, facing the angry crowd made me feel like I had a target on my chest."

Over the next hour, the Superintendent sets about defusing the bomb. First, he honors the group by showing up and listening.

Then—when they demanded to know *why* the band director was fired, Jim tells them, "It's a matter of confidentiality. Our Human Resource Department is handling this, and I'm not going to compromise the band director's future by breaking trust. But I will tell you this, his behavior was totally unacceptable."

Jim's position—where he is willing to take the heat to protect the fired teacher—cools the crowd a bit.

Next, he tells them, "As all of you are aware, my mission is *Leading Children to Success*—all children. After reviewing the band director's behavior, we did what we thought was best for the children."

That further calms the crowd. The remainder of the time is spent building a bridge—putting two boards up and taking one board down. Enough progress is made that—though the problem is not technically resolved—everyone agrees that we can let it go.

Before moving on, I want to emphasize the importance of Charlie England standing at Jim Simeon's side. Now deceased, he was one of the most influential African-American leaders in Lexington at the time. He coached numerous formidable football teams—winning championships year after year. And he changed hundreds of young lives.

For example, when Lexington's own Hiram Jones, Jr., is honored as a Living Legend by the Historically Black Colleges and Universities (HBCU), he specifically shines the spotlight on Coach Charlie England.

England was the first one to highlight his potential on the tennis courts and it was England who helped him put things into perspective when he said, "Jones, that's one of your problems. You don't like to make mistakes. You've got to make mistakes in life."

Still, even as people like Jim and Charlie work to pull the community together—greater forces are at work. The textile and furniture markets are beginning to shift. Some companies decide to send some of their work to China—where lower manufacturing costs will result in greater profits.

In the midst of this, immigrants from Southeast Asia, including Hmongs, Cambodians, and Laotians, begin to move into Lexington—seeking work in the factories and complicating the education system, which begins serving 19 dialects.

At the same time, one of the second-generation furniture owners sells his business and moves out of Lexington.

STARTING OVER

Not immediately recognizing the serious implications—I keep moving forward. With great excitement, I ask the Chamber of Commerce: Why don't we clone the Project Uplift program in Greensboro, NC. A preschool model, it's helping over 240 low-income families in the Ray Warren Public Housing community.

Launched by former U.S. Congressman Robin Britt—grant money and donations provide nutritional and health services to at-risk children from birth. This supports our overall goal for helping *all children* reach their potential.

Here is where we can have our most impact on the future citizens of Lexington. Research show that up to 90% of the brain's *capacity* has developed by age five. Think about *Quality Assurance* and measurable outcomes if we start when it really counts! We can't go wrong with this.

Once again, my idea is met with lukewarm enthusiasm. After giving the option "due diligence," the verdict is the same. We don't have the money.

Then, I understand. Even though—for several years now—the businesses in Lexington have funded virtually every good idea that the school has requested, those days are over. The global economy is threatening their very survival.

However, even if we set the money issue aside, the community is not yet ready to change. (See diagram next page)

Eventually, I come to appreciate that change, much like a lever that is mounted on an axis, such that whenever you exert the pressure of progress on the front of the lever, it always results in some negative recoil. However, if handled correctly, the lever of change can actually lock-in the forward progress—much like a ratchet. Timing is everything!

Repeated over time, small increments of change add up to significant change. Likewise, when supporters and resisters (top and bottom of the lever) align for the betterment of all—significant and permanent change can happen rapidly.

Lever-Ratchet of Change Management

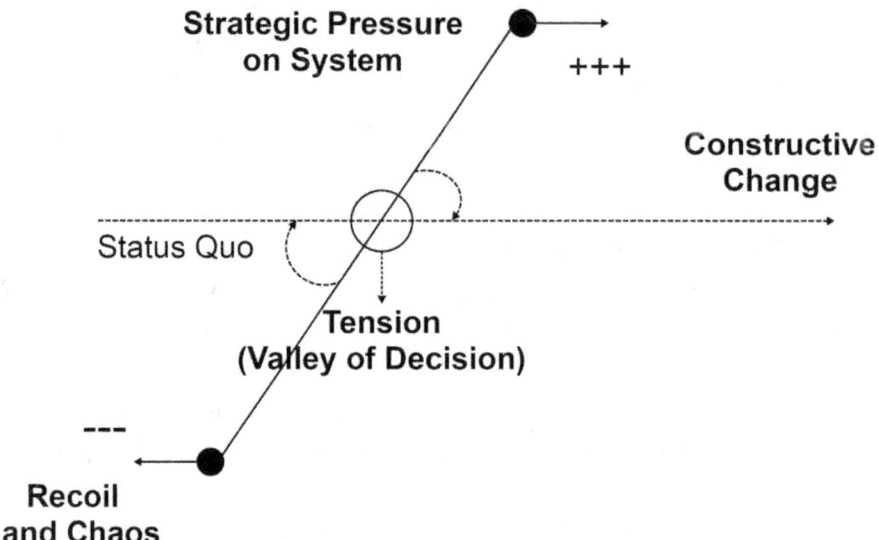

LEVER OF CHANGE

Positive pressure on the top of the lever, also known as progress, always creates negative movement on the back of the lever, also known as chaos.

The goal is to keep the valley of decision as narrow and shallow as possible (small changes) so that it can be managed. Once managed, each increment of change can be locked in— like a ratchet.

For more information visit www.JohntheCatalyst.com

STARTING OVER

As I meditate on this, I realize that Dr. Thompson moved the lever forward—at least twice. This allowed Jim and me—and the greater community—to move the lever significantly, in a relatively short period of time. For a few years, Lexington City Schools really is a model for the nation.

However, by the winter of 1989, I can see the community is now missing two key ingredients for change—the money and the moral imperative to do what is right for *all*. So, in January of 1990, I go into Jim's office. We sit at a table.

"Jim," I say looking him straight in the eyes, "I think I'm going to leave the system."

His chin begins to quiver. I feel bad, because by this time I have learned to love him like a brother. It feels like I'm abandoning him. But I have to move on.

My calling in life is to impact a city in a positive and significant way. I've done all that I can in Lexington. Though I'll be leaving 20 years of powerful relationships in Davidson County—it's time for me to make a change.

Learnings from Sector I

1.) Enjoy work. Be spontaneous, but within reasonable boundaries.

2.) You don't have to have money to make things happen. You do need relationships.

3.) Always, always, always add value to the lives of those you serve.

4.) Life is short. Make sure you are consistently stretching and developing your own potential.

5.) Develop a daily habit of lifelong learning.

6.) Realize that you are always leaving behind fingerprints and should be constructing some blueprints.

7.) There is more to life than your current vocation, station, or season.

8.) Textbooks are necessary, but it really is more about "who" you know, than "what" you know. Build relationships
.

Sector II

Religion

Organized religion—a mega church with 3,000 members—might have more moral imperative to do what is right, because it's the right thing to do. Here Bost discovers that if you have the vision, provision (money) will come around to find you. Once again, he and his team experience unprecedented success by becoming the catalyst for multi-sector engagement. In the process, Bost discovers boundaries—his, other peoples, and those of this sector.

Chapter 10

A Deeper Calling Yet

Six months before saying goodbye to Jim Simeon, a pastor asks me a question. We are talking in the parking lot at First Assembly of God in Winston-Salem. I have one foot in the parking lot, the other on the brake, ready to fire up my engine.

He says, "One more thing before you go. I've been meaning to ask you if you had ever thought you might be interested in doing the same thing for a large church as you now do for a small city?"

He has not only my attention, but has me wondering if he has been reading my mail!

Without pausing for me to answer, he lists several challenges weighing on his mind. The principal of their day school is nearing maternity leave, the parents want a middle school program, the congregation is growing rapidly—demanding better organization—and the older facilities need renovation. In addition to this, debt is high and parking is at a premium given the most recent expansion.

Before sharing my answer, let me tell you how I end up at this church in the first place. In brief, though raised fourth generation Pentecostal, I take the all-too-common teenage detour. Then, three years after beginning my teaching career, I come to Christ.

My principal, Doug Elmore, then invites me to an Interdenominational Prayer Breakfast. Eventually, I would lead this and in the following year—1974—my wife and I attend church, specifically the Assembly of God, under the loving encouragement of "Brother Woodrow Oxner."

The next big leap comes in 1978. Three others and I are completing the construction of First Assembly of God in Lexington—debt free. Brother Oxner names me as Associate Pastor. And, in an unusual way, I receive a clear sense of my calling, bi-vocational of course!

A CATALYST FOR CHANGE

While meditating for months on the Bible's book of Acts, I prayerfully ask God, "Why aren't Christians changing their cities *today* like they did in the First Century? That's what I want to do."

As best I can recall, my words were, "If a creature can give the Creator permission, I give you permission to change me in any way that you see fit, so that I might have impact on a city."

It is then, that I hear my calling, "Wherever I send you, seek that city, if not that city; the next. I will give you a city."

Assuming the 'city' is Lexington, I wholeheartedly jump into my dual-vocation as an educator and associate pastor. My mind and heart are firing on all eight cylinders. Between my two jobs—one paid and one not—I'm working about 16 hours a day.

"In fact, Brother Oxner is so pleased that he calls the Superintendent of the North Carolina District of the Assemblies of God. In 1978, I'm ask to serve as Education Director for the District and then by 1980, promoted to Men's Director.

Shortly after this, Brother Oxner moves on and a new pastor comes in. The new pastor likes to travel, giving me even more opportunities to pastor the congregation and organize programs. Think leadership training!

However, in 1986—I'm now Director of Community Schools—the new pastor seems increasingly irritated with me. Perhaps, because I have less time to fill the pulpit while he's away.

I'm busy bringing the schools and the business leaders together to strengthen the community. So, one evening, during another one of those casual parking lot conversations, I suggest that we truly open the church to the community. Specifically, during off hours, we can invite non-profits and businesses to discuss city-reaching ideas. His reaction shocks me.

"You need to forget this 'city dream,' settle down and serve God," he says sharply.

What he is really saying is that he wants me to use all of my volunteer time serving one community sector—the church. But I wasn't put on this earth to only serve the church, but rather to learn community and to reach cities. I'm not about to put his will for me over God's.

Driven by that sense of calling, I respond, "What I'll need from you is a good reference."

He asks, "What do you mean by that?"

I say, "I'll be moving on, changing churches."

He suddenly thrusts his hand from east to west and says, "You just crossed a line in the sand."

My reply, "What do you mean by that?"

"You know very well that with your divorce, you should not even be in the position that you're in. I'm telling you that you are done!"

I'm dumbfounded as he references the then-standing provision, that a man who'd been divorced could not be ordained as a minister in the Assemblies of God. Years later, it was determined that if a man was divorced prior to his coming to Christ—as I was—he could be ordained. I have now been ordained by two separate church organizations. Religion is an interesting sector.

You see, one month prior to my 20th birthday, I married my first love. She was a young lady I had met my sophomore year in college. Less than a year later, tragedy stuck. Her mother committed suicide and my young wife was now called upon to care for her aging father.

Under the extreme burden of loss and pain, something broke inside of her; "irreconcilable differences" was what was recorded on the divorce papers. My divorce had happened 15 years before this conversation with the pastor.

Further deepening my wounds, I receive a call from the Superintendent—Dr. Charles Cookman—at the District office. The pastor has called and reported our conversation. He is pressing the fact that I am a divorced man with undue privileges in church leadership.

Though the Superintendent has long known my past—and is fully aware of my wholehearted love for God and church—for the sake of peace, he asks that I step back from my duties as Men's Director and my volunteer post as Associate Pastor.

However, the Superintendent applies a healing salve to hasten my recovery, by saying, "John, when a spacecraft is launched to the moon, there is a little window of time where contact is lost between the astronauts and earth. It seems like an eternity, but then, contact is restored. Give this some time."

I have never forgotten his wisdom and tact.

Ironically, my Dad, who seldom calls my home, would call that very night as well, to offer encouragement.

When I pick up the phone, his first words are, "Son, not sure why I am calling. Just felt inspired to tell you, don't give up your dream!"

That's just how I was raised! By now, my dad's been a deacon in Winston-Salem at First Assembly for several years. The church is only a 30-minute drive from our house. But most importantly, I like the leadership style of Senior Pastor Ron McManus.

I'd met Pastor Ron four years earlier. He is beginning his second year as Senior Pastor at First Assembly. I invite him to speak at one of our Men's Retreats, and I'm pleasantly surprised. The way he turns his faith into words inspires our group and moves our men to action.

When I see my dad on periodic visits, he tells me what a wonderful church he attends. First, there are 300 members. Then, under Pastor Ron's shepherding the flock grows to 1000. A year later, it doubles to 2000. By late 1986—when I'm looking to make a move—First Assembly is having five services and serving 3000 attendees.

I have a heart-to-heart with Pastor Ron.

After hearing my story, he says, "John, allow me to pastor you a while, then maybe sometime in the future you can return to Lexington."

We had by then bought a wooded lot—in Lexington—upon which I would build LaDonna's dream home. We plan to retire there.

So, we make First Assembly our new home church. For the next year, I spend the extra time—created by a lack of duties—giving LaDonna and Summer well-deserved attention.

I've learned considerable organizational skills by now—having participated in the three year construction of the church. This also gave me a chance to get to know inspection staff in Lexington. So I applied for a permit to be my own contractor!

Before long, Pastor Ron invites me to teach a Sunday school class. Within two years, he's become a kindred spirit.

It's at this point—the summer of 1989—that we had the aforementioned parking lot conversation.

In response to his invitation, I say, "I'll have to think about that."

Then, I add, "Have you ever thought of putting all of that into one basket—the school, the renovations, and the organizational changes? Because that's the kind of work that I like to do."

Now we each have something to think about. It is during the next five months that the declining economy, a municipal leadership lacking moral imperative—all within a challenged educational system—provide the undeniable "writing on the wall."

So, when Pastor Ron shows up at my office at Lexington City Schools in December—I am ready to make a move.

Except, the job—with all the hats put into one basket—only pays $35,000 a year. That means I'll be taking a $25,000 a year pay cut, while carrying more responsibilities. Plus, we've already begun construction on our new home.

Financially, this move makes no sense at all. But after considerable, prayerful deliberation—there is no doubt in my mind that this is the right thing to do.

In fact, my imagination explodes when I think of the impact that 3000 passionately evangelical people—all driven by a deeper-still moral imperative—can have on this "next" city, Winston-Salem. I accept the job.

A CATALYST FOR CHANGE

Chapter 11

Different Hats

I try on the first hat—Director of Academic Education at First Assembly—my official title upon hire. It soon becomes apparent that the preschool—University Daycare—is rock solid.

It owes its beginnings to a neighborly gesture by former Pastor Carl Connor in the late 70's. Upon hearing that the daycare has flooded at Winston-Salem State University (WSSU)—a historically black college—he offers the brand new facilities at First Assembly until their university facility is repaired.

Once WSSU restores its operations, several of the parents that had become accustomed to the convenience of our site suggest that we attempt our own facility.

Pearl Kautz, affiliated with Assemblies of God institution Southeastern University, takes the lead and grows the Daycare into a remarkable, sustainable, and culturally diverse program that attracts even more neighboring parents from Wake Forest University, along with other professionals.

Parents are so pleased, that they eventually request First Assembly to provide a K-5 Day School. However, unlike the Daycare—which is founded on solid economic principles—the Day School is founded on good intentions and the parental pressure for an affordable private school.

So, what I inherit is a school that is not accredited. The only certified teacher—Rachel Lewis—is also filling the role of principal and she is preparing for maternity leave. The remaining teachers—uncertified—are earning a meager $1,000 per month for only 9 months. This is at a time when the average starting teacher salary in the State is about $20,000 per year.

Additionally, the Day School as a stand-alone—*First Assembly Christian School*—is not sustainable. The church is reaching into its pocket every month to supplement the "affordable" private tuition.

A CATALYST FOR CHANGE

Plus, parents are clamoring for a middle school and the building is too small for the students we are currently serving. We actually have kids in every large storage room!

Thinking my next hat might be a better fit—facility expansion and renovation—I quickly learn that the church had come out of its last building program $350,000 over budget, while carrying $3 million in debt.

Additionally, the "God Dome"—as the octagonal worship center is fondly called by Wake Forest University students—is in dire need of repair even though it's only three years old.

Unfortunately, the contractor —who later serves time in prison— used inferior or insufficient materials and multiple subcontractors—that ultimately resulted in shoddy workmanship.

For instance, I'm soon faced with a $195,000 renovation to fix the masonry parapet walls that adjoined the metal roof. After a hard freeze, snow pushes against the walls and we discover that the required 12-inch walls were only 4-inches.

Even with the new facilities, we are growing so fast we still need to expand. We had been holding five services each Sunday in the old chapel as we awaited completion of the new sanctuary.

Trying to get out of the parking lot while the next crowd is attempting to get in is like trying to navigate traffic during the playoffs at a Major League Baseball stadium.

To make matters worse—we are landlocked. The campus is limited to 11 acres. Those 11 acres are now occupied by the footprints of the original 1979 church, and the new worship center recently occupied in 1987, containing barely enough parking spots for its certificate of occupancy. To expand this growing congregation—by law—we have to find more parking. That means more land.

My third hat—organizational development—proves to be most shocking of all. I enter my first leadership meeting with my version of a strategic planning model—expecting that we will implement some long-term goals. Instead, I find the leadership team –which includes up to 17 senior staff and pastors—passively comfortable with a week-to-week plan.

DIFFERENT HATS

In fact, the big plan seems to be: "If it ain't broke, don't fix it."

Unlike the senior pastor and board, somewhat exhausted from what has now been a five year growth phenomenon, the team is so focused on Sunday service and Wednesday night youth programs—that it is blind to the looming sustainability, maintenance, and growth challenges.

In short, the team has little vision beyond its senior pastor. This moment is the first of several that will eventually bring awareness to the challenges of church growth, built around charismatic personalities on isolated campuses.

A CATALYST FOR CHANGE

Chapter 12

Vision 2000

"Dad," I say to the man who has laid brick in Winston-Salem for over 30 years and now serves as a Deacon in the church, "I want to help First Assembly integrate better into the community. So, who is the person in the sanctuary that will understand that?"

Keep in mind; this is an atypical Pentecostal congregation, now averaging about 3000 in attendance. It seems the more it grows, the more inward an institution can become!

My dad—Ben R. Bost—having served for about a decade quickly answers, "John Holleman. He's Chairman of the County Commissioners. He knows this town like the back of his hand."

Holleman—a very liberal Democrat—could be a bit of a challenge for our very conservative congregation that he periodically visits. However, together—I'm a conservative, right of center Republican—we make a dynamic duo.

He comes on board—as a paid consultant—in 1991. We study what First Assembly is doing well and where the greatest opportunity for improvement lies. In doing our research, we are quick to ask the leadership team—of roughly 20 people—for their ideas.

By listening intently, we soon discern that the oldest and the youngest members of our congregation—and our city—need the most care. Also, as word and excitement leaks out, other members come forward with ideas.

For instance, John Stubblefield—a reporter with WXII—corners me with a video tape one day.

He says, "John, do you think we can work this into our plan?"

"What is it?" I ask.

"Watch and see," he says as he pops it into the VCR.

Immediately, I recognize Congressman Robin Britt, and tell Stubblefield, "I know all about Project Uplift. I tried to interest our Chamber of Commerce in this when I was in Lexington. I even had

A CATALYST FOR CHANGE

Robin Britt come in to talk to them. This is a great idea, John. I'll see what I can do."

This gives us a reason to reach out to our city. Holleman and I take a trip to the Forsyth County Department of Social Services.

We ask, "How can a large church have the greatest impact on our city?"

We are told, "We need a preschool program—like the one you have in your church. But we need it in Southeast Winston-Salem. It needs to be accessible to our at-risk population. Also, it needs to be free or at least very affordable."

Holleman and I are excited about this challenge. We both grew up within a few miles of this area. Following *white flight*—when whites moved out in droves as people of color moved in—Southeast Winston-Salem is now predominately populated by African-Americans and Hispanics.

Holleman and I want to take action immediately. However, as the African proverb warns, "If you want to go quickly, go alone. If you want to go far, go together."

Therefore, our next big challenge is to bring the leadership team on board. As expected, there is some resistance. Foremost is this question: How can we take on another responsibility—as noble as it is—when our own Day School is yet to become sustainable.

The typical church approach, "Maybe we'd better take care of our own problems first," had now met its match!

Excitedly, I explain, "I'm not suggesting that we do this alone. I'm merely suggesting that First Assembly become the *lead innovator* –the catalyst—to make this happen. This is our time to *dream*—not the time to stay trapped in our programs and budgets."

Realizing that we are still in the "what if" stages of our visioning, the team is comfortable to ask very candid questions.

Someone asks, "Is this really on mission. I mean, are we a church or a preschool?"

"Good question," I say earnestly. "What is a church? It's a place of like-minded people—Christ-minded people. What is our mission? To bring the Kingdom of God to our city. That means that out of sheer moral imperative—doing what's right *because* it is the right thing to do—we make our city better for *everyone*. So isn't helping our *most needy citizens* right on target?"

Okay," someone says as we wrestle this out. "Let's say that is true. Let's say that we are here to make our city better, after all, our motto is "The Church that Love Built". But we still need to answer the question: Are we a church or are we a preschool."

"What if," I ask—pausing for emphasis—"we can be both? Instead of seeing ourselves as a church *or* a preschool—can we see ourselves as a church *and* a preschool? I mean if we want to have a *real impact* on our city—we will be hard pressed to come up with a better way to change the future of our city."

This is the first stir in the pot. Everyone in the room is open to doing the right things for the right purposes, in fact long before I arrived, or the church would not be growing. However, doing the same successfully now for years—it has settled for a relative "good" when *great* is a possibility. We are slowly changing our recipe from status quo—to having a significant impact outside our church walls.

The next big stir involves the other end of the spectrum—our senior citizens. We have a sizable 55-plus population who wants to live as independently as possible, before considering assisted living.

Someone asks the obvious question, "How can we possibly fund a senior living complex? We are looking at millions of dollars here."

Holleman carefully explains that he has worked with HUD (The Department of Housing and Urban Development) to convert a Fire Station into housing. He has walked through the process from the application to the open house celebration. Federal monies are available for senior housing.

Another team leader asks, "What are the odds that the Federal Government will give HUD money to a Pentecostal church?"

Again, I implore the leadership team, "We are brainstorming here. *Imagine the joy* of our seniors, living in high quality apartments in close proximity to their church. They will have access to transportation and shopping so that they can live on their own for as long as they possibly can."

A CATALYST FOR CHANGE

Once again, giving the team permission to dream—outside the bricks and mortar of our church campus—shifts the mood and builds momentum.

At yet another meeting, I address the necessity of expanding our Day School. Now, I already know from my fund development experience—during my master's degree program—that raising money to expand educational facilities is one of the most difficult concepts to promote.

People have an instinctive "not my child" reaction. In other words, why are we raising millions of dollars to expand our private Day School, when my child—and most of the children attending our church—do not attend there? In fact, let the parents and the people who directly benefit raise the money themselves.

Frankly, this is exactly the attitude that I encounter. Once again, various members of the leadership team ask the anticipated questions—almost as if I'd given them a script! And once again, I call on brotherly love, being others-oriented, and reaching our city as the motivators for action.

In short, First Assembly needs to expand the Day School facility so that we can help more "under-resourced children" receive a quality Christian education. In turn, those children will sustain the investment that previous generations have platformed.

Just like clockwork, someone challenges, "Even if we wanted to, how could we do that? You know that there's no more room on campus for another building."

By now, they know that Holleman and I always come prepared with the answers. So, it is with upmost confidence that I take out my roughly drawn sketch of the addition. It snaps right on to the existing school—also known as the Family Ministries Center—like Legos.

Here too, it takes some time for the team to see what I see. As this professional drawing of the expansion shows—I propose Phase I and Phase II in an oddly curved addition that comes to within eight inches of our mandated setbacks from the road.

VISION 2000

However, it is the *team* that suggests Phase III and Phase IV—a second floor to our administrative offices as well as a Prayer Chapel! Now we are all on board and ready to move forward.

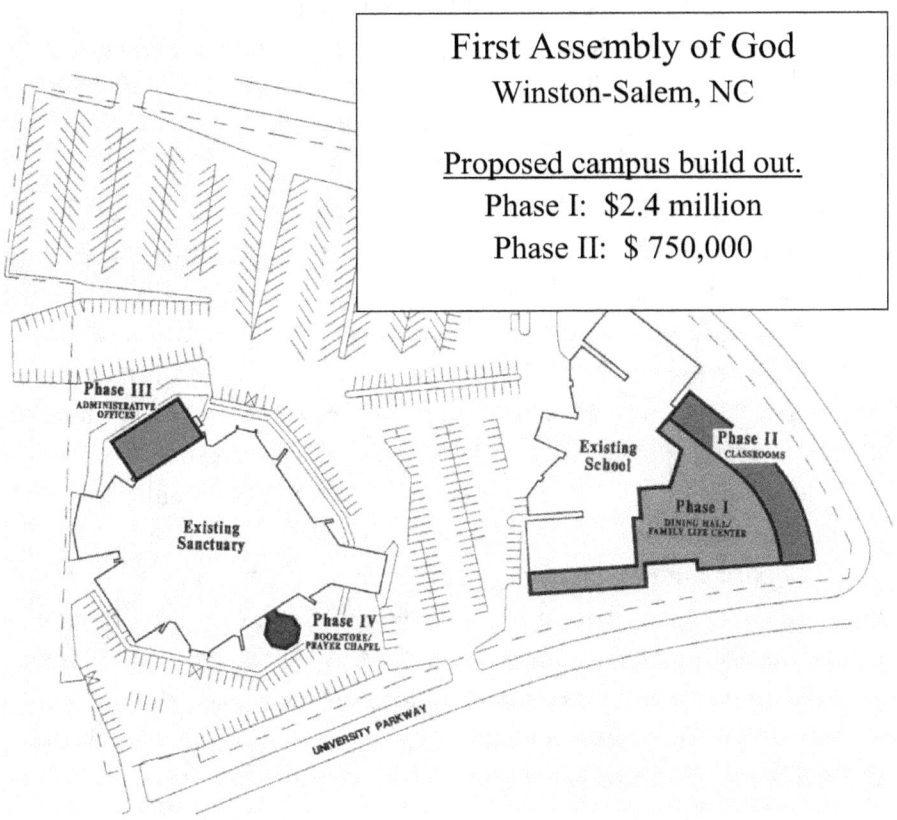

Someone openly insists, "The city is never going to approve this unorthodox design!"

I smiled and gently countered, "Why not? They approved the 'dove' back in 1979."

Everyone knows what I am talking about. Looking carefully at the "Existing School," it's clear to see the wings of the bird, the tail feathers, and even the head. In my drawing, I simply remove the "beak" to make room for a new media center.

Incidentally—the initial architect in the late 70's designed this dove very purposefully. Our campus lies in the flight path of Piedmont

A CATALYST FOR CHANGE

Airlines, so it is a "witness"—the sight of a "Holy Spirit-like dove"—each time a plane flies over.

My proposition is that we add 56,000 additional square feet to the existing 36,000 already existing. However, to make this more palatable, I remind the team that this new space—which includes a 500 seat dining hall—will also be used for church functions.

Gradually, over the next year and with the added help of Ernie Tompkins—a gifted organizational development consultant who was raised among Pentecostals—our stirring creates alignment. Think lever-ratchet and the advantage of supporters and resisters putting the *good of all* ahead of personal agenda or status quo.

And then it happens. By shifting our focus—from "me" to a collective "we"—and then wrestling in the "darkness" to overcome our fears and doubts, our pupa-like team grows the wings necessary to take us to our dream. It is as though the *vision*—of who First Assembly can be in our community—seizes our collective hearts. Suddenly, we are convinced—as a team—that nothing is impossible.

With our "compelling cause" and commitment in-hand, Holleman and his team creates a beautiful, full-color, 20-page brochure. Its title: *Behold, I have set before you an open door,* which is commonly known in Christian circles as the words recorded at Revelation 3:8.

Notice—the city-reaching language on page 12, which is dedicated to *The Vision...The Dream.* "Envision a congregation that by the year 2000 (eight years hence) has succeeded in positioning itself as a PRIMARY COMMUNITY LEADER by providing significant opportunities of spiritual, mental, emotional, and physical growth *from the cradle to the grave* for its fellowship of believers *and the community at large.*"

With that, we launched a $3.1 million capital campaign—urging all to participate. Our charts show that even a child, who contributes $6.41 a week, will give $1000 at the end of three years.

In fact, one of my first donations comes from a kindergarten student who gives me "two bollars." Unbelievably, her handwritten note inspires hundreds to give thousands.

VISION 2000

The Power of Sincerity

Letters of support and testimonials serve as priceless catalysts to move people to action. They don't have to be long or fancy—just genuine.

This unsolicited handwritten note by a kindergartener inspires hundreds to give thousands.

For more information visit www.JohntheCatalyst.com

A CATALYST FOR CHANGE

Pastor Ron McManus encourages all to give— "not equal giving but equal sacrifice." He also urges, not a comfortable sacrifice, but one that stretches one's faith.

The *Vision 2000* brochure contains a removable donation card, to be signed by the member and submitted to the church's business office. The brochure ends with the quote, "Show me your vision and I'll show you your future," by Pastor Paul Cho in Seoul, South Korea.

Chapter 13

Be Careful What You Ask For

By 1993, I'm managing two $3 million building projects. HUD awards First Assembly a $3.4 million grant to build a 60-unit senior complex—now known as Assembly Terrace—across the street from the church. At the same time, we raise our first $1million in our capital campaign. Fowler Jones Construction breaks ground in January to begin Phase I of our Day School expansion.

However, before retracing the important obstacles in these projects, I want to circle back to the earlier challenges of the Day School. Upon accepting this job—three years earlier—the Day School is neither accredited nor solvent.

Oddly, when I investigate the accreditation requirements for private Christian schools—they are minimal and insufficient to attract matching gifts from local employers. Adequate standards have yet to be written. This changes my task from complying to composing. Thankfully, someone refers me to a Catholic Sister from the Charlotte Diocese—some 80 miles south of Winston-Salem.

Typically, Catholics and Pentecostals mix about as well as oil and water. However, we share a common vision. She seeks for Catholic schools what I seek for First Assembly. Together—and with the help of North Carolina Division of Non-Public Schools—we are able to write the needed guidelines by 1992. That same year, the North Carolina Christian School Association (NCCSA) forms.

The accreditation does more than assure a quality education. It moves us one step closer to sustainability. Accreditation allows us to qualify for matching grants from some employers of our parents, such as Reynolds Tobacco, AT&T, and Wachovia Bank.

By 1993, we are making great strides in qualifying. We have 16 certified full-time faculty and two certified administrators serving our 220 students. However, it will be another two years—January 27,

A CATALYST FOR CHANGE

1995—before we get our official letter of accreditation from the North Carolina Department of Public Instruction.

Incidentally, my daughter, Summer, attends our Day School from sixth grade through eighth grade. Then, because we have no high school, she seeks and receives a scholarship at Salem Academy—one of the oldest girls' schools in the U.S.

Simultaneous to all this activity, I had spent considerable time at my new job developing relationships. By now, at the age of 42, I'm fully convinced that it is relationships—not money—that change the world. And if money is needed, it always *follows* relationships.

So, I quickly set out to meet all the neighbors of First Assembly. Literally, I knock on the door of each homeowner with property adjacent to the church.

"Good afternoon," I say with a smile. "My name is John Bost. I'm with the church across the street. Actually, I'm *new* to the church and I want to meet our neighbors. How long have you folks lived here?"

With that or a similar introduction, I meet Mr. A.C. Motsinger, a bi-vocational, urban vegetable farmer. Yes, he has a full-time job, but loves to garden. Year after year, he plows five acres, and then carefully plants and nurtures some of the best veggies in town.

In the summer, he sells his harvest under the shade of a large tree. This man is seasonally consistent and folk expect to purchase his produce annually. His family actually owned a large portion of the property initially purchased by R.J. Reynolds for the campus of Wake Forest University.

Around a corner live the adorable and elderly widowed sisters—Nettie and Lois Swaim. They originally built identical brick houses on adjoining lots after World War II. Each time I visit, they share a little more of their story. In time, they affectionately nickname me their "Preacher man."

Their brother—I.B. Swaim—owns the third house on the corner lot next door, along with multiple rental units and a convenience store off Polo Road. He's all business.

On another street, I come to know some renters. Like the rest of the neighbors, they are not particularly interested in church, but they are nice folks. At the time, I don't realize that they are renting from the Beulah Mathis family. This is the family that sold the church its original property in the mid-70s.

Across Polo Road is a world-class center of higher learning—Wake Forest University. When I talk first with the Chief of the Campus Police and later Vice President, John Anderson, we discover that we share common needs. We each need more space for growth and for parking. This conversation in the early 90's will precipitate a huge shift for this congregation in 2020, but that's a later story!

Lastly, there is another church-affiliated missional headquarters—Pilot Mountain Baptist Association— which sets on about two acres, next to the vegetable farmer. Though they don't actually hold services at this location, their regional church growth is stable and they plan to sit tight.

But why am I doing this? Why am I meeting my neighbors? Actually, that's the exact question that one of the associate pastors at the church asks me. To him, it seems like a waste of time. After all, I have many hats to wear and much work to do.

As he points out, we cannot afford to buy any more property. In fact, we are $350,000 over budget. So why am I "wasting" my time?

However, my primary objective in meeting my neighbors is not to buy property. It is to engage in neighborliness. My objective—my standard mode of operation, as you have now heard repeatedly—is to be others-oriented. I genuinely want to know who they are and what they value.

And yes, while I did leave them a letter asking them to call me if they ever want to sell—they can sense that my main mission is to come to know them as people. As time marches on, I become part of their story and they became part of my story and the story of the church. It's called community!

In fact, I will eventually bury some of these people and even care for their surviving loved ones. My others-oriented concern continues for their lifespan and beyond.

But, I'm getting a little ahead of myself here. This same year, I use the annual United Way campaign as a stepping-stone to help my peers see the benefit of my others-oriented approach. This is a technique I learned from Donna Black, the UW Executive Director in Lexington.

We will become the first *Pacesetter* Church campaign in the city. Though spearheading this campaign is only one of the many official tasks, I encourage the staff to increase their giving.

This is met with resistance. The common attitude is: We give enough. We support *our* missions and help *our* members. Why should we give our assets to United Way?

My answer: We want to *be good neighbors*. Neighbors reach beyond their own households. United Way reaches people we can't reach.

Eventually—the staff is persuaded to increase their giving by 95%—but Pastor Ron's letter to me is telling of the struggle.

He writes, "Although the staff has given you a bad time, I'm grateful…and believe that it will be a wonderful testimony and an open door for us in the future."

The following year, much of my hard work begins to pay off. Remember in 1986, when my privileges were curtailed at the District level? Contact is finally restored as promised. District Superintendent Charles Kelly invites me to serve on a committee to study "employee workload and compensation" at the District Headquarters.

Equally important, I'm beginning to understand the moving pieces that need to come together so that we can turn our vision into a reality. Once again, it all begins with relationship.

Chapter 14

Reaching Back to Move Forward

We are still landlocked. As Pastor Ron and I sit in his office, we realize that the Day School expansion will displace 75 parking spaces. Unless we can replace those spaces, the municipal authorities can't give us the green light on our building plans.

Suddenly, while gazing out his office window, I ask, "Why don't we own those houses right there?"

He turns around and briefly studies three well-worn rental houses adjoining our property.

Then, he says, matter-of-factly, "We don't have the money."

"What if I can find the money? Can we buy them?"

Pastor Ron says, "Check with the church board. If it's okay them, it's okay with me."

The board agrees—as long as I find *new* money to meet the cost.

My first stop is to make a second call on the property owner—Mr. I.B. Swaim. He tells me that since our first meeting—when we had no money—he has placed his property on the open market for $225,000.

He then asks, "What are your immediate plans for the property?"

I say, "We need it for parking."

Suddenly, as if nudged by a higher power, he says, "I will finance $125,000 of the purchase price for one year, if the largest unit can remain a rental until you need it."

Then he adds, "I have another potential suitor, so if you are serious, I'll need you to come up with the remaining $100,000 by Monday."

This is Thursday, so there is not much time. My first thoughts go to Dr. Lois Reich. She took me under her wings when I was teaching at the Davidson County Schools. Old enough to be my mother—she continues to treat me like the son she never had. In fact, Lois and her husband didn't have any children.

A CATALYST FOR CHANGE

Over the course of her career—50 years in the public school system—her passion for helping children only grows stronger. After she retires at 70, she begins a second career as an Amway distributor.

In fact, it's in her Lincoln Town car—back seat packed with Amway deliveries—that I have this conversation with Lois. One thing she loves, is that her Republican "son" is now working closely with a yellow dog Democrat—John Holleman.

Also, it's important to note, that she has just pledged $2 million to fund Appalachian State University's Reich College of Education in memory of her late husband, Edgar Reich. So, I know that Lois has the means if our vision touches her heart.

Oddly, when I mention expanding the Day School, she is not interested. My sense is she doesn't see a need to fund a private school, when her entire life has been dedicated to children in public school.

Her excuse, "John, I don't have $100,000 available right now. I just loaned $75,000 to a former first grade student so that he could buy his first home."

We drive around a little more. I share with Lois our vision of helping the two most vulnerable segments of society—disadvantaged preschoolers and seniors citizens. Now, it seems her heart is touched as I detail the conversations John and I have had both with HUD and with Robin Britt.

"John," she says as her face lights up with a smile, "I just remembered that I have $25,000 that I can spare. Check my mailbox in the morning and there will be a check waiting for you."

Next, I reach forward to a lady I barely know. Unlike Lois—who never stepped foot in First Assembly—this lady has been in and out of membership over the years. We meet at the city's premier private restaurant, the Piedmont Club—thanks to a favor from a friend—to discuss the vision of the church.

I think the discussion is going quite well, when she abruptly says, "Mr. Bost, I've heard nothing thus far that would cause me to contribute in any way."

Wow! Those words hit me like a slap in the face.

Quickly, I ask, "Can I briefly share one more opportunity that might interest you?"

Without hesitating, I continue, "We have an opportunity to purchase those three dilapidated rental units behind the church, but we need to find 75,000 more dollars by Monday. Then, we can turn that land into much needed parking."

To my surprise, she volunteers, "I have $80,000 in CDs (certificates of deposit) maturing on Monday. First Assembly can have them."

That gives us $5000 more than we need for the Swaim purchase. So, with the leadership team's approval—I use the extra $5000 to enter an "option agreement" giving First Assembly the right to purchase the nearly eight acres of the Beulah Mathis' property at $35,000 per acre.

I had earlier been tipped off that the property was coming up for sale, frankly on a fluke call from Realtor, Paul McGill. The option allows us to tie up the property for three years and is dependent on HUD's approval of a grant to build the senior complex. Note the momentum that always follows vision and commitment!

A CATALYST FOR CHANGE

Chapter 15

Others-oriented—Put to the Test

Small communities can have a big voice. So it is with the Neighborhood Association in the University Parkway community. It's one of the strongest Associations in Forsyth County. I thought neighbors would automatically embrace a high quality senior complex. After all, everyone is getting older and most of us have aging family that we really care about.

If our HUD grant is approved, people aged 55 or older with an income of $21,000 or less can apply for subsidized rent in a top-flight housing complex situated near public transportation, shopping, and medical facilities. Could we ask for anything better for our own aging parents?

However, the Association—mainly driven by two heirs to the adjoining property—is fighting us for reasons other than what is best for seniors. In a nutshell, they are hoping that their father's corner property might one day be zoned commercial and draw a higher value down the line.

If, however, we build a 60-unit HUD complex—a seemingly giant residential building—this will likely bias future zoning toward residential.

Of course, the municipal planning staff—from a technical ordinance driven perspective—wants to do what is best for the community. So, if the community really doesn't want a development, the planning board—at their staff's advisement—will deny it. If, on the other hand, the development will be good for the community—once the concerns are addressed—then the planning board will recommend the development to the Board of Alderman (City Council).

Now, here is where it gets a little sticky. Here is where I know we better have some strong relationships—if we want to get this property rezoned. Remember—I'm the new guy in town. All my relationships are in Lexington. So here is how we navigate this.

A CATALYST FOR CHANGE

Going back to John Holleman—now former Chairman of the County Commissioners—he understands the politics of HUD grants, which both local and Federal politicians will demand to be reckoned with.

Holleman knows from experience that our best option is to hire an expert who's been tried and tested. That expert proves to be Perry Craven. She's a certified HUD consultant and she understands all the moving parts.

If any one piece of the puzzle is missing—the whole opportunity can go down the drain. So we hire her for $35,000 to walk us through the process. If we are awarded the grant, First Assembly will be reimbursed for the costs of her services.

She recommends an architect, Ray Troxell. Why? He's designed several successful HUD projects and she knows that he can be trusted to get all the details right.

She looks at the board of our newly established 501(c)(3) for Assembly Terrace—arm's length from First Assembly Church, though sharing a majority of board members. She praises us for having a diversified board—with African-American representation—but warns us that our application will never fly with just one Democrat on the board.

Who would know that? Perry Craven. We remedy this hurdle by appointing seasoned members of the NC Housing Foundation.

She also recommends that our board include at least one medical professional who understands the needs of senior citizens. In fact, the strength of our board will be instrumental in winning the grant during the annual shark feed when grants come available.

Thankfully, one of our members—who manages our prayer room—steps into my office on a holiday in search of a missing phone. Honestly, you can't make this stuff up! Though we've never met, I've heard about her. She's a nurse, newly retired from overseeing a senior facility. Once I share our need for the board, she gladly fills that role.

With all these pieces in place—and Perry Craven keeping the media on the right side of our story—it's my job to appear before the planning board for rezoning. Typically, I might be accompanied by the board or some staff from First Assembly— demonstrative of public support. Numbers matter!

OTHERS-ORIENTED—PUT TO THE TEST

However, once they see how difficult it is to qualify for a HUD grant— further complicated by the fact that First Assembly is a Pentecostal church—their faith wanes.

Either way, it's just me and our attorney Steve Calloway. Attorney Calloway is essential for our success for several reasons. First, the fact that this seasoned man of integrity accepts our case, assures the board that Assembly Terrace and the HUD grant are viable. Additionally, he's been before the planning board so many times that he has a personal *relationship* with the members of the board.

Lastly, and equally important, Attorney Calloway knows in advance all the questions that the planning board will ask, all the answers, and the exact language to use in presenting those answers. That having been said, he can only control his half of the equation. The board, on the other hand, must balance our request with the will and needs of the community.

At the hearing, aside from the perceived threat that our building may lower property value, other Association members speak up about the size of our complex. They use such terms as "large," "looming," and "overshadowing."

Now, I need to practice what I preach. I often remind the leadership team to be others-oriented, by showing "brotherly love", such as during our Pacesetter United Way campaign. This is my chance to be others-oriented. It's my chance to step into the shoes of my opposition—to see this development through their eyes—as the planning staff has encouraged.

I ask sincerely, "What is it that you don't like about the building design?"

One person says, "The roof. A metal roof makes it look commercial and we are a residential community."

Now, in my mind, I know that the reason we chose a metal roof is that it will match our roof at First Assembly. After all, we are birthing this complex and we want it to carry some complimentary traits of our church across the street. But that's not what is important to us.

To them, it is important that it carries some traits of the surrounding homes. At this time and in this neighborhood, most of the homes have asphalt shingle roofs.

Another person says, "It's too large. Four stories is simply too tall. It doesn't match anything else in the neighborhood."

"That's true," I admit. "Let me see what our architect can do. We need to have a certain number of units to make the numbers work, but we will try our best to make adjustments."

Then, I add, "Just to be certain, our main objections are the roof and the appearance—especially the height of the building?"

It is agreed. So, I go back to Perry Craven and the architect. Nicely, this is not the first time they've encountered this. So, together, we come up with a nice compromise. The roof is changed to asphalt shingles. Then we remove one floor—now making it a three-story building. In doing so, we lose five housing units, a mechanical room, and one of two elevators, but the numbers still work.

Lastly, and most ingeniously—I think Ray Troxell thought of this—we place a beautifully landscaped berm in front of the building facing University Parkway.

Already sitting high above the road, the berm—from the curbside—reduces the sense of height and Assembly Terrace looks more like a two-story building, than its actuality of three! This better aligns with our two-story worship center across the street and our forthcoming two-story classroom addition to our Day School.

At the planning board meeting—it is clear that we were making every effort to be good neighbors. We not only listened, we took action to mitigate any perceived injury to our surrounding neighbors.

Still, the neighbors are not really happy. Now, the planning board has to decide what to recommend to the aldermen. On the one hand, we have proven the need for more affordable senior housing in this part of the city. All the required amenities already exist. So, it is an easy match—the need, the location, and the Federal funding. All that adds up to a "yes" vote by the board. It would now move to the City Council—the aldermen at that time.

However, if the neighbors really are against the project—and they have plenty of political connections—the aldermen can end up sacrificing their re-election if they move against community will.

Chapter 16

Thank You Carl Conner

As mentioned earlier, former Pastor Carl Conner had no idea how simply doing what is right because you can and because it is the right thing to do—would affect the church over a decade later.

When I take our site plans for the Day School's odd-shaped addition and our now 53-unit HUD complex to the city aldermen —we are met with a cool response.

To complicate matters, a bizarre requirement had come into play. It would require establishing the back of the church as the front of the church. This is the only way we can meet the setback requirements. Even at that, we are within eight inches of our legal proximity to the roadside curb.

And yes, that twist is what created this somewhat unorthodox—if not odd—looking building that followed the setbacks of Long Drive. However, once sketched, the curves look rather elegant. Long Drive would become a street of most critical importance in the days ahead.

Nonetheless, just before we are ready to be denied, African-American Board Member Mayor Pro Tem Dr. Vivian Burke—who wields considerable power in Winston-Salem—asks if she might speak.

"What you don't know," she says to her fellow board members, "is that when our Daycare flooded at Winston-Salem State University, First Assembly opened their doors to us."

After pausing, she says coyly, "Let him build his little school."

Amazingly, we receive approval to move forward. It was my involvement in these early meetings, that would eventually provide an appointment to the Unified Development Ordinance Committee and later the City/County Planning Board.

There are other unforeseen benefits from "opening our doors" to this predominately African-American University. Professionals at neighboring Wake Forest University realize the wisdom of a multi-cultural daycare experience for their own children.

A CATALYST FOR CHANGE

Then, when children age out, many of the parents—black and white—want First Assembly to continue its multi-cultural/multi-denominational school through middle school.

In the meantime, many of the African-American parents decide to join our church. So, whereas Sunday—church day—is typically the most segregated day of the week in the U.S., we actually would become one of the most diverse congregations in the city.

This too mitigates concerns surfaced as well for our $3.4 million senior housing complex, as the Board's decision teeters. Being a majority white congregation in a neighborhood where the older deed actually forbade "Negroes", our attorney brings to light that some of the resistance from the neighborhood could also be racial. Affordable housing, even for seniors, often surfaces racial bias.

When he shines the light on this, City Councilman Nelson Malloy Jr. reacts visibly. Just a little background: Malloy begins representing the North Ward of Winston-Salem in 1989. However, this African-American change-agent cut his teeth 20 years earlier as a founder of the Winton-Salem Chapter of the Black Panther Party in 1969.

He practices unprecedented *moral imperative*—doing the right thing even when he is vehemently and sometimes violently opposed. In fact, he's wheelchair bound to this day from a gunshot wound incurred while involved in these reform activities.

In Winston-Salem, the Black Panther movement boasts many accomplishments. Most notably, free school breakfast for underprivileged children and free ambulance rides for those in need.

So, at our hearing, Malloy asks one simple question, "What I want to know, Mr. Bost is: If we help you build Assembly Terrace (the name chosen for our senior complex), will people who are white, red, black, yellow, or purple, have a chance to live there."

What my Momma would have called a Holy Ghost moment, allows me to confidently reply, "Mr. Malloy, with the exception of purple, they all worship together right across the street."

He says, "I move that we approve this project." A resounding second is offered, followed by unanimous consent!

Chapter 17

The Children—Our Future

Building Assembly Terrace and expanding First Assembly Christian School is important to me, but my heart knows there is more to be done—especially among the most underprivileged of preschoolers.

I start searching for like-minded people. Little do I know, but that same passion will eventually spread across the State of North Carolina and then into all 50 states in the US.

In addition to John Holleman, Dr. Mark Corts joins us as a partner in progress. He's pastor of another mega-church in town—Calvary Baptist. Like First Assembly, his church also has a Day School—but it's solvent due to higher tuition.

When I share our vision of helping underprivileged children in Winston-Salem—he jumps on board. He's already aware that the first five years are critical and that Southeast Winston-Salem—his birthplace—needs a little help.

We don't know quite what our preschool will look like, but we know that it will need funding. To be able to collect funds from as many sources as possible—churches, foundations, and businesses—we need to set up a non-profit. Because it's going to help preschoolers with their first introduction to education—we name it First Start, Inc.

In a short time, five churches pledge $12,000 each to the program—First Assembly, Calvary Baptist, First Presbyterian, Ardmore Moravian, and Reynolda Church. Then, Holleman suggests that we knock on doors—church doors—up and down Sprague Street to find a church willing to lend space for our preschool.

We are willing to pay rent—and this should appeal to the struggling historically white churches now surrounded by a community of color. Their loyal parishioners are still driving to the Sprague-Waughtown area—while living elsewhere—but, numbers have dwindled.

It costs money to heat and maintain a church. We could benefit each other with this partnership. However, the response of each and every church—and we visited more than a dozen—is always hesitancy and from some a solid "no."

Excuses range from "we don't want fingerprints on our newly painted walls," to "we don't want *those* children (of color) in our church."

Holleman and I have lived here long enough to recognize that this is nothing more than blatant racism—from people who say that they believe the gospel and want to help underprivileged children.

But in reality, they only want to help underprivileged children that look like their membership, unless "those" children live far away in a foreign country.

When that fails, we simply continue to work our way down Sprague Street. Once again, there's no shortage of churches—the city has over 600 churches—but not a single "yes," so far. Holleman shares his frustration with his extended family, and one of his uncles decides to give us a large two-story house on the corner of Sprague Street and Urban. It's right in the middle of our target community.

With a house in hand, Congressman Robin Britt—Project Uplift—agrees to shepherd us through the process. In the meantime, Holleman pulls on some contacts at the County Office and Kevin Fitzpatrick—assistant County manager—receives authorization to help us look at possibilities for transforming the home. Now, energy is running high.

Dr. Corts says to me, "John, you should talk to Dr. Mac Ernest. He's a physician at our church. He may be able to bring medical services to our program."

In talking with Joseph M. "Mac" Ernest III, M.D.,—professor of obstetrics and gynecology at Wake Forest University School of Medicine—he suggests that we use interns to staff a birthing suite on site. After all, with a high Hispanic population—mainly migrant farm workers from Mexico who decide to stay—there is a high need for prenatal and childbirth care.

Dr. Corts also puts me in touch with a dentist, Dr. Fred Smith. He, too, is willing to bring services to our preschool program. So, now our preschool will make sure that each child is healthy and academically ready for kindergarten by the time the child reaches age 5.

THE CHILDREN—OUR FUTURE

However, after completing a few sketches of possible renovations on the house, it becomes clear that this well-intended gift is a "money pit." We will need a new location. By now, our team of visionaries has grown to about 15 people, to include a small Board of Directors.

During a team meeting in this house, John Holleman shares that there is a church—right across the street—almost hidden by a large, overgrown hedge. We never knocked on that door, and at the moment, there is a car in the driveway. Holleman excuses himself, walks across the street, and knocks on the door.

In a short time, he comes back to tell us the good news.

Apparently, Holleman shared our vision for a Family Resource Center (the concept had matured) to include preschool, dental and health center.

On hearing this, African-American Pastor Howard Daniels says, "We have been praying about what to do with our church. We'd like to help. You can use our church basement for your program."

It is shortly after this, that Kate B. Reynolds Foundation awards First Start, Inc. a $60,000 grant for our new preschool at Living Water Church. Later, we will name the preschool Living Water Family Resource Center.

All of this happens by 1993. It will be some time before we get the basement suitable for our program—but in the meantime, Dr. Corts calls a fellow Baptist pastor, a friend of the family of North Carolina Governor James Baxter Hunt Jr.

Pastor to pastor, Dr. Corts tells about the amazing educational outreach happening right here in Winston-Salem. Churches of various denominations, predominately white, have joined forces with Wake Forest Baptist Health, dental professionals, and a local foundation—to fund a preschool in an African-American church that will help under-resourced Hispanic and African-American children. This is nothing short of a miracle in a racially divided city.

As intended, Dr. Corts' friend encourages Governor James Hunt to visit, not knowing that the Governor would go on to establish himself as a national leader in education and serve an unprecedented four terms. Before our program is even up and running—Governor Hunt pays a visit to our preschool at First Assembly where we introduce him as well to parents who will soon benefit from our First Start initiative in the Southside community.

A CATALYST FOR CHANGE

There he shares his thoughts with me, "John, the best childcare in North Carolina is in the churches and the worst childcare in North Carolina is in the churches. The difference is whether they are doing it for mission purposes—to really help the community—or for new revenue streams."

That settles my thoughts as to why we will do it!

On July 9, 1993, Governor Hunt signs into law the North Carolina Partnership for Children and all that it entails. The mission of this public-private partnership: "To provide high quality early childhood education and development services for children and families."

The law limits the number of pilot programs to 12 for the first year. Here is how we manage to get a piece of the pie. Governor Hunt hires Congressman Robin Britt, local Womble Carlyle Attorney Ashley Thrift, and Kevin Fitzgerald to drive the new North Carolina Partnership for Children (NCPC)—also known as Smart Start. Dr. Dean Clifford—the godmother of early childhood education in Forsyth County then calls a meeting at the Womble Carlyle Law Firm in Winston-Salem.

Pastor Ron McManus receives a letter notifying him of the meeting, hands it to me in passing—and neither of us marks it on our calendars. In fact, the letter does not read like an open invitation, even if I had wanted to go.

When the meeting begins, I'm across town in a restaurant courting a donor—Lee Jackson—for our Vision 2000 campaign. Midstream in our conversation, that letter pops up in my mind. Suddenly, I feel a need to show up at the meeting.

So, in a courteous but impromptu fashion, I excuse myself, knowing full well that he will understand my urgency. Incidentally, it was Lee that later introduced me to A.C. Motsinger. This is the farmer who would eventually give his five-acre vegetable garden to the church.

After arriving at the law office, I quietly take a seat in the back of the large board room.

Following a few minutes of discussion about funding a local Project Uplift to support early childhood education, Dr. Clifford looks at me and asks, "Aren't you from First Assembly?"

"Yes, Ma'am," I reply. She later shares that she visits sometimes on Wednesday nights.

THE CHILDREN—OUR FUTURE

"Aren't you already doing this at Living Water?" she asks.

"Yes, we are," I confirm.

She then says to the committee, "There's no need to reinvent the wheel. I don't see any reason to find anyone else."

So, I walk out of that meeting with a commitment for $280,000. When you add that to the $60,000 promised from Kate B. Reynolds and the $12,000 from five churches, that equals $400,000. I know that we can make this work, now!

We've already had a big hotdog/hamburger cook out for volunteers from our sponsoring churches. Together, we gut the basement of Living Waters. We put on a new roof, assume a $100,000 note against the church, put in a new drainage system, and a wheelchair ramp. Then, we set up our classrooms, along with state of the art birthing and dental centers. We eventually liquidated the property across the street, though it served us well as a catalyst for the center.

Our grand opening takes place on Sunday, November 24, 1996. Our preschool program is a partnership between First Start, Inc., The Kate B. Reynolds Poor and Needy Trust and Forsyth Early Childhood Partnership—the local partner with NCPC Smart Start.

Soon, we are serving 35 families in the preschool program, while providing a birthing suite and dental services that will eventually accommodate approximately 1000 families. We truly are helping the most needy in our community—by now, mostly Hispanic.

They are so appreciative and so are our local public schools. Under the direction of our new Executive Director, Audrey Davis (formerly assistant to Mrs. Kautz at First Assembly's University Day School), we aid the preschoolers and their parents in learning English as a second language. We also help the children practice the skills needed for success in kindergarten.

Like a pebble dropped in a pond—the realization of our dream has far reaching consequences. North Carolina comes to be the first State in the US to fund a statewide early childhood program that includes health, education, and parental support. By 2000, the program is established in all 100 counties in NC. In the course of a few years, all 50 states visit Smart Start programs in North Carolina.

A CATALYST FOR CHANGE

Chapter 18

Time to Make a Change

Meanwhile—on the home front—grumbling in the ranks is escalating. I am now serving as executive pastor and I'm expected to manage the molehills before they become mountains.

However, in a church this large—now bumping up to about 5000 attenders—each associate pastor has his own constituency. While there is some rivalry between them—they seem to unite on one front. They don't like the way I'm doing things.

"Maybe you're not the right person for this job," Pastor Ron McManus says to me.

Rather than take offense, I reply honestly, "Maybe I'm not. But, I'll tell you this. If I find out that this isn't a good match, you won't hear it through the grapevine. I'll tell you directly."

Maybe a little terse, but I was banking not only on my productivity but the trust developed over five years.

After giving it some thought—on April 19, 1995—I hand him a letter listing the accomplishments to date—the Day School accreditation and campus expansion, the $3.1 million capital campaign, Assembly Terrace fully occupied with a waiting list, expanded parking and land acquisition, and, of course, the Living Water Family Resource Center preschool program. The letter includes an option for me to move on.

When Pastor Ron reads the letter, he says, "You can't quit, John. We still have too many fish to fry. Let me rearrange the staff. You can serve as Development Director, where you do your best work. I'll have someone else manage the pastoral staff."

I wait another 18 months, before turning in my next and final letter of resignation. However, let me pull back the curtains on *why* I feel the need to move on.

During my first two years with First Assembly, I am mainly working with projects. However, in 1993, Pastor Ron—noting how efficiently and effectively I can build a team around an idea—asks me to serve as executive pastor.

There is no big announcement, we are simply placing multiple issues "in one basket" so I can work through them at my own pace (our original agreement). Think parking lot discussion in 1989. In this new role, I'll be reorganizing the staff so that it best serves the needs of the church.

To serve in this capacity, I'll need to be ordained. Unfortunately, the Assemblies of God Church has not yet reached its new decision on pre-salvation divorces. So, I go to a friend of mine—Reverend Max Shoaf at the Psalm 91 Church— and take along Ernie Tompkins as a witness, to receive my ordination.

With ordination in hand, in lieu of another raise, Pastor Ron can now approve my tax-free housing allowance. I'm now realizing a near match of my Lexington City Schools salary. As appreciated as it is, this can't possibly compensate for the resistance that I'm about to incur.

As an early improvement, I respectfully consolidate Pastor Ron's administrative assistant with a person who can coordinate all the secretaries of all the associate pastors. In doing this, much duplication of duties—wasted time—can be avoided.

In a word, it's called accountability. This goes 180-degrees against the current laissez faire culture. My wakeup call came when an administrative assistant put the feelings of the staff into words.

She says curtly, "You're running this thing like IBM. We're not a business. We're a church."

"Really." I say matter-of-factly.

Though I don't address it then, a church is a business. It's just a business that doesn't pay taxes and at least in this case, it seems resistant to what I feel is customary accountability.

In little snippets of conversation with associate pastors, we try to sort this out.

One young pastor notes, "Churches operate on the law of love—not business-like accountability."

I respond, "Isn't the law of love all about boundaries? It's really the same thing as accountability. Called by either name—we are trying to account for the best use of our time and money so that we can accomplish our ministry."

I am learning my second lesson as to how leaders think differently within each of the five sectors—education, faith-based, business, municipal governance, and the social sector.

A few months later, after the groundbreaking at the new Day School addition—I am asked by the contractor to alert the staff, "No one is allowed on the construction site. It is off limits without Bost's permission."

When I make the announcement, someone objects, "Why? Why do we need *your* permission?"

I shake my head, smile, and assure the team, "It's nothing personal. Fowler Jones Construction asked me to do this for safety reasons. That way, someone will always know who's on the site. It limits liability."

Instead of agreeing with me, I see sideways glances.

It is during this construction phase, that I get a call from the senior pastor notifying me that he has met with a group of youth leaders on a Sunday evening. At that meeting they change the library at the Day School to a youth suite."

"What?" I ask.

"Is it going to be open as a library during school hours?"

"Nope. We're going to use it on Sundays and Wednesdays and then it will be off limits the rest of the time."

"You've got to be kidding," I say in frustration.

A few days later, I meet with a trusted associate for a frank discussion. I come to realize that my leadership style has now become a personnel issue with my peers.

In a large church setting, associate pastors each have a body of supporters. Alone, they have some power. Together, they wield considerable power.

This proof hits me like a slap in the face. But it is like the slap of a good friend, who demands that you face reality. I now clearly understand the most necessary skill set of a senior pastor—conflict management.

A CATALYST FOR CHANGE

For the first time, I am able to connect the dots of church culture. Looking back, I came to First Assembly with a dream for city-reaching. My assumption being that a large church—comprised of over 3000 members—would be helpful in my mission.

Until this moment, I didn't fully understand the filters that sector leaders use to manage risk and chaos. Whether in education, faith based sectors, nonprofits, marketplace or municipalities, each have their limitations when it comes to community. With the church: the best way to make a community better, is to enable the work of Christ in the lives of the community. People are at their best when they love God—and love good—and when they love other people.

The church, under the pressure of growth, can easily lose sight of its true mission—"to spread the Gospel." This always assures social justice. The church then, over time, can be lured into the need to attract attendees for revenue's sake, designing programs in order to bring people into the doors of the church.

Again, as my friend George Bullard would say (Life Cycle diagram is at the end of this chapter.), program and management have gotten into the front seat, where vision and relationship should better be! As long as the programs feed the church revenues, they are continued. When they cease to cause attendance and offerings to rise, they are often eliminated.

If I am allowed to be somewhat direct and to overly generalize, it can unknowingly become a matter of nickels and noses. The more noses at Sunday worship, the more nickels. The more nickels, the more on-campus programs, mostly necessary to meet the needs of the membership. It's a corollary perhaps to the public school's "Books, Buses and Butts." Neither truly engenders community.

Pretty soon, there are programs for single moms, youth sports, drama productions, men's ministries, puppets and clowns, five choirs, a book store, a prison ministry, a shut-in ministry, prime-timers seniors, support groups, foreign ministries, and more.

Churches mean well, with their Wal-Mart approach! All of these programs are wonderful—and there is nothing more moving than praise and worship with large choirs, full orchestras or even praise bands at a mega-church on Sunday morning. But churches can experience mission drift—if the programs or management slip into the driver's seat where community vision and relationship more rightfully belong.

When that happens, it is as if the church grows blinders—or becomes siloed. The church, though possibly offering lip service to community needs, may no longer see the need to serve *outside* of its walls. Eventually, she forfeits her role as PRIMARY COMMUNITY LEADER in nurturing cradle to grave "justice for all."

So, yes, it's helping thousands of people. But mainly, it's helping itself. It's helping the people that work for the church and that attend the church. This is not meant to sound as one standing outside throwing rocks at the church windows, for I understand the carrying costs of facilities brought on by standard church culture. If the nickels and noses begin to diminish, the very survival of the church may be at risk.

Admittedly, First Assembly does make some remarkable strides in social justice before, during, and after my seven years of full time employment. However, it is not without discomfort.

Like the proverbial new wine poured into old wine skins, these social reform programs—the senior complex and especially the outward-bound Southeast Winston preschool program—and yes, eventually the Day School, just never fully fit within the inward-bound nature of church culture.

A quote from Sam Pascoe, an American scholar comes to mind, "Christianity started out in Palestine as a fellowship; it moved to Greece and became a philosophy; it moved to Italy and became an institution; it moved to Europe and became a culture; *it came to America and became an enterprise.*"

I am beginning to understand that it is time for me to leave my post. Though I would be engaged by all three future senior pastors, my next window of service is coming into focus.

This time, Pastor Ron McManus supports my decision. He himself will eventually leave his charge.

The Life Cycle and Stages of Congregational Development

Phase One: Early Growth
- Birth (Vrpm)
- Infancy (VRpm)
- Childhood (VrPm)

Phase Two: Late Growth
- Adolescence (VRpm)
- Adulthood (VRPM)

Phase Three: Prime/Plateau
- Maturity (vRPM)

Phase Four: Early Aging
- Empty Nest (vRpM)
- Retirement (vrPM)

Phase Five: Late Aging
- Old Age (vrpM)
- Death (m)

Growth | **Prime** | **Redevelopment** | **Aging**

V: Vision/Leadership/Mission/Purpose/Core Values
R: Relationships/Experiences/Discipleship
P: Programs/Events/Ministries/Services/Activities
M: Management/Accountability/Systems/Resources

Copyright 2001, Rev. George Bullard, D.Min.

Courtesy of George Bullard   BullardJournal@gmail.com

TIME TO MAKE A CHANGE

Learnings from Sector II

1.) Remember to use your 3 brains. First, listen to your "gut"—that hunch some call discernment. Then, make sure it aligns with your "heart"—your sense of values and calling. Lastly, check in with your "head"—to evaluate your risk tolerance. Then act accordingly!

2.) Look for a cause, an opportunity that is meaningful to you. You should always be growing as a person and as a professional.

3.) When you enter a new sector—listen intently, especially among your peers—know that all sectors come with their own risk filters and tolerances. It takes time to learn the new "language," so be patient with yourself and others.

4.) In all organizations, pay attention to the people just as much as assigned tasks. For a quick study, read *Situational Leadership* by Paul Hersey and Kenneth Blanchard.

5.) Move at the speed of the group. Consensus is critical.

6.) Real leaders tell the truth—even if it means taking a hit.

7.) Life's not about equal giving—it's about equal sacrifice. The more you've been blessed with—talents, assets, ideas—the more you share.

8.) "Impossible" problems require a both/and solution.

9.) Plan your exits as well as your entries.

Sector III

Business

Bost takes his values to the marketplace—commonly known as the world of business. Realizing that his position as owner of Master Counsel, Inc., makes him the product— Bost takes action to raise his self-awareness and define his quest—thus improving his potency as a catalyst for positive change. He specifically seeks out business opportunities that align with his core value to make life better for everyone. In the process, Bost builds a tight and trusted network with leaders in all five sectors.

Chapter 19

A Call for Courage

When I place my letter of resignation on his desk, my good friend and pastor asks, "How are you going to feed your family?"

Pastor Ron asks this in all sincerity. He knows that I need to be true to my calling—to foster significant community impact in our city. However, he also knows that this is the worst possible timing for me to make a move.

I'm in the middle of building a house—so it will be very difficult to secure a mortgage without a job. Plus, I'll be losing my tax-free housing allowance—a perk for ordained ministers working in a church—and I'll be paying my own gas from now on.

I tell him, "I have a company that's called Master Counsel."

What I don't tell him is that this name—Master Counsel—comes to me in the middle of the night. As always, I grab the pen and paper next to my bedside and write it down. Later, Attorney Ed Green helps me incorporate the company. What I really have—at this moment—is a corporate shield or a shell, with absolutely no contracts.

"What does your company do?" he asks.

"I'll do the same thing for others that I have been doing for you," I say confidently.

He stands and flexes his shoulders as he tries on this unexpected idea like a new sports coat.

Then, he walks around to the other side of his desk, sits in his chair, and asks, "Can you do something for me?"

"What do you have in mind?"

"Can you continue to give oversight and secure funding for First Start (Living Water Family Resource Center preschool program)?"

"Well certainly," I say matter-of-factly, "this is the kind of work that Master Counsel will be doing."

"How much will you charge me?" he asks.

A CATALYST FOR CHANGE

"I figure that I'll need $4000 per month to live on. So, I'll charge $1000 a month for each contract. My goal—with the help of an administrative assistant— is to manage 10 contracts," I explain.

"Only one thousand dollars a month?" he repeats more to himself than to me. He then adds, "I have another request as well."

He and another benefactor of the church have been engaged in the prospective relocation for the Assemblies of God District office to Selma, NC.

He asks, "Do you think you could also manage the Selma project?"

"Sure," I say with a smile. I had no clue what was in store.

Now, you'd think that I'd be really happy. I'm fully committed to my new career. Additionally, I not only have Pastor Ron's blessing, I have his full financial support. Interestingly, about a year later, he'll leave First Assembly to join John Maxwell's non-profit business—EQUIP—which develops "Level 5" church leaders.

Soon, though I had acquired two other similar contracts—the dagger of doubt begins to stab at my heart. What have I done? Did I really trade an $80,000 a year job—when I account for the tax perks—for $48,000 a year? Where do I plan to operate this business? I don't have my house finished yet, my current home has sold and I can't afford to pay rent for office space.

Suddenly, Master Counsel's bright sunny prospects look as dark as a moonless night. In panic, I search for solid ground—another job that I can count on while I grow Master Counsel on the side.

Almost as if by a miracle, I hear that Jim Simeon is leaving his post as superintendent of the Lexington City Schools. With my Ed.S. degree in hand, along with 20 years of relationships and a stellar reputation in that town—I make up my mind to apply.

However, before submitting my application, I make one phone call.

"Becky, this is John Bost," I say to Assistant Superintendent Bloxom. She grew up in the Lexington City Schools, has a real passion for education, and I'd helped her advance from assistant principal to a place on Jim Simeon's leadership team before I'd left the district.

I can hear genuine joy in her voice as she responds, "John, how are you?"

After a bit of catching up, I pop the question, "Are you planning to apply for the superintendent's position?"

"I am," she says excitedly.

After assuring her of my support, I hang up. I will not compete against my mentee. That would go against one of my core values—others-orientedness. But it would also go against my moral imperative—doing the right thing, because it's the right thing to do. If I go back to public education knowing full well that it cannot further my calling—well, that's the wrong thing to do.

And in that moment, I realize what I am doing. I am flirting with the idea of choosing comfort over courage. In doing a quick reexamination, I find that my three brains align—in regards to moving from the religious sector to the private sector, the marketplace. Master Counsel would remain a for-profit company!

And yet, the dark side—the period of time when one door closes (resigning from First Assembly) and the other door has yet to open (Master Counsel as a sustainable business)—can be nearly unbearable.

So, I try yet another quick fix. Wake Forest University School of Divinity posts an opening. I'm on good terms with the administration and we begin a conversation. However, in short order, it becomes apparent that I'm—again— running away from my calling.

I make up my mind—that like an unhatched chick within the darkness of the shell—I will stay true to my calling until a breakthrough occurs. Almost instantly, providence moves in my favor. Lester Burnett—a wealthy businessman who owns the nearly vacated Wachovia Bank building—has heard about my city-reaching mission. He offers me a glassed-in corner office on the 24th floor—complete with telephone and furnishing—*at no charge*.

Why does he do this? Simply put—he believes in my mission and he knows my reputation. That's called *social capital*—which has little to do with money. Actually, there's more to that story and you can find it in my first book entitled, *Repo: The Church in Foreclosure*.

I'd met Lester a few years earlier when Dr. Mark Corts and I were trying to establish a private high school—via First Start, Inc. We were looking at the old Arista Mills property in Southeast Winston-Salem—

A CATALYST FOR CHANGE

so that like our preschool program—this high school could have the greatest impact.

It turns out that our idea was simply ahead of its time. Today, the Carter G. Woodson School—a K-12 public charter school—graces this site. Owing its existence to the unwavering determination of African-American Attorney Hazel Mack— this school serves a student body that is 41% African-American and 57% Hispanic.

About 90% of the students are eligible for Free Lunch—indicating that it is attracting the traditionally under-resourced population. This is exactly the population that Attorney Mack fought for during her 35 years at a non-profit law firm. There is no doubt in my mind, that she was the right person for this opportunity.

Back to my perch on the 24th floor—as I look out the floor-to-ceiling glass—directly below me rooftops and roads at first appear to be fixed—like a giant jigsaw puzzle. But this topography is alive. Sometimes slowly, like when someone plants a tree, and sometimes quickly—like when a fire devours a building—change is always happening.

As I level my chin, I can see First Assembly of God, past Wake Forest University, and all the way to Pilot Mountain—26 miles away. Suddenly, any bumps and bruises I've suffered in the past pale into insignificance when I realize all that lies ahead.

Lastly, I gaze heavenward.

I hear that voice again in my heart that I first heard in 1978 saying, "Wherever I send you, seek (the welfare of) that city! If not this city, the next."

In prayerful contemplation—I seek clarification. What does it mean to *seek* or *reach* a city? How can I best invest my time and resources to *unite* the community? And, how can I make a significant difference in the *social justice*—improving opportunities for people of all colors and creeds to excel.

The answer, it seems, is buried in the past. The secret is rooted deeply in the founding of Salem, which later becomes Winston-Salem.

Chapter 20

A Quick History Lesson

One year prior to my resignation from First Assembly, Kevin Frack—the pastor at Ardmore Moravian Church— and eight of his church elders request a meeting.

After we are seated in the boardroom, I ask, "Why are you here?"

Kevin responds with a question.

"Can you teach us how to reach the city?"

I weep.

Kevin explains that from their vantage point, it looks like First Assembly is growing, diversified, and making a difference in our community. Ardmore, on the other hand, is desperate, dying, and distanced from its changing neighborhood—with a substantial Hispanic influx.

Over the course of the next several months, Kevin takes me on a virtual pilgrimage—later serving as my guide in the Czech Republic —to trace the roots of Winston-Salem. As a descendant of the town founders, he is the best man for the job. From this exploration, we crack the code on how to reach a city—how to bring social justice for all. Hint: It has little to do with churches.

Salem—the root-stock of Winston-Salem—is founded on November 17, 1753, when 15 Moravians—German-speaking Protestants—arrive on foot from their settlement in Bethlehem, Pennsylvania. They purchase 100,000 acres of land—the Wachovia tract.

Their purpose in coming to America is simple. They are missionaries from what is now the Czech Republic. Their objective is not to build a church, but rather a sovereign city. In fact, *they find organized religion to be oppressive and divisive.*

Instead, they want to *build a vocationally sustainable community* founded upon solid principles. In their minds, the best road map to justice is inscribed in the gospel of Jesus. Specifically, they believe that if everyone practices the love of God (adhering to the Bible's moral/ethical standards), and imitates Jesus' self-sacrificing love—in which he even loves his enemies—the result will be social justice for all.

This vision—that ultimately moves the Moravians to cross the Atlantic Ocean—is forged centuries earlier, by many oppressive blows over several generations. Ideologically, John Wycliffe—of England—takes the first beating in the 1300s.

Wycliffe commands an international platform. He's a professor at Oxford University, a Catholic priest—the only legal religion in the Holy Roman Empire— and chaplain to the King of England.

From that stage, he preaches the following messages of reform: The Bible is the only source of truth—not the Pope or Church hierarchy. The Church should give away its wealth—even as the apostles were poor—and feed the sheep rather than fleece the sheep. The sale of indulgences—paying money to have punishment for sins shortened or eliminated—is unscriptural. Justice is only possible when all people can read the Bible in their own language.

To make that a reality, John Wycliffe leads the *first translation of the Bible into English.* Then, his followers—poor priests labeled Lollards—preach and distribute sections of the English Bible to the common people in England.

In retaliation, the Church labels Wycliffe a heretic, removes him from his post at Oxford, and threatens any and all who preach his message or even listen to it. Offenders are labeled heretics, excommunicated from the Catholic Church—and sometimes tortured and murdered.

Wycliffe dies from a stroke in 1384, leaving behind hundreds of documents that convict the Church. Seventeen years later, his teachings fall into the hands of John Huss—850 miles west in what is now the Czech Republic.

Huss, a Catholic priest and dean at the University of Prague, picks up where Wycliffe left off. In fact, a lithograph—in the still standing Huss house—says, "Wycliffe struck the spark. Huss lit the candle. Luther wielded the torch."

Like Wycliffe, Huss makes the Bible available to his people in their Czech language. However, instead of taking the Bible to the countryside, he focuses on *the marketplace.* Under his tutelage, common businessmen

A QUICK HISTORY LESSON

can hear the gospel and *apply its ethics to their business practices and daily life.*

In an effort to support Huss, his followers build Bethlehem Chapel in Prague. This isn't so much a church—with traditions, songs, and tithing—as a gathering place to learn. At times, Huss speaks to over 3,000 people.

As they did to his mentor, Wycliffe, the Catholic Church continually hammers Huss with harassment and accusations of heresy. This only makes him bolder—though he does flee to the safety of the countryside. There, he continues to write and speak for the common man.

Unfortunately, he is lured back into harm's way, when the Church—presumably wishing to heal its religious dissensions in England and the now Czech Republic— invites Huss to *The Council of Constance* in Germany.

Sadly, instead of allowing him to defend his beliefs—via the Bible—the Catholic Church gives him an ultimatum. Recant, repent, and cease to oppose the Church or be burned at the stake. Huss chooses to stay true to his conscience.

On July 6, 1415, John Huss is burned at the stake. Strategically, the Church uses the writings of John Wycliffe as kindling for the Huss fire and sends a strong message. Anyone owning a Bible—other than in the dead language of Latin—or promoting Church reform will not be tolerated.

Before breathing his last breath, Huss utters, "In 100 years, God will raise up a man whose calls for reform cannot be suppressed."

Legend plays upon Huss' last name—which means goose in the Czech language—for he likely prophesies as he speaks to the crowd, "They will roast a goose now, but after 100 years they will hear a swan sing, and him they will endure."

Either way, true to his prophecy, in 1517, Martin Luther nails his 95 points of protest against the Roman Catholic Church onto the church door at Wittenberg.

In the meantime, Huss followers—called Hussites—prove to be as tenacious as their namesake. In response, the Church hounds Hussite reformers, driving them underground and unknowingly hardening them into one of the sharpest swords against injustice.

In fact, in literal sword craftsmanship, using the shita-kitae method—by repeatedly heating, beating, and folding steel into itself—impurities are eliminated, the ability to endure stress and resist bending is maximized, and an unmistakable grain pattern graces the entire blade.

Within 40 years, vicious persecution pummels these people into one of the most formidable societies—formally organized as "Unity of the Brethren."

As the name implies, *they are determined to avoid a hierarchy of religious power.* Instead, *each person* will be guided solely by "the gospel and example of our Lord Jesus Christ and his holy apostles in gentleness, humility, patience, and love for our enemy."

Additionally, proof of being a Christian does not depend on doctrine or stated belief, "but that a person lives(d) his or her life according to the teachings of Jesus Christ."

By the time Luther comes onto the world scene, the "Unity of the Brethren"—now known as Moravians—numbers 200,000. Bitter persecution continues—climaxing in the brutal Thirty Years' War from 1618-1648—and eventually driving some Moravians north to Saxony, Germany.

There—in 1722— they find refuge on the estate of Count Nicholas Ludwig Von Zinzendorf. The Moravians build the community of Herrnhut –meaning "the Lord's Watch"—but they are fraught with conflicts and divisions among themselves.

Count Zinzendorf pleads with them to focus on their points of agreement and pray about everything else. They begin a 24-hour prayer vigil—in which various brethren sign up for one-hour of prayer around the clock. Amazingly, this continues—unbroken—for 100 years.

The result is similar to the final step in forging a sword. The hammering stops. The steel is plunged into cold water. That sudden cooling brings the molecules—in this case the brethren—rapidly together, creating an unprecedented *bond of unity* among the people.

That moment in time is commemorated today as the Love Feast. It was in a very extraordinary spiritual moment duly recorded in history,

A QUICK HISTORY LESSON

that the "Holy Spirit descended" so much so that those praying refused to leave the small Lutheran Church, food being brought in for their sustenance.

They create a model theocratic community—where Bible principles permeate every aspect of daily life—marketplace, family, governance, education, worship, and outreach. Then, they duplicate that model as they spread their message around the world.

Their goal: "To bring the good news of God's infinite love to the poorest, most despised people of the world." That includes slaves and Native Americans. Hence, their arrival in North Carolina in 1753.

It should be noted that at this time, these mission minded followers of Huss have spoken out against the racism of slavery; some even selling themselves to slave ships to minister on the treacherous journey that lay ahead for souls stacked belly to belly like cord wood! This explains the disproportionate numbers of Moravian descendants in the islands that served as ports of entry for slave ships.

Back to North Carolina—bonded by shared values imprinted on their hearts deeper than any DNA, the Moravians establish Salem, North Carolina. It is a *marketplace community*—based on the Herrnhut model—where *love of God is expressed by excellent workmanship and placing the good of all above the interest of the individual.*

In this Moravian community of craftsmen—carpenters, tanners, jewelers, farmers, tailors, millers, and more—"everyone contributes(d) according to ability and takes (took) according to need."

Residents are cared for from cradle to grave—with housing, meaningful work, education for *girls* and boys, healthcare, art, music, and spiritual edification. Native Americans and African Americans are vital to the congregation.

Within 20 years, Salem establishes itself as a regional center for trade. Outsiders travel 50 miles or more to purchase Moravian goods from people who believe that *the quality of their work and the way that they treat their fellowman* is their worship to God.

By 1849, the county of Forsyth forms. Being the largest and most prosperous city, Salem is offered the opportunity to serve as the county seat and establish the Court House. However, it declines to bring "worldly" or "political" entities into its spiritual sanctum.

Instead, the town elders sell 31 acres—one mile north of Salem—to the County Commissioners. The new city of Winston—named after Revolutionary War Colonel Joseph Winston—is born. Winston will serve as the county seat.

However, it seems that in less than 100 years, the Moravians—who detested the control and manipulations of the Catholic Church—has gradually grown top heavy with unscriptural rules and hierarchy that so dominates the common man.

For instance, the Church owns all the land, sets price controls on goods, and plays a role in where you live, your trade choices, and even who you marry! Essentially, Salem devolves from a *successful faith-based marketplace community* to a restrictive Church-dominated town where power and money are in the hands of a few.

Inevitably, Moravians begin to move to nearby Winston. With the handwriting on the wall—in 1857—the Church elders divest control of the city, allowing residents to purchase property. In doing this, shrinking Salem becomes a legal municipality—destined to become a living history museum.

Thus, the Moravian Church settles into denominational life—with worship more defined by what happens within the *church walls* rather than in the *marketplace*. Sadly, the original mission— *where the love of God is expressed by excellent workmanship and placing the good of all above the interest of the individual*—fades into virtual non-existence.

Note, it is *this original mission embraced in each person's heart*— and NOT the church—that holds the key to sustainable social justice.

In the meantime, the young city of Winston proves to be a magnet for capitalism. This is especially true once the railroad reaches the town in 1873. The following year, Richard Joshua "RJ" Reynolds—a 24-year-old entrepreneur in tobacco—moves to Winston and begins building his empire.

Soon after that, James Alexander Gray, Sr. and others found Wachovia Bank—which becomes one of the largest banks in the area.

A QUICK HISTORY LESSON

Then, in the early 1900s, the P. H. Hanes family boldly moves out of tobacco and into textiles—manufacturing hosiery and underwear.

Lastly, Bowman Gray, Sr.—a college dropout—works his way up the ranks from salesman in 1895 to president of RJ Reynolds in 1924. His trust fund will later bring Wake Forest University (initially named Bowman Gray School of Medicine) to Winston-Salem (the twin cities officially merged in 1913).

In the midst of this (1890), Winston is so progressive that Simon Green Atkins—an African-American leader—founds Slater Normal and Industrial School—a school for African Americans—which became Winston-Salem Teachers College— now known as Winston-Salem State University.

In 1925—chiefly due to the successes of the Hanes, Reynolds, and Gray families— Winston-Salem is declared "The City of Millionaires." It is the largest city in North Carolina. And, America's spotlight shines proudly on its achievement: Winston-Salem is home to the largest manufacturer of tobacco products and men's knit underwear.

The Twin Cities success continues until the 1980s. At that time, textile manufacturing begins to move offshore. Then, in 1988, RJR Nabisco (a merger of Nabisco Brands and RJ Reynolds Tobacco Company) falls victim to Wall Street's largest hostile takeover—a $25 billion leveraged buyout—by Kohlberg Kravis Roberts & Co. In the following two decades, manufacturing jobs—the driving force in the economy—plummet by 39%.

It is in the midst of this economic decline—1997—that I begin Master Counsel. Having already proven to myself that public education and church alone are not the roadways to social justice—I'm determined to reach the city the John Huss way. I'm taking *my Christian values to the marketplace.*

However, before going too far—I take steps to strengthen my business network, understand human nature, and define my quest.

A CATALYST FOR CHANGE

Chapter 21

Sharpening My Saw

"You invited the fox into the hen-house! Why did you do that?"

John Anderson—VP of Finance and Administration at Wake Forest University—chuckles as he recounts the conversation between himself and WFU President Thomas K. Hearn Jr.

Anderson has invited me to attend his graduate-level negotiations class, at the very time that the university is attempting to purchase First Assembly.

Anderson and I—each involved on opposite sides of this soon to prove premature transaction with First Assembly—want to each see how the other man thinks! (About 23 years later, WFU did purchase the church property.)

It had been a few years earlier—in 1995—that Anderson and I first met. The campus Chief of Police had inquired about shared parking for off campus students. By 1997, I had resigned from First Assembly, but would be a primary negotiator when the next senior pastor took serious a conversation about acquisition. In fact, I would serve as a consultant to the church for about 18 years through four senior pastors.

In the throes of framing a new business, any tools within my reach are treasured. At this point, I am the only product my company has to offer. The challenge is to prepare, position, and package myself! It's all about communication, and my experience at First Assembly has made me acutely aware of my blind spots.

So as Warren Buffet would later advise, "Invest in yourself. The one easy way to become worth 50 percent more than you are now at least is to hone your communication skills—both written and verbal. If you can't communicate, it's like winking at a girl in the dark—nothing happens. You can have all the brainpower in the world, but you have to be able to transmit it. And the transmission is communication."

In response, I'm actively seeking self-awareness training and awareness of others at the very time that Anderson is offering an

Enneagram class. So, I enroll in that too, not only for the content but to enrich our relationship, which continues to this day.

The Enneagram inventory, much like the DISC and Myers-Briggs from my graduate study days, isolates nine distinct personality types based on shared perceptual filters, focus of attention, and funneling of energy. By understanding these personality types, I gain more awareness of my own "type" and the eight other types that I will be potentially coaching in my business.

Based on my responses, I am —Type-1, a Reformer with an almost balanced wing of 9. As Anderson explains this type to the class, it is as if he is reading my mail.

It's true: I feel most loved and worthy when I'm being good, righting wrongs, and meeting or exceeding expectations. At the same time, I resent "bad behavior" and impulsiveness—which can actually trigger feelings of anger inside me.

Of course, similar inventories were a part of my graduate work, such as the DISC—**D**rive, **I**nfluence, **S**teadiness, **C**ompliance—four behavior types of typical people.

I'm a combination of both D&I, Initiator (DI) — "likely to be an assertive, optimistic leader, who is comfortable with taking necessary risks and can drive others to take action." Adding yet another layer of understanding, is the Myers Briggs Assessment. This system identifies 16 personality types using the following code. **I**ntrovert/**E**xtrovert; **S**ensory/I**n**tuitive; **T**hinking/**F**eeling; **P**erceptive/**J**udging.

On the Myers Briggs—my score is evenly split between EN**T**J—known as the "commander"—and EN**F**J, known as the "teacher." Both are leaders, but the latter is more concerned with leading people than leading projects.

Now you would think that this would be enough research to fill my need to "do my business right"—but the same year that I take the Enneagram class, I reach out to George Bullard.

Bullard—a tried and true Baptist—is already doing what I want to do—coaching and organizational development—but on a global scale. He understands the importance of identifying personalities and uses Self-Awareness profiles as one of his coaching tools.

SHARPENING MY SAW

Enneagram

The best summation of the Enneagram is: *"Every single person has access to all nine numbers. Based on nature, nurture, and discipline, you express the values of each number at varying degrees of intensity based on your lived experience."*

TYPE	PRIMARY VALUE	CORE MOTIVATOR
1 Reformer	Justice	Being Good / Right
2 Helper	Appreciation	Being Loved / Wanted
3 Achiever	Accomplishment	Being Valuable / Successful
4 Individualist	Creativity	Being Authentic / Unique
5 Investigator	Clarity	Being Competent / Capable
6 Loyalist	Guarantees	Being Secure / Safe
7 Enthusiast	Experiences	Being Satisfied / Content
8 Challenger	Autonomy	Being Self-Governed / Independent
9 Peacemaker	Serenity	Being at Peace / Harmonious

DISC

Four behavior types of typical people.

Drive—outgoing and task oriented
Influence—outgoing and people oriented
Steadiness—reserved and people oriented
Compliance—reserved and task oriented

Myers-Briggs Type Indicator

16 psychological preferences based on 8 personality indicators

Introvert/**E**xtrovert   **S**ensory/**In**tuitive
Thinking/**F**eeling   **P**erceptive/**J**udging

(Free tests are available online. See Appendix for more details.)
For more information visit www.JohntheCatalyst.com

A CATALYST FOR CHANGE

In one of my early Internet searches—pre-Google—I reach out to Bullard. Though he typically limits his assessments for groups that he is coaching, Bullard agrees to do an individual assessment for me for $90. That's a bit pricey for my startup budget, but my gut told me to proceed.

My biggest discovery is some people mainly think with the front quadrant of their brain, where *conception* takes place. Here the brain compares concepts, creates meaning, asks "why," sees the "Big Picture," and imagines future possibilities. This is where I do my thinking.

Other people think with the back of their brain, where *perception* takes place. Here is where the brain processes information from the five senses, identifies "what is," stays in the present, and decides what is practical and "real."

Still others predominately think with the left-side of their brains. Here the brain makes judgments based on *logic,* analysis, reason, calculations, and scientific methods.

John Bost
Master Counsel, Inc.

Lastly, some people are more right-brained thinkers. Here instinct, intuition, gut-feeling, sensitivities, needs, free associations, and values yield decisions in the form of *feelings*.

The big takeaway is that all four thinking patterns are valuable and all four patterns have blind spots. So Bullard recommends that people "stretch" to practice using the three patterns that feel less natural, and build a team of differently dominate thinkers.

Interestingly, about this time, I'd reconnected with Rick Smyre—an internationally known futurist and current president of the *Center for*

Communities of the Future. He comes from the opposite perspective of Bullard. Whereas Bullard is all about church, Smyre—though raised Presbyterian—is leaning toward agnosticism.

Out of curiosity, I invite them to dine with me in Charlotte—on my dime. Then, I sit back and listen. Both are interested in transformation, but Smyre believes that it can happen without religion. In other words, truth is truth no matter where you find it.

Bullard disagrees. Though he does use coaching—rather than disciplining—his work is still God-centered.

Amazingly, that "chance" meeting eventually leads to the three of us serving on a nine-member board. With Bullard at the helm, in 2001, we are able to secure a $1.6 million dollar, three year, Lilly Endowment Grant for *Sustaining Pastoral Excellence* at the Hollifield Leadership Center near Hickory, NC. *Sustaining Pastoral Excellence* is a certification process in Christian Leadership Coaching—serving virtually all Christian denominations

As you might guess, I earn my certification and begin coaching pastors and later business people—as part of Master Counsel. However, if my ultimate goal is to bring social justice through the marketplace, then I need to establish better connections with marketplace leaders.

A CATALYST FOR CHANGE

Chapter 22

Networking

Shortly before leaving my post at the Church, I enroll in Leadership Winston-Salem, class of 1997. This program—sometimes called "a community MBA"—attracts emerging leaders and lets them interact with key community leaders.

In the process, participants come to understand the city's biggest challenges around race, geography, and economics. Additionally—as you might guess—the program includes self-awareness, conflict management, and leadership opportunities.

Though I'm 48 and have worked in Winston-Salem for seven years, this seems to be the best way to learn more about the community. Simultaneously, it will facilitate the development of high quality and enduring relationships. After all, if I'm going to be a player in social justice to the city—through the marketplace—then I'd better clearly understand the issues.

So, as a class of 56—the number of people that can fit on a city bus—we meet from 7:30 a.m. to 5:00 p.m. once a month—splitting our time between the classroom interaction, and meeting corporate and community leaders.

In the process, we visit what is often most promoted on behalf of Winston-Salem—the arts, the parks, the universities, the marketplace, and the historic heritage. And we see what is often unseen—sadly mostly east of Highway 52—the impact of poverty, racism, crime, underemployment, inadequate housing, and the lack of a clear path to change.

Some say that this division was unintentional, given that industrial communities were normally built on a topographical ridge. In Winston-Salem we call that Main Street. Because factories were coal fired and prevailing winds blew the smoke eastward—the "haves" settle in the west. That left the less desirable east for the "have-nots" and

A CATALYST FOR CHANGE

warehouse like facilities. This didn't just happen in Winston-Salem. It happened across the country.

The question is: How can we change such a deeply entrenched problem? In one of our Leadership Winston-Salem class session, this is expertly addressed by Barry Johnson, Ph.D. He tackles *Identifying and Managing Unsolvable Problems* and proves to us that unsolvable problems—with opposing solutions—can be *managed*.

To illustrate this, Dr. Johnson, uses the example of inhale/exhale polarity. If we decide *only to inhale*, we will get much needed oxygen, but carbon dioxide will build up. If we decide *only to exhale*, we will clear out the carbon dioxide, but we won't have sufficient oxygen. The problem of breathing can't be *solved* by choosing one OR the other. However, the problem can be *managed* by choosing to engage in inhaling AND exhaling—first one, then the other, and repeat—thereby *managing* the problem with a both/and solution!

Applying this to social injustice: Privileged whites want to maintain stability—to keep things as they are—but this results in missed opportunities and social unrest. The under-resourced, predominately African-Americans in our city, want to change the system—to work for livable wages and to have increased opportunities to contribute to their town—but change results in loss of continuity and altered core values.

The problem of social injustice *can't be solved* by maintaining the status quo (stability) OR by enacting radical change. Instead, it can be best *resolved* by incremental small changes, stabilized over short blocks of time by means of evaluation and adjustment—repeated over and over again.

This education-based program—Leadership Winston-Salem—traces its roots back to Wake Forest University. Way back in 1983, Julius Corpening, Development Director at Wake Forest University, and local business man, Ed Pleasants spearheaded a task force to see if a community leadership program would benefit the town, particularly with regards to the racial challenges of this city. In fact, to this day, we struggle as to whether their goals have been attained.

NETWORKING

In 1984, the Chamber of Commerce acted on its recommendation and offered the first class of Leadership Winston-Salem. Thomas K. Hearn Jr., the newly hired president at Wake Forest University—who began a leadership program in Birmingham—signed on as the first chairman of Leadership Winston-Salem.

The University continues to believe in the program, supporting it not only financially, but also in manpower. I am so benefited by the program, that I also stay involved for the next 20 years.

In fact, in 2009, when current Vice Chairman Bob Parker—a vice president of Wake Forest University Baptist Medical Center—can no longer serve, he says, "Put John Bost in my spot."

So, I fill the post, later serving as chairman in 2010-2011. It proves to be perfect timing for a Reformer who likes to fix things.

Earlier, in 2003, corporate sponsors begin to pull funding from the program. Why? The man who's hired to inform, educate, and motivate participants about white privilege and racism—which affects minorities including women—is challenged by those who feel he is using his soapbox to brutally humiliate and alienate the whites. Hence, funding from corporations, most led by white males, dries up.

In all fairness, most local C-level people had by now participated in the program, or if new to the community, had experienced similar programs now available in most cities. Others may have not have felt the responsibility to mentor grassroots leaders—those who would one day fill critical leadership roles—to the degree of the programs' original founders.

We take a year off—a hiatus for 2003—to "address the challenges." Some would call it conflict avoidance when it comes to race, still the problem to this day. In short, we replace the presenter, establish mandatory Action Learning Projects—pairing teams of participants with non-profits facing a real-time dilemma—and look for new funding sources. But we never quite solve the problem!

So, in 2011, instead of going out to solicit funding, our then Executive Director Jo Ellen Carson and I, seek permission from the board to meet with top corporate executives to solicit their advice. In other words, *I'm building relationships—trusting that the money will follow.*

In the midst of our 12-month listening tour, it becomes apparent that virtually all the corporations have in-house leadership programs.

So, I begin to ask, "What is it we can do that will give your direct reports an opportunity to learn our community—because they are coming in from the outside?"

The answer: A 12-week program—versus the 9-month flagship version—that is invitation only for senior executives and their direct reports. Additionally, they want facilitated peer-to peer dialogue centering on *gap visioning*—where we are, where we want to be, and how to get there—with a bias toward action. We name it INSIGHT.

When Carson and I take this recommendation to the board, we are met with resistance. In essence, the board asks, "How can you ask for another program, when we can't even sustain the one we've got?"

However, once we crunch the numbers—with tuition for our premier INSIGHT being considerably higher than our flagship tuition—it becomes clear that INSIGHT will pay for itself and part of the Flagship program too.

INSIGHT is launched in 2012 and continues to bring together some of the best hearts and minds in Winston-Salem—for the betterment of the community.

In between all of this—just to highlight the value of relationships –it was a Leadership Winston-Salem connection that saved my hide in 2008. Who could guess, that on the very day that my partners in an initiative were scheduled to close on a $2.5 million loan with Wachovia Bank—the bank would be acquired by Wells Fargo. All impending deals are canceled. So there I sit—with Wachovia's top loan executive from Charlotte—and she is as devastated as I am.

As the clock is ticking on my much needed venture capital, I'm scanning my memory bank for a Plan B. Suddenly, an official from Lexington State Bank comes to mind. We'd formed a budding relationship when he attended Leadership Winston-Salem, because we both have an interest in leadership and my old stomping grounds—Lexington.

NETWORKING

Based on that relationship—and the personal trust established—he "walks" or should I say "runs" the loan through the approval process and closes the deal. I'm convinced that without our LWS relationship, we never would have gotten through the door.

Back to launching my business, by 1998, it's all systems go—except that I have not built my rocket. In other words, I have all my new tools, marketplace connections, experience, and ideals, but my vehicle for delivery—Master Counsel—is still undefined.

However, as happens so often, when we take action and do all we can—Providence comes around to find us. Seemingly out of nowhere, I receive an invitation to attend a Quest conference.

It calls to mind a quote from William Hutchinson Murray who said: "Concerning all acts of initiative and creation, there is one elementary truth the ignorance of which kills countless ideas and splendid plans: that the moment one definitely commits oneself, then providence moves too."

A CATALYST FOR CHANGE

Chapter 23

Defining My Quest

"John Bost?"

"Yes."

"This is Jim Lord. You purchased 30 copies of my book *The Raising of Money*. I'm curious as to why."

Utterly astonished, I briefly describe the Selma project—one of the two contracts from Pastor Ron—and our desire to acquire and convert a vineyard into The Southland Leadership Center for Excellence for the North Carolina District of Assemblies of God. I distributed his book to everyone on our team.

In response, he says, "I want to invite you to a Quest Gathering in Sedona, Arizona in March (1998). Our mission is simple: Quest is a consortium of change agents with a profound reverence for the high calling—which is philanthropy. Its agents are known for their integrity and respect for the human spirit, compelled by a passion and hope for a better, more secure future. Can you attend?"

He's ringing my bells. Still, I ask, "Why are you inviting *me*?"

"I'm inviting change-agents from different religions— and even some non-religious leaders— and I don't have a Pentecostal. The idea is to find our common ground, get beyond the issues that divide us, and share best practices so that we can create the world that we want. I want your point of view as part of our process," he says.

In doing a quick self-check, my three brains—gut, heart, and head—all line up.

"Okay, I'll be there," I confirm.

Then, he says, "There's only one catch, John. You have to have skin in the game. It's going to cost you $3500—plus transportation—for the five-day Quest. That includes everything—meals, rooms, and materials."

Suddenly, my "head" drops out of the lineup.

A CATALYST FOR CHANGE

My internal risk manager is telling me, "You only have $15,000 cash to your name. That's your *entire* safety net. You have a wife and your daughter has already planned a mission trip to Mexico. NOW is not the right time for Quest."

However, instead of listening to my internal voice, I confirm, "I'll be there."

Then, my heart joins my head in growing resistance to this decision.

A voice within me says, "How are you going to explain this to the love of your life? Just last year—when you quit your job—LaDonna gave you that special Valentines Card. The one with the little boy—dressed like a man—and the little girl—dressed like a woman, walking down the sidewalk with a suitcase. She wrote on the card, 'The Journey Begins.' But this—expecting her to agree that spending $3500 on a "gut feeling"—is asking too much of her."

So, I didn't tell LaDonna. Instead, I waited—without telling a soul. A few days later, Chris Shandra—whom I'd come to know while he was starting a restaurant in Burnette's building, the Winston Tower about a year earlier—came to see me on the 24th Floor.

He said, "I feel like I'm supposed to give you this."

"What is it?"

"It's $3500. My business is doing well and I just felt like the Lord laid it on my heart to give this to you," he said.

Immediately, my head and heart jumped back into alignment. With the money in hand, I have no problem explaining Quest to LaDonna and garnering her full support.

Quest proves to be everything and more that Jim Lord promises. We arrive as 20 strangers from around the world. There are leaders—true gurus—as lofty as the World Relief organizers, Buddhists priests from Scotland, and a Shaman from South America. And then there is me—lowly John Bost. I feel like a lion in a den of Daniels.

This actually was my first exposure to Appreciative Inquiry, a term that would later be reinforced by the Action Learning Process with Leadership Winston-Salem. Our assignment for the week: We must share our beliefs, but we must refrain from proselytizing or in any way

DEFINING MY QUEST

Appreciative Inquiry (AI)

When we genuinely come to know other people's dreams, goals, and desires—something called Appreciative Inquiry—*we add value to their lives and to their calling. AI can also unite people in a shared vision.*

Discovery: Open your eyes and really see the best of what is—the strengths, the practices, the accomplishments.

Dream: Open your imagination to envision the possibilities—the future you want by being true to your core values and strategic objectives.

Design: Gather the resources to build the bridge to close the gap—guided by the **d**iscovery and the **d**ream.

Deploy: Assign who needs to do what, by when—and take action.

Repeat and revise (adaptive planning) as needed.

Six AI Questions

1) What led you to where you are now?
2) What are your mountaintop moments?
3) What do you value most?
4) What is changing?
5) What is the best future you can imagine?
6) What will it take to bridge the gap?

https://en.m.wikipedia.org/wiki/Appreciative_inquiry
For more information visit www.JohntheCatalyst.com

disrespecting another person. Over the course of the five days, we use the 4-D Appreciative Inquiry Method in teams and in groups.

We are told, "Resident in you are images, ideals that must be lived out, yet will only be found through inquiry—using the best of the past to inform the future. Build your future first in images, then live it."

These are powerful tools—tools for sustained transformation—not rubber band stretch and shrink exercises. Then, right on cue—just as I'm beginning to see the blueprints for Master Counsel—Jim Lord tells us to "dump on paper" what we want to do and who we will need to be to do that.

Though I never planned on sharing this with the world—here are my handwritten notes.

WHAT YOU DO: *Master Counsel Inc. is a for profit consulting firm committed to understand best practices in Organizational change and advancement yet focused on people and the processes necessary to achieve the highest ideals of those involved while allowing the images released by those beings to become the action steps which they find themselves naturally doing. This reduces the stress from the fear of failure while assuring resources appropriate to the highest aims.*

WHO I NEED TO BE TO DO THIS: *John Bost, called by God toward his image, seeing with his Father's eyes, loving with his father's heart, touching with the Father's hands the soul of those entrusted daily to my being. I will not be distracted by the snare of necessity or the alarm of the urgent, but rather be about releasing the highest ideals and images of men.*

Think John Huss and the Unity of the Brethren commitment to take Christian values into the marketplace—*where excellence in workmanship and love of others is my worship to God.*

Jim Lord then walks us through the rest of our Adaptive Planning process, because his intention is not to forge us into a team. His only intention is to send us back to our mission or calling—better equipped to realize its highest expression.

In short, he has us make the following lists: assets (not limited to financial, but also relationships), sources of funding, constituencies/domains, next steps necessary, who needs to be involved, and personal reasons "why" we are doing this.

He wraps this up with a commitment plan, strategic steps, and a method for integrating Quest ideas into daily life.

On the final day—we take a sunrise hike. As planned—trekking from the red desert lowland to the brilliant snow-capped mountain peaks forever freeze-frames the entire Quest experience.

As I fly back to Winston-Salem, I'm thinking, "Houston, we are ready for lift off!"

A CATALYST FOR CHANGE

Chapter 24

One Man's Trash

"What is that awful smell?" I ask myself as I step out the front door.

LaDonna and I had moved into our transition home several months earlier. This was the house on Murray Road in Winston-Salem—the house between the now sold dream home in Lexington and the soon to be built dream home on the outskirts of Winston-Salem, in Clemmons.

I sniff the air again. Clearly, the stench is coming from the east. So, I follow my nose to the Hanes Mill Road Solid Waste Facility—better known as a garbage dump. Most shocking of all, I didn't have to drive too far. The landfill is less than three miles from my front door.

Obviously, I never would have bought a house so close to a garbage dump and my realtor should have disclosed it. But how could I have missed this—when I grew up a mere 20 minutes from the site?

The answer is: In the 1970s, when I was off to college and then settled in Lexington the first section of this landfill was opened. This section—as one might predict—bumped right up against Highway 52. This proverbial ribbon of road seems to always separate the "haves" from the "have nots."

And, with prevailing winds typically blowing from west to east—it separates the *occasional* smell of garbage from the *consistent* encroachment of foul air in residential areas.

This experience seeds one of my first entrepreneurial ventures under the shield of Master Counsel. After all, if my mission is to make the community a better place for everyone—this challenge has all the right ingredients.

So, even though we move out of this neighborhood in 1996—a few months before I start Master Counsel—my commitment to help the residents remains intact.

Adding to my awareness, in 1997, I'm appointed to serve on the City County Planning Board. We'll do a deeper dive into that later—as it leads to an opportunity to explore the "politics" of municipal governance. For now, suffice to say that the issue of garbage is a consistent concern at our meetings.

Basically, the Winston-Salem Forsyth County Utilities Commission operates the landfill. The landfill is blocked to the east by Highway 52, so they want to expand the site westward—toward Murray Road. This will further encroach on residential properties.

Wanting to solve the problem, I begin a multiyear investigation—we'll call this a "less than appreciative inquiry" of sorts—around the topic of waste management. It's more complex than meets the eye. Here is what I discover about the Hanes Mill Road Solid Waste Facility.

- The old section of the landfill (1970s) did not have a protective liner to protect against groundwater contamination.
- Protective liners were first used in the mid 1990s.
- To keep odor and pests down—a six-inch layer of soil is applied to the top of the garbage.
- Space is running out. A solution must be found.

At the same time, I'm sharing my curiosity and concerns with various people in my life—one of whom happens to be Tim Beeman. I'd met Tim when his wife began attending First Assembly.

He's struggling with a new "We do dirt" business he has named White Oak Transport. I admire his entrepreneurial spirit—one man and a truck—so I bring in an accountant to help him write a business plan. He soon expands to thirteen trucks. Also, he is encouraged to bid on the mulch and dirt work around the church.

A few years later, Tim introduces me to Jim Bryan from the Public Health Department. Over lunch, I voice my concerns about the seemingly *unsolvable* and growing waste problem.

Then, Jim asks, "What about a transfer station?"

"How does that work?"

"You bring in three trucks of garbage, compact it into one truck load, and then haul it to the landfill," he explains.

"Is anyone doing that?" I ask.

"Not in Forsyth County. But I could show you a couple of places about an hour away that do this," Jim says.

So, we take a field trip to Uwharrie Environmental Inc. Landfill about 70 miles south, and then cut across to see a facility in Charlotte—which is also about 70 miles—from Winston-Salem.

The operation is pretty simple. You need a metal building on concrete, and a piece of heavy equipment to compact the waste. The transfer station pays for itself because you charge for three incoming loads of garbage, compress it into one load, and then haul that single load to the landfill. At the same time, you are also saving *environmental capital*—landfill airspace. It's a win-win.

As we continue to grow this seedling idea, Tim offers, "I'll put the dirt under it."

He's recently sold his White Oak business and has taken part of the payment in land.

With a viable idea in hand, I approach Paul Norby, City/County Director of Planning and Development Services of Winston-Salem.

Paul hears my idea and says, "There's only one problem. The (Winston-Salem Forsyth County) Utilities owns all the garbage."

"What!" I ask in disbelief.

"It's true," he says. "So as it stands, the planning board could not approve of this."

I step off the planning board—now having a conflict of interests—and call in my old friend—Steve Calloway. Attorney Calloway has been approaching the planning board for years.

Within a short period of time—he cracks the code. We need to have garbage declared a "commodity"—a material or product with value that can be bought or sold.

Attorney Calloway sets to work on the "text amendment" to present to the planning board. At the same time, the necessary "proof"—that this will benefit our community—is revealed right before their eyes when I take a few planning board members on a field trip to Uwharrie and Charlotte.

So, our "day in court" at the planning board meeting proves to be a landmark success. This is an answer that everyone wants to hear—a means to reduce the need to expand the landfill, a way to reduce the encroachment on residential neighborhoods, and a way to minimize the footprint of each load of garbage.

Everyone is happy except Winston-Salem Forsyth County Utilities. To be fair, landfills are huge investments. They require a minimum influx of waste to pay for the manpower and operating costs of the facility. And, *change is often resisted*—even by the best of us.

If waste is reduced too much, they either have to raise their prices per load, or close their doors. Either way, they do not accept waste from our transfer station. So, we haul it to Uwharrie—and still make a profit.

In 2004, Tim is bought out by Republic—now named Republic Services Overdale Road Transfer Station—located at 5000 Overdale Road in Winston-Salem.

In the end, I earn a consulting fee. However, my biggest payoff rests in having fed my heart's desire—*to make my community a better place*. And it didn't take money to do that. It took relationships—Attorney Calloway, Tim Beeman, Jim Bryan, and the planning board, to name a few.

Jim Bryan—who brought intellectual property to the venture—and Tim Beeman, who owned the land, split the profits from the sale of the acreage to Republic. Jim takes his share of the profits in adjoining land owned by Tim.

Then, we begin to brainstorm other waste management ideas. After all, as Yotam Ottolenghi said, "One man's trash is another man's treasure."

Growing waste continues to be a challenge. The *Winston-Salem Journal* stated, "The landfill took in 233,786 tons in 2014-15." But here, too—by paving the way for the first transfer station, we made a positive impact in local waste reduction.

The *Journal* went on to say, "There is also *competition for garbage*, with private hauling companies transferring some to their landfills outside of the county. In 2014-15, about 70 percent of the disposed residential and commercial waste from Forsyth County ended up at the Hanes Mill Road Landfill, with the rest going to landfills outside the county."

That is a *30% reduction in local landfill waste*! But we aren't done yet. We have another idea to help the city.

ONE MAN'S TRASH

Hanes Mill Road Solid Waste Facility
Operated by Winston-Salem Forsyth County Utilities

This is a reminder to do your homework before proposing a change. Be sure to map—literally and strategically—all known facts and a plan of action.

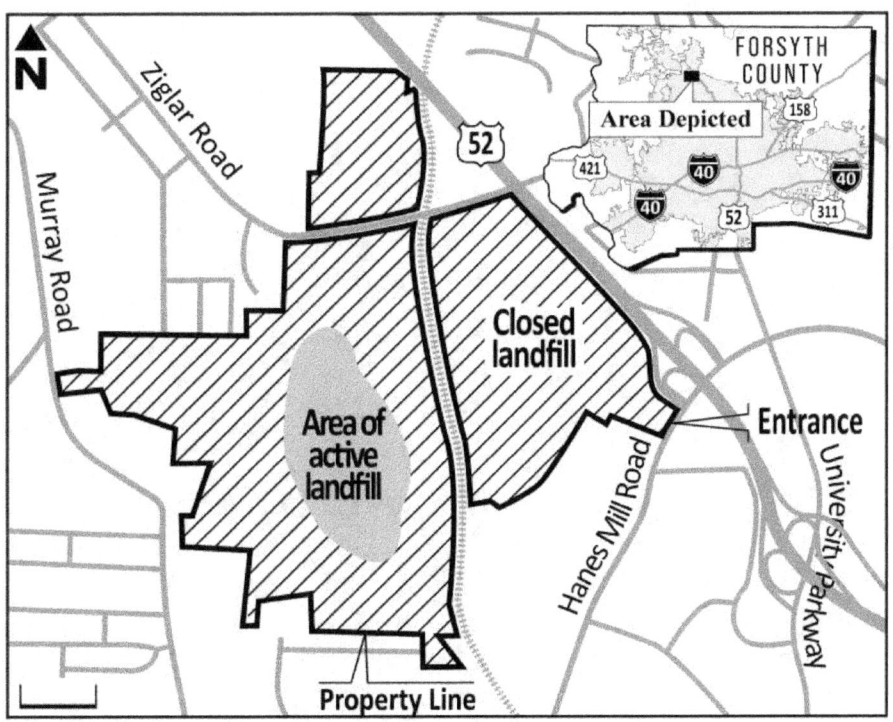

For more information visit www.JohntheCatalyst.com

A CATALYST FOR CHANGE

Chapter 25

Two Birds with One Stone

"What can we do with the remaining 40 acres of Tim's land?"

Jim and I roll that question around for some time. We try on the possibility of opening a private construction debris landfill. Forty acres is inadequate for burying the debris.

In fact, Jim and I assemble 300 acres in Walnut Cove sufficient for the task, but the gentleman whom we were working with passed away unexpectedly. Fortunately, we were able to sell the land to another person in that industry.

Then, one day, Jim hits on an idea.

He says, "Instead of burying construction debris, why don't we recycle it."

Immediately, gut, heart, and head line up on this. Recycling is a genuine solution to the growing waste problem. Collect, sort, and then cycle construction debris back into the marketplace.

Additionally, I've been working with ex-felons for a few years now—more on this in the section on social outreach—and one of their toughest challenges is to find employment once they exit the prison system.

A construction debris recycling company will create an excellent first step for this clientele, while reducing the need to expand the landfill. Proverbially speaking, we'll be killing two birds with one stone.

Mission: Recycle product back into the marketplace—to conserve landfill airspace and environmental resources—while simultaneously creating entry-level jobs for ex-offenders trying to restart their lives.

The more I think about it, the more exciting the idea becomes. Perhaps our new company can be what is now known as a B Corp.

Borrowing from the website, www.bcorporation.net, "*Society's most challenging problems cannot be solved by government and nonprofits alone. The B Corp community works toward reduced inequality, lower levels of poverty, a healthier environment, stronger communities, and the creation of more high quality jobs with dignity and purpose. By harnessing the power of business, B Corps use profits and growth as a means to a greater end: positive impact for their employees, communities, and the environment."*

In short, it's not all about money. B Corps—though taxed like any other corporation—are designed to balance *profits* and a greater *purpose*—to make the local and global community better for everyone.

Suddenly, my mind takes another leap forward. I make a personal commitment to use my share of the profits to fund additional outreach programs that matter to me. Before shopping for equity stakeholders—we have the idea but not the money—we do an informal feasibility study.

The 40 acre piece is already zoned for general industry, so we pay a visit to our nearest neighbor—Corn Products (now Ingredion, Inc.) at 4501 Overdale Road. There we inquire of Bruce Hedrick who explains *what* they do—about 100 employees manufacture corn syrup and corn sugar.

He tells us *why*—there is a strong market for the products. We can see *where*. And then, he shows us *how*—wet corn milling using boilers heated by wood. Again, we see the benefits of appreciative inquiry and others-oriented conversations!

Just before we leave, Hedrick—who believes in our mission—agrees to buy our wood chips as long as it meets his "dry" standards. He also assures us that the roads can handle the heavy trucks that our operation will demand.

Next, we try to find a market for crushed cement block, and brick. Initially, we think this can be sold to paving companies. However, we are told that—though crushed cement may look like gravel—it behaves very differently in asphalt. Apparently, it's been tried.

When gravel-sized cement is added to asphalt, it will not bond properly to the substrate. Over time, the asphalt surface can actually "slide" and create potholes. Eventually, we find a market with farmers—North Carolina is a national agricultural leader—who put down the grindings to make gravel-like access roads to their fields and buildings.

Then, there is the dirt—a natural consequence of sorting tons of sheetrock, wood, bricks, and other debris. Initially, we plan to sell dirt to the landfill, which uses six-inches or more to cover the waste. However, by the time we actually get our business operating, the landfill's need for dirt has been replaced by latex products.

Our dirt dilemma leads to another idea—another business—that we'll save for the next chapter. As for recycling metals—there are plenty of scrap yards to buy our bounty.

Now at the very time that I'm looking to move forward on this recycling business—I also have two other promising business ventures. Realizing that I'm in over my head, I call in an expert—Randall Baker—to help me pick the "best" business to pursue.

I'd met Baker through his employer, Dr. Merwyn A. Hayes. Hayes attended First Assembly for a short time and I picked him out immediately. He's the kind of man that has an unmistakable presence about him.

He knows who he is and where he's going. And he can help you figure out who you are, where you need to go, and how to get there. In fact, he is the founder (sadly he died August 21, 2017 on his 79th birthday) and CEO of the prestigious Hayes Group International—training corporate leaders around the world.

After our first conversation, Hayes decides to help me "reach a city." He'll do this by personally mentoring me—inviting me to free leadership trainings—and ultimately instilling in me his personal motto: "Good, better, best never let it rest until your good is better and your better is still best." As a Reformer—I'm a ready follower.

However, when it comes time to bring in an expert to sort out my business ventures—I insist on paying. So, Randall Baker is hired as a consultant for $10,000 with the Hayes Group receiving 5% of the capital raised.

After investigating all three businesses options—opening a waterpark at I-85 near Highway 8, building a self-sustaining village in

A CATALYST FOR CHANGE

Nicaragua (future chapter), or developing a construction debris recycling business—Baker chooses the recycling business.

He writes up a business plan and then shops equity stakeholders among the Hayes Group's extensive list of investors—mainly Fortune 500 and Fortune 100 companies. None of them are interested. They just can't seem to get excited about "garbage."

So, Baker takes the idea to a businessman he knows from his homestate of Pennsylvania. He's the CEO of a global dye manufacturing company. And guess what?

His company hires people who need a second chance—including ex-offenders. It seems to be the perfect match.

Before long, we are up and running. The company purchases a million dollar piece of equipment that conveys material over a set of 10 containers—where workers and magnets sort the material according to type—such as wood, aluminum, sheetrock, and concrete. This is where the aforementioned loan through my Leadership Winston-Salem connection came into play.

Here are the 2015 stats. Abbey Green can recycle 450 tons per day. It serves 18 counties. About 70% of intake cycles back into the marketplace. Their top three recyclables are crushed concrete, compost/soil, and wood chips.

Their revenues—2/3 come from tipping fees and 1/3 from product sales (cycling products back to the marketplace). In that, Abbey Green is doing as we planned—reducing the need for landfills, creating jobs, and going green!

Abbey Green—a construction and industrial debris recycling center—is located at 5030 Overdale Road, Winston-Salem, NC.

TWO BIRDS WITH ONE STONE

Figuring that Jim has a handle on the recycling aspect, I shift my energies to helping the ex-offenders. Realizing that they will need housing and mentoring, I invest in a nearby home and hire Kevin Frack—having recently left his post as senior pastor at Ardmore Moravian—to supervise the restoration of the home.

Before the group home restoration is complete, our principal partner informs me that we won't be hiring entirely ex-offenders. He realizes that he has tied up a lot of debt in this operation, and he needs to get it up and running quickly.

He clearly explains that only one in 25 ex-offenders work out and he can't afford that kind of turnover at Abbey Green. So, I relinquish the house to a non-profit focused on re-entry, but hold my equity shares in hopes that my share of the income stream will eventually fund my other outreach programs.

However, in the course of a couple years, several challenges occur. One regarding funding, lesson learned about the difference in an investor bringing debt versus equity.

Secondly, the challenges of reentry and the time necessary with each employee, as well as the requirements of managing a halfway house.

I interpret all this as *personal mission drift*—straying from one's original purpose. My DI, *Initiator* personality type now seems on point. I cash out.

Good or bad, my gut decision seems to have panned out, as the project was eventually sold to another firm who was better able to profit from it as a parallel function for recycling and compaction transfer purposes.

This chapter in my life reminds me of a famous quote by Harry S. Truman, "It is amazing what you can accomplish if you do not care who gets the credit."

I will just add to that, "And if you don't care who ends up owning the company."

A CATALYST FOR CHANGE

Chapter 26

Making Dirt

Neil Patel—a writer for Forbes—titles a story *90% Of Startups Fail.* I, too, hold that as a truth, when starting Master Counsel, and yet each failed venture genuinely surprises me. Trust me, it's not due to a lack of effort. Sometimes ideas don't work out.

One unexpected windfall from our early feasibility study for Abbey Green was the discovery of just how much leaf compost accumulates on the city storage facility.

We anticipated that over 20% of the construction debris that would eventually be brought in would shake out to be "dirt." We're not talking topsoil. Instead, it is the particles of sheetrock, wood, and dust—that has to be dealt with.

Once again, Jim Bryan has an idea.

"We can make manufactured soil by adding nutrients and compost," he suggests.

"Good idea," I agree. "And, we can put ex-offenders to work producing this."

After all, a LCID (Land Clearing Inert Debris) recycling facility has to move product off its property by a certain drop-dead date. Otherwise, it no longer meets the guidelines of a recycling facility—putting the company at risk of closure.

Because Jim has a full time job, I bring in my friend Paula McCoy to help us pull this together. In brief, we investigate mixing construction debris "dirt" with organic sludge from the Archie Elledge Wastewater treatment plant, along with leaf debris—both available from the WSFC Utilities—and pond screenings (fine particles washed from gravel) from Vulcan Materials.

Incidentally, James King at Vulcan—after hearing about our B Corp-like mission (we were before our time)—offers to give us the quarry "hole" with 120 acres of land at Butler Street and Reynolds Park Road. This was a working quarry in the 1920s, shut down in the 1970s,

A CATALYST FOR CHANGE

and waiting for repurposing in 1998. However, King insists that we run our ideas past the City, before he'll consent.

The "hole" is breathtakingly gorgeous—with a 12-acre crystal blue lake set like a gem at the base of silver rock cliffs that rise to a height of 150 feet. Stunning!

Quickly, Paula and I do a feasibility study—envisioning premier housing for nearby Winston-Salem State University faculty, even sharing with the Board of Directors, meanwhile approaching Billy Satterfield about developing a golf course. Jim Bryan talks to the University of Arizona about tapping into the geothermal potential of the lake. It is sounding like a plan.

However, when we talk to the City—they delay in answering our request. Some time would pass before we realized that the City—in conversations with Vulcan—had received the property for recreational use, while we were lining up our ducks! But later, I realize that the City may have saved my hide. There is a lot of liability tied up in a 12-acre lake with 150-foot cliffs. One accident could have sunk my entrepreneurial ship.

Nineteen years later, in 2017, we knew the City made the right decision when it invested over $4 million and opened Quarry Park with its magnificent observation platform, hiking trails, and picnic areas—with plans for zip lines, disc golf, an amphitheater, and camping.

In the meantime, Jim finds out that a local tobacco company has been hauling 600 tons of "floor sweepings" to the Hanes Mill Road Solid Waste Facility each year. The sweepings mainly consist of tobacco, paper, and latex glue used to hold the cigarette filters in place.

Jim believes that this organic matter may make an excellent soil amendment. The tobacco company is interested in going green—repurposing its waste—so it supports our efforts. *Jim and I* form a business—*Jimandi*—in which we invest about $30,000 over the course of 10 years.

Early on—as a way to reduce bulk—Jim forms the sweepings into something that resembles hockey pucks. Then—as a favor—a friend at the Wake Forest Institute for Regenerative Medicine—tests them and finds that their nitrogen content is 19%.

This matches the nitrogen content of chicken manure—except that chicken manure is "hot" and has to be composted before applying directly to a vegetation. With these findings in place, we explore production. Because we don't have a facility, we talk to a nearby prison to see if this can be a prison industry.

The Warden takes one look at the pucks—realizes that they contain a high nicotine content—and advises us that these could not be allowed inside the prison. In fact, he tells us that even if they were sold legitimately outside the prison walls, they would soon become a source of contraband and soon sold on the black market as well as inside the prison walls. These guys truly are entrepreneurs!

Of course, the tobacco company doesn't want to carry a liability like that. So, we talk to a chicken farmer. We looked at the possibility of adding chicken manure to our "pucks" to make them inedible.

Incidentally, there's no shortage of chicken manure in North Carolina. This state is the 4th highest producer of chicken in the US.

Next, I put the pucks to the test. In the past, I'd grown hybrid tea roses. So, I set up a rose garden in our side yard and plant about 15 beautiful tea roses. Next to each bush, I take a bulb planter—much like a cookie cutter on legs—and punch out an area of earth the size of a puck. After placing the puck in the hole, I cover it with dirt.

Much to my amazement—the tea roses grow like a body builder taking steroids. They are strong and beautiful—requiring very little pesticides. I'm wondering if the pucks carry a dual advantage of releasing nitrogen while also releasing the natural insecticide found in nicotine. I even go so far as to contact the American Rose Society to share my findings.

Encouraged by their response, I invest to have a company manufacture sleeves that can hold 10 pucks. In the meantime, Jim is exploring ways to extrude a tobacco sweepings in solution made with excess filter glue—so that it can be applied to lawns in the form of pellets. His first attempt produces pellets, but they are so moisture rich that they stick together and mold.

In the meantime, years are passing and the tobacco company wants an answer: Do you have a marketable product? If not, let's move on.

A CATALYST FOR CHANGE

In our conference, one of the tobacco company's researchers says, "John, even if you could produce and market the pucks, you'd have to sell one to every man, woman, and child in North Carolina to move 600 tons of floor sweepings."

He is right. We just aren't set up to mass produce and market this volume of material. Jim pleads with me to invest just $25,000 more—into an extruder that forms a perfect pellet.

It's a tough call—this pellet maker really does produce a viable product. And Jim has even arranged to have a golf course test the product for free to see if it lives up to our hopes. But I've reached my saturation point. Instead of investing any further, we dissolve Jimandi and I give full rights of the project to Jim.

By this time, we have the numbers together on production and marketing. It will cost consumers $400 per ton to buy our "green" product versus $100 to buy an equivalent amount of chemical nitrogen.

As an interesting side point—I laugh at this now—a chemist discovered that the reason my roses thrived was *not* only because of the nitrogen in the tobacco puck. But as well, the mold in the latex glue that held the puck together served as a transport system for nitrogen in the soil that would not typically be accessible to the plant!

Perhaps it's a viable idea for the next generation of entrepreneurs. As for me, I'd simultaneously journeyed down another path, which you'll see eventually leads us to Nicaragua.

Chapter 27

Others-oriented Habits

Shortly after I announce my departure from First Assembly, my administrative assistant Karen Kirby, says, "John, what am I supposed to do? I feel like I was sent here to work for *you,* not for the Church."

Kirby is a very capable assistant, but I've already decided that Master Counsel will not have any employees. On the other hand, if she really thinks that she was sent here to work with me, who am I to tell her no.

After a pause, I tell her, "You can come with me, but you'll have to start your own business. I'll buy services from you. And, I'll help you get started. The first four contracts I sign are for me. The next three will go to you."

So, she sets up an office next to mine on the 24th floor of the old Wachovia building, now known as the Winston Tower. By taking a step of faith—when my business could not even support myself—I had the honor of watching her grow her career over the next 20 years.

Something similar happens in 2000, when Robby Lee comes to see me. Robby is a young married man with four children.

When we meet, I ask, "How did you end up in Winston-Salem?"

He says innocently, "I looked at a map and felt like this is where we needed to be. So, we moved."

Startled, I ask, "Do you have a job?"

"No. My pastor said to come talk to you."

I remember his pastor—I'd done some work for him in Salisbury. However, I don't know what to tell Robby. I don't have a job for him. And, I'm not sure what opportunities are available in the city.

But he is the kind of young man that I like to help. He's got guts. Who would take out a map, throw the proverbial dart, and then move a family of four?

So, we engage in a bit of appreciative inquiry (as a reader you are tiring of the mention of AI or you're starting to believe). In short, it is apparent that Robby is brilliant when it comes to computers. He not only understands them, they fascinate him.

Finally, I tell him, "If I had your brains, I could make a bundle of money. I'll tell you what, why don't I hire you to build me a website and we'll see where it goes from there."

That—being others-oriented and giving someone a helping hand—led to a most amazing 20-year journey as well! Within a few months of building the website—Robby is contacted by a friend associated with Infra Corporation in Australia.

That's right! Someone 9,500 miles away sees Robby's name listed as the creator of my website and wants to meet with him. We scrape together enough money for plane fare and send him over.

Three weeks later, Robby returns.

He says, "They want me to introduce their new help desk software."

"What does that require?" I ask.

"Well, I'd have to have a team," he says.

"How many people does it take to make a team? There are two of us, right! We are a team," I state obviously. Then I ask, "What else does it take?"

"I'd have to get licensed," he says.

"How do you do that?" I ask.

"I'd have to go back over to be trained."

"Is it worth it? Is their product viable?"

Then, I watch Robby light up again as he excitedly tells me about this new ITSM (Information Technology Software Management) that streamlines every form of management in a company—incidents, accidents, service, change, release, and configuration—with a ready set of policies, procedures, and protocol.

Though I only grasp about half of what he's saying—we have everything it takes to make a team. I know people and Robby knows product. So we set up a company under the Master Counsel Shield—Master Counsel Technologies, LLC.

Robby flies back to Australia and earns his license. Next, shortly after the merger of Sony Corporation and Ericsson Telecommunication

Company, our team meets with leadership from the new Sony Ericsson in Raleigh, NC.

Our "team" consists of Robby, Robby's sister-in-law—the exceptionally brilliant Theresa Pappas Stone—a specialist from Australia, and me. At the end of the day, we walk away with our first contract—for $700,000.

Software sales—globally—continue to come in, helped along by prestigious awards such as the 2002 Pink Elephant's PinkVerify ITIL certification, recognition as HDI's Best Business Use of Business Support Technology in 2006, and then the biggie in 2007 when *Network Computing Magazine* names it "Helpdesk Product of the Year."

After a couple of years, Robby senses the need for additional training, "Perhaps, it's time for you to go back to school for your MBA. You're not going to find a better program than right here in Winston-Salem at Wake Forest University."

And he does. As expected, Robby graduates at the top of his class. He continues to service the Infra software clients even after it is acquired by Dell EMC in 2008 and then by VMware in 2010. Though the acquisitions muddy the waters for the clients, Robby rides this shooting star long enough to raise his family and put all four of his children through college.

However, it's back in 2007 that our path takes yet another unexpected turn.

A CATALYST FOR CHANGE

Chapter 28

Nicaragua

In 2007, eleven years after seeking help in reaching a city, Kevin Frack resigns as senior pastor of Ardmore Moravian. He, too, has drawn the conclusion that the institutional church is less interested in taking its values, wealth, and people-power to the community to solve real problems.

Like me—in imitation of the *founding* Moravians—he wants to take his Christian values to the marketplace. However, the day after he resigns—September 4, 2007—Category 5 Hurricane Felix slams into the northeastern coast of Nicaragua with sustained winds of up to 160 miles per hour.

The following day, the Moravian Church sends Frack to Nicaragua to do a damage assessment. They chose Frack because he has lived there, knows the language of the Miskito tribe, and he's Moravian—by bloodline and faith orientation.

"What I found," Frack tells me upon his return, "is heartbreaking devastation. People who had very little—and who suffer with 95% unemployment—now have nothing. They are subsistence farmers who aren't able to subsist any more."

We share a moment in silence.

Then, Frack says, "There might be one silver lining in this dark cloud. In its wake, the hurricane left thousands of felled trees—extremely precious tropical hardwoods like mahogany, various cedars, and Brazilian cherry. These trees are under a moratorium to protect the rain-forest, but right now they are just lying on the forest floor. Maybe we can use those trees to help the people help themselves."

"What is the window on harvesting the downed trees?" I ask.

"We would only have about five or six years and then the wood wouldn't be any good," Frack says.

A CATALYST FOR CHANGE

He knows. He earned a post-graduate certificate in Tropical Agriculture while pursuing a Master's Degree from the University of Florida.

That might seem to be an unusual degree for an American-born man, but then again, Frack is not your usual kind of guy. In 1974, when he was in college—as a math and music major—his roommate's parents invited him to spend a summer in eastern Honduras where they were serving as missionaries.

Frack fell in love with the humble Miskito tribe and their rugged, beautiful land. In fact, he spent his entire junior year of college in eastern Honduras living with these people and learning their ways.

He decided that one of the best ways to help these subsistence farmers was through better agricultural practices. Thus, he went to graduate school. After graduation, the Moravian Church asked Frack to work with the Miskito Natives (formerly called Indians) in Nicaragua.

His job—as agricultural consultant—was to travel to remote villages to teach Miskito women to grow vegetables to counteract the malnutrition common in the area. He also taught people to look at their gifts and to try to use them to live a more abundant life. Additionally, this energetic young man taught music at the high school.

As a side point—the Moravian missionaries arrived in Nicaragua in 1847—about 100 years after they set foot in Salem. Moravian missionaries carried the Gospel to the ends of the earth, so that today, most Moravians live in Africa and Latin America.

Unlike Salem—which devolved from a faith-based marketplace community, to a church-dominated community, to a church that has much less impact on its community outside the church walls—in Nicaraguan Miskito Indian life, the church is still the center of the community. It is the center of worship, education, and even business. And virtually every town, city, and village has a church.

So, when Frack and I begin brainstorming a way to use the tree harvest to help the Miskito tribesmen to start their own businesses—to develop a truly sustainable community—it is only natural that the Moravian Church will help.

NICARAGUA

At the same time, as Frack and I explain the possibilities to Robby Lee—he excitedly shares the growing dream with his professors at Wake Forest University (WFU). It turns out that WFU has a campus where it trains in SMEs (small and mid-sized enterprises) at American College in Nicaragua.

WFU jumps on board—and pro bono, under the supervision of Attorney Steve Virgil—legally establishes our company now named Terra Verde International LLC. (Terra means earth in Latin. Verde means green in Spanish.) WFU also sends graduate students onsite both to advise and to learn as our project unfolds.

Our primary objective is to establish a for-profit business in Nicaragua using downed trees to create an income stream to train a workforce and develop a sustainable community—which will ultimately be owned and managed by the indigenous people.

From the stateside, five businessmen—John Bost, Robby Lee, Mike Cheney, Jay Helvey, and Troy Smith—scrape together $100,000.

The Moravian Church has eight Wood-Mizer sawmills. They've been left in villages during the immediate reconstruction phase after hurricane Felix.

The church then offers, that if we can recover their lost sawmills, we can have the use of two, free of charge. This proves to be quite a dicey move on Kevin's part to recoup the abandoned devices. He alone understands the language and culture, enabling him to convene a team of indigenous Nicaraguans.

Robby Lee, by then engaged in a MBA at WFU, secures legal aid and access to grad students; we even find a guy with a helicopter to lift the trees out of the forest.

That, too, happens in a most unusual way. Baker and I are talking to an investor about Abbey Green, when I notice a boar's head and other big game mounted on this investor's walls.

I ask the man, "Do you hunt big game?"

He says, "Yes."

I ask, "Where?"

He says, "I shot that boar in Nicaragua."

A CATALYST FOR CHANGE

I say, "Really! We've got a project in Nicaragua. We are harvesting the downed trees to help the Miskito tribe develop a sustainable community. The only problem is, we don't really have a way to get the trees out of the forest."

He says, "I heard about the trees. We have a helicopter, but I don't have any people on the ground."

Wow, now another piece of the puzzle slides into place.

The Miskito also have skin in the game. The indigenous leaders in the Village of Sukatpin agree to lease 2500 acres to Terra Verde at no cost, and to share as full partners in the development of a business model that will generate jobs and train Nicaraguans to start their own businesses.

In our vision—when it is all said and done—the 2500 acres will have been cleared, sustainable forestry for harvesting fruit, nuts, and lumber will be in place, sustainable vegetable farming and animal husbandry will feed the people, a Foundation will train Nicaraguan entrepreneurs, and the original businessmen will have recouped their investment and netted a small profit.

Here is what actually happens. WFU helps us obtain the legal documents to harvest the felled lumber and to begin operations. This takes some time, because Nicaragua operates under a Socialist form of government—which discourages foreign investment.

In fact, WFU warns us that Nicaragua is one of the seven worst countries in the world to do business in. However, we decide to proceed because we have estimated that there is $2 million worth of lumber lying on the ground. If we don't use that to help the Miskito help themselves *now*, how long will we have to wait for another opportunity?

Lastly, with such strong support—by WFU, the Moravian Church which is deeply rooted in the culture, the local Miskito tribe, and the expertise of Kevin Frack—surely we have put the odds in our favor.

Obstacle 1: By the time we are ready to use the Wood-Mizer sawmills—they are nowhere to be found. The church in Nicaragua has lost track of them. Apparently, various villages have taken ownership of these, hauled them off, and used these machines for everything but sawing wood. None of them are in working condition any more.

Frack approaches the local Moravian Church and asks, "If we can put the sawmills in working condition, can we use them to put these people in employment?"

The Church leaders say, "Yes."

From the eight broken sawmills delivered by our trusted team of local Nicaraguans, we put two sawmills into working condition and have them delivered to the "farm."

With that hurdle overcome, we put 50 families to work clearing 75 acres of jungle for pastures and farming. We build two cabins for workers, a cookhouse, and a large warehouse.

The Miskito Natives feel a sense of unprecedented joy. They are pulling their future right out of the ground with their own hands. And, it's not all about the future. They are getting paid now—and we pay them above average wages.

Genuine hope is running high. Of our team of five—only Robby and Frack actually travel to Nicaragua—witnessing this real and sustainable change for some of the most oppressed people in the world. The joy that this brings me is immeasurable.

Our project operates smoothly for eighteen months. It is operating from our investment money—not yet from lumber sales—but this is about more than money to our team.

Additionally—keeping with our intent to make this operation sustainable for the indigenous people—we buy four oxen to haul the lumber, versus the helicopter. All this time, Frack is traveling every month—two weeks in North Carolina joining his wife in raising his children and then two weeks in Nicaragua staying alongside the Natives while they get on their feet.

When Frack, CEO of Terra Verde, is stateside, a Nicaraguan forestry engineer trained in Cuba—who is Chief Operating Officer (COO)—and a Nicaraguan who is a trusted attorney, continue to oversee the operation.

A CATALYST FOR CHANGE

Miskito natives haul lumber "their way" using oxen. The goal of Terra Verde International LLC is to create a healthy and sustainable community of entrepreneurs.

Obstacle 2: The first breakdown occurs when we hire a new bus to transport workers. Then we use that bus to send in the payroll with our COO and two helpers. Gunmen hijack the bus, shoot it up enough to scare everyone, and then steal the $3,000 cash.

Even though we later find out this is an inside job—our Nicaraguan company leaders set this up—we learn a painful lesson. Never send money on a new bus. That new bus—so out of place in this poor community—screamed, "Rob me."

Obstacle 3: Not too long after this, we notice that the precious lumber that we've been stockpiling has not sold. So, Frack investigates. All the mahogany and teak planks have disappeared.

It turns out that the COO has sold the first shipment on his own and pocketed the money. It is hard for us to believe that he would do this to his own people.

But he does not see himself as one of them. Yes, he is a Miskito Native. But—and this is a big but—he has been to Cuba, where he earned a Forestry degree. In his mind, that puts him on a higher level. He is *entitled* to take for himself.

Also, he is not from the Village of Sukatpin. He feels no loyalty to *these* Miskito natives. And, even though they share the same faith—Moravian Christians—he doesn't seem to believe that God is watching. Nor does he compassionately care for others as "brothers and sisters" or even as "good neighbors." This *lack of basic ethics* proves to be a key learning piece for us.

So, as Frack says, "The first year, we trust, but verify. The second year, trust no one and verify everything. The third year, I don't even trust myself. By that, I mean, that I can no longer trust my judgement. People, who I am absolutely sure I can trust, betray me and their fellow Miskito natives."

Obstacle 4: In tracing the problems, we find that the villagers have witnessed the COO stealing the lumber. Additionally, he is offending the population by having an illicit relationship with one of the girls in the village. And, he is stealing from the workers. He is cheating them by skimming off the top of the payroll.

So, Frack, with the agreement of another high level Nicaraguan manager with Terra Verde—fires the offending COO. Instead of solving the problem, this action sparks several new problems—much like stomping out a fire in a windstorm.

Obstacle 5: First, the former manager (COO) tries to sneak back onto the farm and steal the four oxen. But oxen don't go quietly. Twenty-three village men hear him in the middle of the night, unite, and confront him.

According to Frack, the thief tells them, "These are mine. I bought them with my money."

They know differently and force him to return the oxen to the farm.

So, then, he sues Terra Verde for stealing his oxen. He is slick. In fact, Kevin had gone with him to purchase the oxen. The COO signed the document *on behalf of Terra Verde*, because we had thought we could trust him. He now claims that the oxen are his because he signed the receipt. His signature is proof that he was now part of the transaction.

As silly as this sounds in the US legal system, foreign courts are rife with bribes and conflicts. Plus, he has a close family member who serves as a magistrate.

Obstacle 6: A court date is set for a hearing. Frack does not want to return—even fearing for his personal safety. The working people are angry at the corruption. And some of the indigenous company leaders in Terra Verde and some of the leaders of the Village—who have now become corrupt—are angry because we are shining the light on their dishonesty.

Even still—though our dream has now turned into the worst nightmare—Frack goes to court. Surprisingly, Frack—accompanied by the Nicaraguan Terra Verde Executive Director, Larry Palmer (who earned his accounting degree at a US university)—is assigned to an honest and fair Judge. We can thank Palmer for that!

According to Frack, she says, "Tell me your side of the story, so we can see what we can do about this."

Frack talks to her for two-and-a-half hours—pouring out his heart— and she finally says, "The man accusing you isn't here, and I like what you've been doing. We need more of that. So, I'm dismissing this case."

So that problem—thankfully—goes away on its own. Or, so we thought. At that point, we decide that due to the "pirate culture"— where greed and power corrupt too many people—we need to close up shop. We pay everyone what we owe and then we turn all the operations over to the local people.

Obstacle 7: This is not what the former manager who sues us expects. He thinks—with $2 million still laying on the forest floor— that we will compromise and even come to terms with the corruption.

In other words—just like people pay the mafia in the US—in some foreign counties, people pay "leaders" to "protect" business. He mistakes us for capitalists where profit is the sole motive. Our motive, our venture was more a proof of concept, however two fold.

First, our intention was to create a sustainable for-profit industry providing local employment and return on our initial investment;

secondly, to develop a working farm which would eventually be turned over to the village as a center for sustainable food production.

Had we been solely capitalistic in our motives, it would have been "cost effective" to pay bribes and fees to harvest the lumber—employing poor Miskito Natives in the name of philanthropy—and then leave the Natives holding an empty bag when the forest floor is cleaned up. And, with $2 million, there would have been plenty for the "leaders" and Terra Verde.

However, we are not capitalists. We are operating under the principles of a B Corp—and our primary concern is helping *people*. When that isn't happening—when our mission cannot be accomplished—we exit.

Unbelievably, after we settle up, he threatens to follow us to the US so he can sue us stateside. He's like a pit bull that won't let go of our pant leg. So, we have to completely dissolve the business.

In hindsight—I feel so bad for the average Miskito Natives. By far, most of them are honest, hardworking, and so hopeful about building a better future.

And we can't blame the breakdown on just one corrupt "leader." Once we start investigating, we find that some of the people's own tribal leaders are stealing from them.

Revisiting this 13 years later, I find an interesting bit of research in *The Harvard Business Review*. In a 2018 article on ethics—titled, Research: *How One Bad Employee Can Corrupt a Whole Team*—authors Dimmock and Gerkon explain "just how contagious bad behavior is."

In their study, financial advisors are 37% more likely to commit misconduct if they encounter a new co-worker with a history of misconduct. And, if they share the same ethnicity—"the contagion effect is nearly twice as large."

In our case, we take the isolated, ignored, and malnourished Village of Sukatpin—*unknowingly* stir in some high profile corrupt "leaders"—and end up contaminating the local village elders.

Now, it is not as though the local population is innocent—what we would consider "high moral character" by US standards. Prior to us ever arriving, we learn that it is nothing for the Natives to accept help from missionaries, and then turn around and steal—petty theft—from them.

However, by bringing money to an impoverished area, we accidentally *attract* the most heinous moral crimes—human trafficking, high-level theft, and the marketing of addictive drugs.

Though I'm sure no one consciously designed it this way, it is almost like *the poor* are bait on a trap. That *bait* attracts well-intended *philanthropy*. However—as proved out in our Nicaraguan Project—the *money* can end in the laps of the *"leaders"* and the poor can end up *worse off* than they were before "*help*" arrived.

I'm convinced that five men, with honest intentions and $100,000—or even $ 5 million dollars—could not bring lasting benefits to the oppressed Miskito Natives. Why? Because it's not about the money.

It's about the current *culture and relationships*. Right now, people in power *want to* continue to prey upon people in poverty. Until they *want to* share the power, share the wealth, and share the care—very little sustainable change is possible.

Do I have any regrets? No. My goal is to make the world a better place for everyone. By being personally involved in Terra Verde, I'm able to test the limits—identify the fail points—in social reform.

I know for sure that it is not a lack of commitment, planning, execution, financing, or collaboration on our part that results in the failure. Additionally, we consistently do what is "right" when we are wronged. So the big lesson: Culture. Culture. Culture.

I carry this learning forward in all my future endeavors.

NICARAGUA

A CATALYST FOR CHANGE

Aerial View of Deacon Place

Deacon Place—*an upscale 328-bed student housing community, complete with a 6,000-square-foot community center which sports a fitness center, game room, a resort-style pool, fire pits, and outdoor BBQ grills. It's directly across the street is Winston-Salem Christian School, formerly a part of WSFirst.*

Chapter 29

Deacon Place

In 2014, developer Mike Kelley invests $500,000 over four years and constructs a 17 million dollar development that eventually sells for 28 million! I, too, make a good chunk of change selling property—sometimes multiple times—and from consulting fees.

However, before we enter into this venture, I ask Kelley, "Where did you learn to take risks like this?"

"On the pitcher's mound," he says nonchalantly.

Kelley—a former major league pitcher for the Cleveland Indians, drafted out of high school in 1970—embodies the nerves of steel and the risk capacity that one might expect. But how did he arrive at that?

"The key," Kelley explains, "is to compartmentalize."

"What do you mean?" I ask.

"When I was on the mound," he says, "I had to be extremely focused. So I trained my brain. One part of my brain focused only on first, if there was a runner on base! One part focused on second or third base as the case may have been. Another, the person in the batter's box. To win you have to keep them separate." Compartmentalization can be positive!

Unfortunately for baseball—a windfall for development community—Kelly is thrown from a horse and breaks his pitching arm. We meet sometime later when I am asked to assemble multiple properties for retail purposes and he shows up!

At the same time—though I'd physically left my post at First Assembly (renamed Winston-Salem First) 17 years earlier—my heart is still tied to it. I want to see this church do well.

I want to grow its campus value, given years of conversation with its prestigious neighbor Wake Forest University. Then hopefully, once this season of now 70 years of lifetime has come to full maturity, the investments of all those who came before us will continue to add value to our city.

A CATALYST FOR CHANGE

So by 2014—when the church has abandoned the idea of closing Long Drive, which would have required a new interchange at Polo and University Parkway (see the previous site map) and have now divested themselves of the concept of a high school across the street, debt retirement is the challenge—I suggest that they sell roughly 10 acres on Long Drive.

The land has limited value—one piece is virtually land locked, with only one curb-cut at the dangerously busy intersection of University Parkway and Long Drive. As well, the neighborhood's Small Area Plan will not accommodate any retail development in this specific area.

While sniffing around, I find out that the gentleman who had previously purchased land behind the afore mentioned HUD 202, Assembly Terrace—in a favorable relationship with Wake Forest University—is thinking about buying the church acreage to expand his tract of New Orleans-like rainbow-colored residential units, which he leases to students.

This type of housing, though fully occupied, would ruin the vision and value for a long discussed future resale of Winston-Salem First church. After a reasonable due diligence period, we find that Wake Forest University is really hurting for housing, with a 110% dorm occupancy.

Kelley, with the help of a newly selected team, steps to the mound! What if we could build a gated community with 328 beds sporting options for townhouses with up to 1,800 square feet and fully furnished four bedroom suites? And, what if we build it to look like Wake, operate like Wake, and even name it after Wake—Deacon Place? Might Wake Forest University or some generous donor buy the finished product for Wake?

However, it's not as easy as it sounds. There are many precarious moving parts—all of which have to align—for this team to score. Among the greatest of these challenges is *culture*.

For our purposes, *culture means the norms, values, expectations, traditions, and stories a group shares, along with the group's perceived place in the greater community.*

Here are the three cultures that we would come to know and honor:

Wake Forest University—A world class university with a stellar record of living up to its motto "Pro Humanitate." This Latin aspiration translates often as "For Humanity" and implies that Wake Forest University exists for the sake of humanity—with a responsibility to serve the local and global community.

However, in 2011, James Powell, Associate Professor of Classical Languages, suggests that the real meaning of the motto might be "developing the fullness of human potential" and "to consider what we are as human beings and what constitutes genuine human flourishing."

I use this as an example of WFU culture. WFU sees itself as a frontline leader locally and globally. It values and expects excellence. And it refuses to step on the toes of the local community. There will be no sale unless we can all learn to dance.

University Area Neighborhood Association (UANA): As defined on its Web site: The purpose of our organization is to support one another in maintaining our neighborhoods as a safe and pleasant place to live. While we are not anti-student, we are pro-neighborhood.

They do dance—but they have had their share of disappointments and broken promises by other developers. These unfavorable incidents have become part of their storyline. The Web site clearly states: Over the years, we have dealt with a variety of issues, including to *rezoning and local permits for construction or expansion of sites of concerned neighbors*, conversion of owner-occupied, single-family homes into rental houses (usually rented to Wake Forest undergraduates), and violations of the local noise and other ordinances by late-night partying at rental houses.

As for their place in the local community—UANA is a family-oriented neighborhood—with high expectations. Written expectations include taking pride in home and lawn maintenance, no parking on lawns, and no violations of the city/county noise ordinance. That means no loud parties between 11:00 p.m. and 7:00 a.m.—prime college party time—with the consequence of a $500 fine and up to 30 days in jail.

Winston-Salem City/County Planning Board: As stated on its Web site: The Planning Board's role *with regard to zoning issues is to conduct public hearings on proposed changes* to the Official Zoning Map (i.e., rezoning requests) and proposed amendments to the Unified Development Ordinances (i.e., text amendments). In addition to these advisory functions, the Planning Board acts as a *final decision-making board in regard to subdivision of land, approval of certain types of site plans,* and certification of areas as blighted for redevelopment projects. A professional planning staff serves the Board.

As noted earlier, the municipal planning staff—from a technical ordinance driven perspective—wants to do what is best for the community. So, if the community really doesn't want a development, the planning board—at their staff's advisement—will deny it. If, on the other hand, the development will be good for the community—once the concerns are addressed—then the planning board will approve the development.

Additionally, Councilpersons Dee Dee Adams and Jeff Macintosh—with crossing wards in the District will show up at the planning board sessions to represent their constituents.

Fortunately, I've already learned the dance of all three cultures. At WFU, I facilitated shared parking between the University and Winston-Salem First church—making the most of the limited land available. And, some of the administrators, faculty, and I have become genuine friends.

UANA knows me well from the 60-unit affordable housing community called Assembly Terrace. UANA taught me to bend, turn, and twist—as we removed a floor, changed the roof, and added a berm—beautifully blending the existing with the up and coming.

Lastly, having served on the City/County Planning Board—and having helped design the UDO, (Unified Development Ordinance)—I understand the limitations, wiggle room, and nuances of the Board.

However—I'm not dancing with just one or even two cultures. For our venture to be successful—I'll have to dance with all three of them simultaneously.

Let the dance begin.

Winston-Salem First originally purchased the land in 1997 to build student housing for a church based discipleship program and potentially a private high school. UANA resisted our idea. Therefore, the planning board approved rezoning for only two acres—with the stipulation that we'd maintain a 100-foot buffer to separate any new development from the existing residential homes.

Thankfully, years before, a former church deacon bought four houses. This afforded us the buffer requirements and the potential for new drive cuts. Also, we had a residential "vote" in UANA.

Additionally, three homes across the street from the four have come up for sale. With hesitancy, but knowing we need support from the community, Kelley—the man with the money—tells me to purchase them. At the time, I think it's a waste of money. Our development will never reach across the street. But it ends up being a most brilliant move.

These houses are actually rentals. Nothing more than cages for the party-animals that insist on breaking virtually every rule of UANA—noise, upkeep, vehicle placement, and general regard for the other neighbors. We are talking college teenagers here, after all!

Now—UANA is ready to dance. The Association is grateful that we own the rentals. They also know that we will eventually resell the units. Even though UANA knows that it is against the law for me—as a realtor—to discriminate, they ask for my assurance that these homes will be sold to individual families where possible, thereby *restoring* the neighborhood. Keyword: restoring.

We assure them that we want nothing less than to leave UANA and the families that it represents, better than we found them. I will make every effort to honor their wishes, as my wish is their wish. In the end, we were able to sell two to families. The third remained a rental.

At this turn, UANA is ready to look at our blueprints, and pleasantly surprised that we want to build an upscale GATED community—that will most likely be populated with *graduate* students. They know that at some point, something is going to be built on this land, and they will be hard-pressed to find a better dance partner.

With UANA's blessing in hand, we next approach Pilot Mountain Baptist Association. We have been in conversation for over 20 years and though they do not use this property—they are holding on to it for "investment" purposes. In a nutshell, their two acres are worth about $600,000 because it has priceless curb-cut on Long Drive.

But they want $900,000. When we do the math—it will cost us $750,000 to build the roads and infrastructure we need—by disrupting the four houses we bought on Barclay Terrace. Doing that—taking away homes from UANA which is the opposite of *restoring* the neighborhood—will kill the deal. The Planning Board would not approve of it. So, we overspend for the two acres to stay in the dance with UANA and the Planning Board.

Once we have the two acres under control—with its precious curb-cut—the Planning Board rezones all 12 acres. Now that everyone on the dance floor is happy, we take our plans to Wake Forest University. Wake gives us their blessing.

In the meantime, Mike Kelley—who has only built Big Box retail stores and a theater—is looking for a company to build the student housing. His brother in Colorado gives him two leads.

We interview both and choose Signet Real Estate Group—a world-class global firm which has built several premier housing facilities.

Simultaneously, Signet interviews us and ultimately, because they can match the needs of Wake Forest University step for step—think dance—Signet chooses to work with us.

Now—after all the relationships are in place—the money follows. Mike Kelley has already spent $500,000. Signet invests $2 million and brings in the remaining $20,000,000 from six investors.

Deacon Place opens in the spring of 2017—complete with a 6,000-square-foot community center, which sports a fitness center, game room, a resort-style pool, fire pits, and outdoor BBQ grills.

By December 2018, this premier community is operating at nearly 100% capacity. As hoped, Wake Forest University cuts in and claims the purchase for $28.42 million.

Everyone is happy. Wake Forest acquires the ultimate in student housing for its upperclassmen and graduate students without taking the risk of managing all the moving parts.

UANA is thrilled to welcome new families—reclaiming three of these houses from student renters—and restoring their neighborhood. Lastly, the City/County Planning Board feels that rare sense of satisfaction when all involved community players move in unity—and the community is better for it.

However, before detailing the social outreaches that have always been in parallel with my growing marketplace experience—allow me to clue you in on a conversation that ultimately leads to a chance to explore governance—sometimes called "politics."

DEACON PLACE

Learnings from Sector III

1.) Everyone is looking for respect and gratitude. Money may satisfy temporarily—but genuine appreciation motivates people to do their best. (See Herzberg's motivation-hygiene theory.)

2.) If you are a Big Picture person, bring people around the table who can make it happen. Any true vision is bigger than the visionary. High impact players know that.

3.) Some dreams take 30 years. Some 30 months. The big stuff takes longer.

4.) There comes a time when the initiator releases the dream. As Kenny Roger's sang, "You've got to know when to hold 'em. Know when to fold 'em. Know when to walk away. And, know when to run.

5.) A few key words to be familiar with in the marketplace: Equity, Debt, EBITA, and Value.

6.) Become a "possibility" thinker—"what if" and "why not?"

7.) If the organization you are with is not aligned with your goals, you will seldom make a lasting impact. Move on!

8.) Life is not about chasing the money—it's about chasing the value.

Sector IV

Politics

Bost accepts an invitation to run for Mayor and in doing so, garners much needed insights into the inner-workings of municipal governance. When conditions are optimal—this catalyst accelerates significant improvements for the Village of Clemmons. Conversely, when political will falters—meaning that change is no longer imminent—Bost accepts a new invitation. It's a reminder that catalysts can't make the impossible happen.

Chapter 30

What? Run for Mayor

"John," my neighbor, Al, asks, "can we have a meeting in your cabin?"

Al Harbury—a retired NASA scientist—lost his run for council prior to moving in next door to me. However, he continues to advocate for Smart Growth—intentional and sustainable development—in Clemmons.

The Old Guard—many of whom swaddled our newly incorporated village in 1986—opposes virtually all growth. They want Clemmons to remain a quiet little bedroom community with low taxes.

As for the cabin—well, that is in my backyard. LaDonna always wanted a mountain cabin, and when that doesn't happen, she suggests, "Why don't you build it here."

So, in 2006—a year before my conversation with Al—Dixon Builders constructs our 720-square-foot cabin. The rustic design uses the best of natural materials to accent our main feature—a handcrafted wood-burning fireplace.

LaDonna and I have slept in "the cabin" a few times, but mostly we use it for meetings—such as the one Al is calling for. So on the appointed day and time, nine people file in. All concerned citizens—they are all capable of garnering community support, running for council, or even mayor.

Al speaks for the group and says, "We want strategic issues addressed by our leadership. But when we approach the Council members—they don't seem to want to resolve the problems."

"What issues are we talking about?" I ask.

"For one," someone in the group offers, "the increasing traffic problem on Lewisville Clemmons Road. Everyone knows that it's been a problem since the I-40 interchange went in, but no one wants to solve it."

"Plus," chimes in Robert Marshall, "when we bring up the Development Guide, they say, 'That's not a plan. It's only a guide.' So, they don't pay attention to it.'"

Then he adds, "Maybe it is only a guide. So, *why* don't we have a plan?"

After listening to their concerns and frustrations, I suggest, "What you are describing sounds like a PAC—Political Action Committee. It's basically a non-profit that raises money to influence the elections. I can help you set that up."

After deciding to name the group Proactive Citizens of Clemmons—PACC—someone hands me a plastic bag and says, "We've already started raising money. We have $119.60."

As momentum builds, someone says excitedly, "You could be our treasurer, John."

I quickly set that straight, saying, "No thank you. I'm not going to be part of your organization. I'm simply going to help you set it up."

So, in the summer of 2007, I head to the local Board of Elections to register PACC. In the course of the conversation, I say, "Oh, they have already started raising money. They already have $119.60."

"When did they collect it?" she asks.

"I don't know. Seems like they've been collecting money for about a month now," I say offhandedly.

The clerk asks, "Where is it?"

I say, "In a plastic bag."

She then demands, "You'll have to forfeit the money."

"Why!"

"You had it longer than 10 days and didn't register it. You will have to forfeit it."

"No," I say adamantly. "These good people in our community have gone door-to-door to collect the money. I'm not giving it up. It might not be much, but it's a matter of principle."

"Okay," she says calmly. "Then just sign here acknowledging that you have the funds."

A few days later, I get a call from Raleigh—someone from the NC Board of Elections.

"Is this John Bost?"

"Yes. How may I help you?"

WHAT? RUN FOR MAYOR

"Sir," he says directly, "I understand that you are in possession of $119.60 from the Proactive Citizens of Clemmons. I'll need for you to write a check for that amount to the State of North Carolina."

His statement hits me like a punch in the gut.

I say, "Sir, let me tell you something. I'd rather go to jail than to give you that money."

Without missing a beat, he says, "I'm calling you because I have the authority to arrest you."

I say, "You're kidding! For $119.60 that was collected in good faith by our PACC members."

"Sir," he says—like he's had this same conversation with 100 other people—"I'm very serious. Do you remember Jim Black? (Former NC House Speaker) They put him in prison. The amount of money doesn't matter. It's the law."

Softening—trying not to shoot the messenger—I suggest, "Surely, there is another way."

He pauses, and offers this helpful advice, "There is one way to avoid forfeiting the money. You can collect affidavits from every individual that gave you money. And, there is a limit of $50 per person. So, if someone gives you $60 and he is married—have the husband and wife sign that they each gave $30."

When I share this story with the PACC group—Al speaks for the group and says, "If you can do *that*—we want YOU to be our Mayor."

"Sorry guys," I say shaking my head. "I'm up to my eyeballs in work and other outreach programs. I'm not your man."

I didn't detail my involvement in Abbey Green, Nicaragua, and some social outreach ventures.

Al pleads, "It's not a full-time job, John. And, you're the one with the planning board experience and the heart to do this. What would it take to interest you in this?"

"Let me think about it," I say.

At a certain point, I recall my mission to impact cities and realize that this might be part of that. Therefore, I start doing a little investigating. First on my list is a visit with Village Manager Gary Looper.

A CATALYST FOR CHANGE

Briefly, I confess that I've paid little attention to Village politics—even though I've lived in Clemmons for 10 years. Looper graciously brings me up to speed.

The Village is governed by the Council/Manager form of government. The Mayor and one Council member are elected for a two-year term. The remaining four Council members are elected to four-year terms.

The elected *Council* adopts the annual budget, hires the Village Manager—Looper—passes ordinances, and appoints citizens to various boards. The *Village Manager* then carries out the Council's wishes and manages the daily operations of the Village. And, the first ever *Village Planner*—Megan Ledbetter hired just months earlier—advises the Council on how to best preserve, prepare, and protect the community by making best use of the land.

After meeting with Ledbetter, attending a few Monday evening Village Council meetings, and even meeting with the current Mayor—I'm still wavering.

Then, one day, one of the potential candidates says to me, "I hear you're thinking of running for Mayor. Don't waste your time. This is my year and I have the necessary support. If you run, you're wasting your time, you'll simply lose."

I feel the hair stand up on the back of my neck. Nobody makes decisions for me, at least with that approach.

I say plainly, "Sir, you just helped me make up my mind. Thank you!"

Incidentally, I would come to know this gentleman much better in the days ahead, and come to respect his often tongue in cheek comments.

The next day, I register as a candidate for Mayor. Lastly, I need three viable candidates for Council members—people who believed in the PACC vision. Two PACC members—my neighbor Al and Robert Marshall—sign on, along with existing Councilman Larry McLellan. Chris Jones and Mary Cameron remained as Council, totaling five.

When ballots are tallied—over 60% are cast for John Bost. My "Council team" wins too. It's time to navigate yet another sector of community—municipal governance. My duties begin January 2008.

Chapter 31

We Need a Compass

One of my first official acts as Mayor is to plant a Historical Marker at U.S. 158 and Bryn Mawr Lane. This marks the approximate place where the first stake was driven by Moravian surveyors of the Wachovia Tract 256 years earlier, in 1752.

The public ceremony is consistent with my platform—in which I promise to promote Clemmons' history and heritage.

My Moravian friend, Kevin Frack, presiding at the event says, ""I hope that instead of looking back at the past to recover something that's there, that we actually build on the past."

In those few words, he summarizes my challenge—to honor our past, embrace our present, and plan for our future. This mission stirs in me a new sense of adventure.

Now, age 60—with years of experience in planning and development, coaching and leadership development—what is possible? I know one thing for sure; we want to go 20 years into the future.

Thus begins a two-year journey that ultimately results in a 136-page plan—*The Village of Clemmons COMMUNITY COMPASS 2030 Comprehensive Plan.*

Here is what we find—and when I say "we," I mean 2,500 residents who weigh in by participating in polls, community forums, and workshops. That alone—having more than one out of 10 residents participate—proves that the people of Clemmons care.

We are in the midst of tremendous growth. In the planning area (Village boundaries plus the edges that might be annexed)—the population of Clemmons has grown as follows:

- 1990—9,235
- 2000—15,941
- 2009—23,010

A CATALYST FOR CHANGE

Stated differently, in the past 20 years (1990-2009) the population has skyrocketed by 150%. So, when we—the part of the community that chooses to engage—excavate the layers of Clemmons' problems, we reach this bedrock.

Unplanned growth. If that is the problem, then we have the solution—planned growth. Hence, our *Compass* or 20-year plan.

Here are our main issues:

- Clemmons—though rich with agrarian and village history—has no clear sense of self. It's lacking a consistent community "brand" and visitors have no sense of "arrival" or "destination."
- The traffic on Lewisville Clemmons Road is no longer a nuisance—it's dangerous. As the main artery from the I-40 exit—full of incremental (unplanned) developments from fast food to hotels to retailers—it lacks sufficient supporting roads. It is rife with accidents.
- More people require more municipal services—water, sewer, trash—and yet the Village tax rate remains one of the lowest in Forsyth County. Clemmons tax rate is .0985 per $100 value of real property (2009), while the average tax rate in North Carolina for a similar sized town is .29 per $100 valuation. Additionally, Clemmons ad valorem tax rate is capped at .15 per $100.
- The Village of Clemmons has no "heart"—No Village Center—culturally, socially, economically, functionally, but *not* geographically. Optimally, the Center is *the place* of mixed use—such as post office, hospital, library, along with restaurants, retail, and parks—with pedestrian friendly sidewalks. It's *the go-to place* for parades, events, and for showing off the Village to our out-of-town visitors.
- Quality of life—the opportunity to work, live, and play in our own Village—is greatly restricted. The only real park is Tanglewood—1200 beautiful acres on the west side of Clemmons. However, it's owned by Forsyth County and

requires a $2.00 admission free. The people of Clemmons want connected green-ways, bike paths, open spaces, and parks allowing for recreational opportunities throughout the village.
- The current commercial development—strip development (think line)—has resulted in visually unappealing curbside presence, lack of walkability, and definitely *not* proud focal points of the Village. Instead, like an envisioned Village Center—Clemmons wants several Activity Centers (think circle) where families can shop, recreate, receive professional services in areas that complement the surrounding neighborhoods and are visually appealing.
- Clemmons wants to be a good neighbor. In moving forward, Clemmons desires to work closely with its bordering communities—such as Bermuda Run in Davie County and the town of Lewisville.

The community offers some amazing solutions and as their newly elected Mayor, I truly want to act on their collective goals, dreams, and desires for our Village.

They, in turn, appreciate my experience from previous work on the UDO—Unified Development Ordinance, a multi-year appointment to the City/County Planning Board, and ultimately, my work on the *2001 Legacy Plan* for Winston-Salem.

Legacy is a larger and more comprehensive version of the forthcoming *Clemmons Compass*. Incidentally—studies found that 90% of the zoning decisions adhered to the *Legacy* plan—a success story in itself.

With this mutual respect, my role as Mayor becomes like that of a master chef. By extracting and combining the insights and observations of the Village Council, Planning Board, Steering Committee, Village Staff, Clarion Associates (our primary consultants) and the people of Clemmons—we reach consensus.

Before I know it, two years have passed and it's time for re-election. In November 2009, I run unopposed. Then, in the Spring of

2010, the *Clemmons Community Compass*—Clemmons' plan through the year 2030—is approved. It's time to celebrate.

5th Annual Clemmons Community Day
On behalf of the Chamber of Commerce, Jody Peske presents John Bost with an award to recognize his service and contributions as Mayor of Clemmons.

Chapter 32

Clemmons Community Day

Enthralled by the community spirit of the people of Clemmons—I want to give them more than a paper *Compass*. After all, what makes our community special is not its geography, it's our people.

However, when I run the idea past the Council—they are less interested—the response is more of a "tried and failed," perhaps lessons learned on behalf of the longer term members.

Undeterred, I talk with our Village Planner, Megan Ledbetter. Ledbetter is full of energy and ideas, and yes, very skilled. I've learned much from her—during Council meetings—as she waits patiently for just the right moment to speak.

"Megan, we need to have a community celebration! Our people are special and we need to stir up our community pride."

"You're right, Mayor," she says, always cheerful. "Our people are our greatest asset."

"Well," I explain, "the Council doesn't seem very interested in putting legs under this idea."

"That's because it's not their job," she says plainly.

Then, she adds, "It's not the Mayor's job either. Your job is to take care of the water, sewer and trash—stick to the *Compass*. But community celebrations are beyond your jurisdiction."

She then gives me a little hope, by saying, "I'm not saying that it can't be done. You'll just have to find a different way to do it."

When that door closes, I look for a window. That window proves to be fellow Realtor and active member of our relatively new Chamber of Commerce, Brad Hunter.

"Brad," I ask, "how can we pull together a celebration for our Village? We don't have a single event—no parade, no movie night, nothing. We need something to bring us together."

"What do you have in mind?" he asks.

A CATALYST FOR CHANGE

"Well, something family-oriented—that the whole community can embrace. Food, music, games—maybe we could get our business community behind it. I'd spearhead it myself, but from Council's and Town Hall staff perspective, it better fits the function of the Chamber of Commerce.

"Hmmm," Brad says audibly. "If we can use this as a chance to showcase our local businesses, then it would make sense to involve the Chamber of Commerce. Why don't we go see Jody Peske at the Chamber?"

That is the match that lights the fuse. Peske—another Realtor—loves the idea and garners the support of her fellow Chamber business members, such as Frank Samuelson of the Civic Club, eventual councilman and Realtor, Jack Ingle, Joanna Lyall from Wake Forest Baptist Health, and numerous of other key volunteers to form the first Clemmons Community Day committee.

Together—with my Mayor's hat off—we secure vendors, a venue, games, food, and music. Then, early in May 2010, we host our First Annual Clemmons Community Day on the Broncos Football Field—directly behind Clemmons Elementary School. It proves to be a big success—with 50 vendors and a large crowd of neighbors.

The next year—as word spreads—it's even bigger—now with even partial funding from the Council itself. By the third year, we've partnered with the Jerry Long Family YMCA in Clemmons. Of all the YMCAs in northwest North Carolina, this one gets the most daily visits. So, it is a perfect location. And, the YMCA sponsors its YMCA Healthy Kids Day as part of our festivities.

By our 10th Annual Clemmons Community Day (2019), visitors come out in droves—rain or shine. We've added a NASCAR Show Car & Simulator, poetry and live music, a rock climbing wall, gem mining, trackless train rides, fitness demonstrations, a giant slide, bounce houses and more. Also, everyone is encouraged to bring a can of food to donate to the Clemmons Food Pantry—to help our neighbors in need.

However, with my Mayor's hat back on, it's time to learn to dance with the giants—Novant Health and the Winston-Salem Forsyth County Schools.

Chapter 33

Village Point

Prior to my being elected as Mayor, the two local leaders in healthcare—Novant Health and Wake Forrest Baptist Medical Center—each petition the State for permission to build a hospital in our prospering Village of Clemmons.

Instead of deciding either/or—the State opts to "divide the baby." Baptist will locate its 53-bed hospital in Davie County—just across the Yadkin River. Novant will build its 53-bed hospital—less than three miles away—in Village Point in Clemmons.

Shortly after this, the community—via the *Compass*—confirms Village Point as the new Village Center.

The *Village Point Small Area Plan* (2003) acknowledges the challenges of limited road access and watershed restrictions. At the same time, it calls for upscale retail, office campus, civic buildings, walking trails and connecting greenways, a lake, mixed residential, upscale town homes, an outdoor amphitheater, a 12-screen theater/entertainment complex, the Jerry Long YMCA, parks and open spaces.

In 2010—as Novant moves forward with its building plans, it offers to give the lake on its property to the Village of Clemmons. Novant wants to support the community's wish for a local park. Therefore, the Council is flabbergasted when I propose that we decline the gift.

My argument: This 7-acre lake is part of the storm water facility—as noted in the *Small Area Plan*. Whoever owns the lake is responsible to make sure that as the water moves downstream, it moves at the same *quantity* and *quality* as the stream it's entering. Managing the flow and the sediments can be very costly. Additionally, if that old earthen dam holding it together bursts, we'll have real liability for the flooded property downstream.

A CATALYST FOR CHANGE

A Plan and a Picture

Writing a plan—honoring all interested parties—and illustrating with pictures is the surest means to garner support and stay on target.

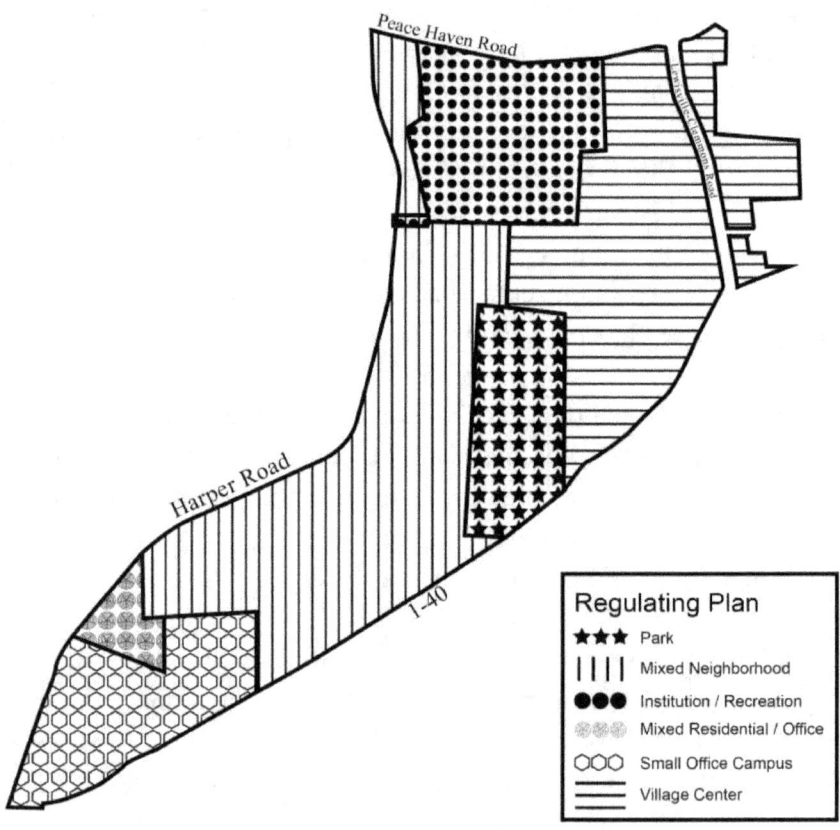

Village Point—the new Village Center—is a 340-acre tract bounded by Peacehaven Road to the north, I-40 to the South, Lewisville-Clemmons Road to the east and Harper Road to the west. Nearly 124 acres are approved for Novant Hospital and a new elementary school.

Map from the 2003 *Village Point Small Area Plan*.
For more information visit www.JohntheCatalyst.com

One of the Council members asks, "So what are you suggesting?"

"We need to tell Novant that we don't want it," I say plainly. "We don't want it *unless* they bring in a consultant and find out what it's going to take for Novant to make it safe for us. And, I can tell you right now—based on other work I've done with storm water—that we are probably talking $1 million, if not $2 million."

In essence—I'm suggesting that we learn to dance with this giant. Dancing is not having the giant—Novant—take all the steps forward, while we are backed into a corner. Dancing requires that they, too, take some steps backwards, while we move forward. And like a dance, this *negotiation* can be pleasant and even awe-inspiring.

One of the Council members objects, "But the hospital is a non-profit. They don't have that kind of money."

"Let me tell you something," I say with a knowing smile, "they may be non-profits, but they aren't hurting. They simply call their excess funds 'surplus income' instead of profits. They have plenty of money and we don't need a white elephant."

As hoped, Novant agrees to dance. It engineers a proper dam with its own sediment facilities—and then it gives Clemmons a true gift. The new Village Point Lake qualifies for the N.C. Wildlife Resources Commission's Community Fishing Program. The Commission stocks the lake with 350 large-mouth bass, 3500 bluegills, and 700 ready to eat channel cats.

Then, the Village steps up to build a state of the art fishing pier. Lastly, the people with poles—sometimes grandparents pass on the art of fishing to grandchildren—populate the park. It's really a beautiful thing to watch—when community cooperates for a best possible outcome.

Additionally, Novant donates land for the park and shares the cost of completing Town Center Drive—also a need highlighted in the *Small Area Plan* and the *Compass*. This road improves access to the hospital, the school, and Harper Road. And, it opens the way for further *planned* growth.

In 2013, Novant gives us our biggest gift. It opens Novant Health Clemmons Medical Center at Village Point. This hospital is a first-rate facility—that sets a high bar for neighboring businesses. Novant really does help our vision—set out in the *Compass*—become a reality.

In 2015, developer Chris Parr steps up and adds upscale residential living to Village Point. He opens the Clemmons Town Center Apartments. Notice "Town Center"—our community vision.

The first 208 units appeal to families wanting one, two, and three bedroom options ranging from 800-1300 square feet. And he has 104 more units on the way. Residents are literally living in a park in the new 'happening place' in Clemmons.

Tenants can walk to the YMCA, visit neighborhood restaurants—including Panera Bread or Dairi-O—bike down the greenways, visit a friend at the hospital, or walk to the *new Frank Morgan Elementary School*. The whole area—Village Point—really is all and even more than we ever hoped for.

However, I'm getting a little ahead of myself. To get that new school, we'll have to dance with another giant—the WSFC School system. We need to negotiate the kind of school that will merit a presence in our new Village Point. Here, too, communities can be too quick to "accept anything" offered in response to such accelerated growth.

When I approach the Council—recommending that we delay accepting the school—they look at me like, "What kind of Mayor are you? Are you for us or against us?"

It is true that Clemmons and Southwest Elementary School, both just off Lewisville-Clemmons Road, are bursting at the seams, and frankly, anything we could do to modify traffic patterns would be a win. We really do need another elementary school and no better place than in the expansive Village Point complex. But that is exactly my point.

I tell the Council, "We don't want a situation like they have at the new Meadowlark campus in Winston-Salem. They've already outgrown their campus and have to use trailers. And the traffic is so congested that parents are often waiting 30 to 45 minutes to drive one-quarter of a mile. So we need to make sure that we get this right. We don't need traffic jams at Village Point."

With their blessing, I have a conversation with Superintendent Dr. Don Martin. I have considerable respect for this community leader—a true forward thinker. And, as a former associate superintendent—I understand his challenges. But, my job is to stand up for the best interests of the citizens of Clemmons.

When we meet, I explain forthrightly, "Before you build *your* school in Village Point, it has to have the appropriate infrastructure (roads) so that it fits our *Small Area Plan* with the hospital and other developments. It has to accommodate the expected *future* growth."

"We can't do that," he counters. "We can only build for current enrollments."

"That's ridiculous," I say. "We both know that once you drop in a school—like Meadowlark—rooftops follow. Then, like Meadowlark, you're soon over-spilling into those ugly trailers and you've got one of the worst stacking (traffic) problems in Forsyth County at the end of each day."

"I know that," Martin concedes. "However," he adds, "we are absolutely constrained."

Agitated—by the narrow-minded laws that restrict both of us—I say, "Then, we don't want *your* school."

Unruffled, Martin replies, "Fine. We'll build it somewhere else."

Now I know that this is not a solution. Our schools in Clemmons are aging. And expanding Clemmons Elementary—as they've considered in the past—isn't really an option. Already with a Walmart proposed and the Post Office in close proximity, traffic jams up on Highway 158.

So, Dr. Martin and I continue our "dance" over the next several weeks. On the one hand, the proposed school has plenty of land—a bargain offer from Novant. It's simply a matter of agreeing to use the land for Smart (sustainable) Growth—creating traffic circles—and ample driveway and parking space around the school.

Also, it is a matter of designing the school to accommodate our *future* growth while meeting our upscale architectural standards for Village Point. Thankfully, all the details are ironed out.

A CATALYST FOR CHANGE

September 2011, the new W. Frank Morgan Elementary School—named for a local 30-year principal and decorated WWII Veteran—opens for classes. The first year, it serves 500 students, with a capacity for 775. The school is everything we hoped for, a true point of pride for Village Point—our new Village *Center*— and for the Winston-Salem Forsyth County Schools.

However, with all this success under my belt, I try to dance with an alligator. Alligators don't dance. It is then, that I learn some hard lessons about the politics of municipal governance.

Chapter 34

Bond Referendum

Before I know it, two more years have sped by. It's time for the re-election in 2011. It's also time to turn our attention to the increasingly hazardous Lewisville Clemmons Road.

This is why PACC insisted that I run for Mayor in the first place. In my defense, just weeks after winning, I met with the NC Department of Transportation (NCDOT) to talk about an interchange at I-85 in Lexington. This is personal business—regarding a possible national waterpark venture.

However, before leaving the meeting, I say, "Let me ask you a question. I understand the Council in Clemmons has been asking for a feasibility study on Lewisville Clemmons Road since 2004. This is 2008. What's the hold up with that?"

The group looks at me as if I'm suddenly throwing my weight around.

Then, a division engineer for the NCDOT tells them, "I need to share something with you before anyone responds. You may not realize that John Bost is the newly elected Mayor of Clemmons."

Before he can continue, I say evenly, "I am very politically naïve. And I will say whatever I need to say to whomever I need to say it. We really need that feasibility study."

Three months later, we have our study. It has five options—ranging from $55 million to $165 million. Though the NCDOT owns the road—it declines to pick a solution. Instead, it recommends that the Council sort it out.

However, in 2009, I receive a letter from the NCDOT telling me in no uncertain terms that the State will put in a median—to improve the safety of Lewisville Clemmons Road. The letter strongly suggests that we devise a plan to compensate for the slowed traffic. I know from experience that we will have to mitigate consumer frustration. People will no longer be able to make left turns into businesses. As it stands, they will have to employ a U-turn to access businesses on the opposite side of the street.

The NCDOT is less concerned about the economics. For the DOT—it's all about safety. A median will decrease accidents. It's proven. However, having to navigate a median causes alarm among business leaders—in their eyes, it will decrease business. Ironically, unmitigated traffic and high accident rates are more the detriment to traffic volume, and thus business income.

The problem and the solution are found on pages 92 and 93 of the *Compass*. It's important to remember that the *Compass*—approved in 2010—represents the will of the people.

Page 92 says in part, "NCDOT has plans to improve the (Lewisville Clemmons) roadway from four driving lanes with a fifth continuous turn lane to four driving lanes with an *11 foot landscaped median*, sidewalks on either side, and consolidated driveways, as feasible. These improvements will improve traffic flow and provide better access management along the corridor."

Page 93 says in part, "Create a *parallel street system* by linking cross-access driveways between adjoining properties to create an urban street on either side of the Lewisville-Clemmons Road." Our plan is to connect backstreets off of Lewisville-Clemmons Road just south of Interstate 40.

So, I talk to the Council. It's going to cost us, but we need to have our parallel roads in place *before* the NCDOT—who owns Lewisville Clemmons Road—builds the median. They are giving us fair warning—lets be proactive and follow our *Compass*.

Additionally—in 2011—this is still what the people want. Earlier in the year, we surveyed 700 residents and found that 55% favor improving the flow and safety of the road.

At the same time, let's be smart about this. We just came through a scary economic recession in 2008. Now we know recessions can happen. To be on the safe side, let's float a bond as a safety net.

That way, if we start construction and have an economic downturn—we won't be stuck with our streets torn up. We can access the bond to complete our project. Additionally, if we access the bond and there are funds left over, we can use those funds to build a much needed connector road—Village Point Drive—in Village Point.

Three of the Council members agree—now is the time to act. Two, are more reluctant. I let them know that it's very important that we take a united stand on this issue. After all, Clemmons is extremely debt and tax averse. This will be the first bond in its history. So we will need to present a solid front. We eventually come to a labored consensus.

First, we try the easy route. If our legislature will support the bond, we can avoid a bond referendum (letting the voters decide). However, our House Reps decline. They know that debt is a controversial issue in Clemmons and they plan to run again.

Not wishing to wait, we hire a consultant to guide us through the referendum process. Unfortunately—in the name of frugality (the mayor has no vote)—we hire the lowest bidder.

I know we are in trouble when he calls me the next day and asks, "Mayor Bost, what do you think we should do?"

He doesn't have a plan, nor does he have much experience. However, we decide to move forward. Our consultant issues one warning: Elected officials cannot *advocate* for the bond. Unfortunately, we are not told that we can *educate*. We truly are novices at this!

Nonetheless, we "leak" our dilemma to key supporters at the Chamber of Commerce. The Chamber, in turn, starts an advocacy group named *Friends of Clemmons*. Then, by means of signs, newspaper stories, and information sessions, *Friends of Clemmons* spreads the word.

Just to verify—according to the 2011 Village of Clemmons Annual Financial report, "The Village *has no general fund debt* as of the fiscal year ended June 30, 2011. However, there is *a bond referendum on the November 8, 2011 ballot for a $6,000,000* general obligation bond for streets and sidewalk improvements. Voter approved debt repayment is calculated outside the tax cap limit."

As stated earlier, funds from the bond will be a safety net. They are earmarked for constructing parallel roads on each side of Lewisville Clemmons road—as outlined in the *Compass*— with an allowance that any unused funds can be used to build a connector road at Village Point.

A CATALYST FOR CHANGE

As the bond referendum gains traction—the opposition takes a stand. Mainly the Old Guard—these business leaders are concerned that if we build parallel roads, the business center will quickly shift from "Historic Clemmons" to Village Point. That will likely decrease the value of property that they are personally holding in the south end of the Village.

However—that is not how they sell it to the public. First, they use gorilla marketing—waiting until the Thursday before the voting Tuesday to "drop a bomb" on the voting public. This only muddies the waters and scares the voters.

To accomplish their mission, they create a rival group called *The REAL Friends of Clemmons*—an anti-bond group that matches our signs tit-for-tat. Then they do a media blitz—investing $5000—in anti-bond advertorials.

Using aggressive tactics seemed to me a little un-neighborly. But where I draw the line is when trusted public leaders *purposely mislead* the very people they are supposed to be protecting.

Their false claims are as follows:
1) Mayor John Bost is a tax and spend RINO—Republican In Name Only.
2) Mayor John Bost plans to use this $6,000,000 like a line of equity—using it at will.
3) Most deceptively—Did you know that once the bond is in place, the Council can actually borrow back the amount it pays off each year in principal? They perhaps never ever intend to pay this off.

Regarding point three, what they fail to tell the public is this: In order to borrow the $50,000 a year in principal paid, we would have to float a $100,000 bond referendum. No one is going to pay $100,000 to borrow $50,000. So "real friends" *intentionally* paint a false picture for the public.

Then, on the day of election—at the polls—the "real friends" follow voters up to the doors while giving them sample ballots of write-in candidates and encouraging them to vote against the bond.

BOND REFERENDUM

As we wait for the ballots to be counted—I am livid. I don't know and I don't care who wins the election. What I care about is my perception of *corruption* of our political process in the Village that I love.

Two minutes before midnight, Dwight Sparks—the editor and publisher of the Clemmons Courier—calls.

He says, "Well Bost, looks like you won again!"

I snarl back, "Let me tell you something, Dwight. Nobody won in Clemmons tonight."

He says cheerily, "Tell me about it. This is going to be fun."

I should have hung up.

Instead, I say, "What they did to Clemmons is criminal."

I go on to tell him about how the "real friends" pressured the voters right up to the election doors. They basically handed out a ballot that for all practical purposes misled the community as to the purpose and the payoff of the bond.

I'm sure in what was my least ever leadership moment, it must have sounded as if I no longer wanted to be Mayor. The *Winston-Salem Journal* called next and apparently picked up on that as well!

I lost all three of my Council members—meaning that I no longer had the three necessary votes to follow the *Compass*.

The next morning—life goes on—I speak at Leadership Winston-Salem. A reporter from the *Winston-Salem Journal* approaches me.

She tells me that when the *Journal* called the night before—they had me on speakerphone. I was so angry—and rightfully so—that the reporters didn't even recognize me. They said to themselves, "Who is this guy?"

She says, "If you give us an exclusive interview, we will give you the headline tomorrow."

By this time—I've had a chance to calm down, and have talked with wise counsel. I know that I want to be part of the solution, rather than add to the problem of distrust of leadership in Clemmons. I agree to the interview.

Journal Reporter Paul Garber titles the story: *Clemmons Mayor Staying*. He notes my reasons for stating that the "election was corrupted."

A CATALYST FOR CHANGE

Paul conveys my concerns and my capacity for working with the three new Council members who were against the bond. I've worked hard to build a united Council—so this will be challenging.

However, I eat crow and promise, "I believe that is my skill set (building a team) and I believe I can build another one. I'm trying my best to build bridges and not burn bridges."

Interestingly, the *Journal* contacts Forsyth Elections Director Rob Coffman about the anti-bond volunteers following the voters up to the polling doors.

He says, "Being aggressive in a campaign is not illegal. It's kind of the *American way*."

This is further confirmed when I later meet one of the anti-bond opponents—a locally respected leader.

I say to him, "Why did you *knowingly* miscommunicate to the public?"

Without missing a beat, he quips, "That's just small town politics."

Lessons:
1.) Don't wrestle an alligator. When people are willing to give up their values—the very thing that sets humans apart from the beasts—don't be drawn into a fight.
2.) Test the water. We knew that 55% of our polled population favored fixing the traffic on Lewisville Clemmons Road. In hindsight, we should have polled more pools of people—in various neighborhoods and employment.
3.) Don't float a bond in an election year. When it's time, have a bond referendum as the only issue—with plenty of time and *education* available for the public. Also, anticipate and neutralize any purposeful or unexpected misconceptions.
4.) Remember that people are easily led and misled. Usually, it's the loudest and most negative voice that people remember.
5.) Never answer the telephone when you are angry—justified or otherwise!

Chapter 35

Churning Concrete

Churning cream in a butter maker is hard work—I did it as a child. But the results are worth it. Everyone gets to enjoy fresh, creamy butter.

Churning concrete in a butter maker is even harder. But the difference is: Nothing good comes from it. So it is with my next two years in office.

True to my nature—a reformer—I genuinely take on the challenge of building a united team with the three newly elected Council members. Knowing that nothing fortifies team spirit like a victory—I ferret out an opportunity.

My intent is to put a play in motion, hand the ball to the town manager—Gary Looper—and then let the Council take it across the goal line.

Hence, I meet with Matthew Dolge. He's an Appalachian State University alum, a resident of Clemmons, and the Executive Director of the Piedmont Triad Regional Council. Think relationship.

In digging around, I discover some money in the Appalachian Regional Commission (ARC).

I ask Dolge, "What would be necessary to access funds from ARC?"

He says, "It's designed for funding economic development in rural areas."

I acknowledge, "Clemmons is not considered a rural area."

Then, he adds, "If you have a development that creates significant jobs, then geography is not an issue. That is an exception that's written into the program."

We put our heads together and figure out how many jobs will be created if we use the funds to put in Village Point Drive—our new "center" of Clemmons—which will then pave the way for more development.

A CATALYST FOR CHANGE

With those stats in hand, Matthew works out a conversation with the Governor's office. A few of us from the village and the hospital meet to nail down logistics. When an agreement is reached, I get a call from the Governor's Chief of Staff. Of course, we will have to apply officially—but that will be a simple formality.

I call a closed session meeting and explain everything to the Council. This can be our first touchdown as a team. As the discussion continues, one of the Council members speaks up. He had earlier "called a contact from the Department of Commerce that controls the grant funding and they don't have any idea what you're talking about."

That call—motivated by a lack of trust—ruins the entire opportunity. When he makes the call, it puts the Governor in the hot seat because the decision was not yet official.

From there, things only deteriorate. Without a team and a common vision—I am stripped of any real power. It seems that the pendulum has swung from sheer joy in my first four years to sheer misery in my final two.

Not yet ready to give up serving the people, I decide to run for County Commissioner in 2012. The other eight candidates sign the marriage amendment. I don't sign it, not because of the issue at hand, but because I see it as partisan political ploy. It's a calculated means to steer voters to focus on a single issue—rather than the greater issues at hand. Need I say here, that I am not a good politician!

In the end, I lose the election—but come in as 4th runner up, the other winners, the three incumbents! That's not bad for a first attempt in the larger arena.

The marriage amendment passes and creates national attention. As the May 8, 2012 *New York Times* story headlines—North Carolina Voters Pass Same-Sex Marriage Ban.

The following year, 2013, friends and supporters pressed me to run for Mayor one more time. With a team—three members of the Council that now support the *Compass*—we can still move the needle and help the vision become a reality.

However, running for County Commissioner sent a message. Some saw this as proof that I really didn't want to be Mayor again. So, though I ran, I lost.

Oddly, in 2019—in preparation for this book—my writer and I meet with Town Planner Megan Ledbetter. As always, she is pleased to see me.

She asks me, "Did you know that we have already met 98 of the 100 objectives in the *Compass?* In fact, we are just finalizing the draft of our updated 2040 *Compass.*"

She then goes on to list some of the other positive changes that happened under my watch.
1) Clemmons Community Day is now a treasured *tradition*.
2) The Community Gardens—21 4' x 12' plots designed by a Girl Scouts troop, rented to residents, with much of the produce donated to the Clemmons Food Pantry, has a standing waiting list.
3) Village Point IS the Village *Center*—and real problems from the lake and potential school traffic have been averted due to passionate and patient negotiations.
4) The parallel roads—they are happening now! We were just a little ahead of our time on some things.

I tell her honestly, "Sometimes I have regrets. I wonder if I could have done things differently."

She smiles and says, "Your biggest strength and your biggest weakness is that you always have ideas. It's impossible to act on all of them. But know this—all the seeds that Mayor Bost planted in Clemmons are in full bloom now."

In hindsight—maybe I did somehow impact the city of Clemmons. But my heart still aches for the growing number of under-resourced in my hometown of Winston-Salem.

Learnings from Sector IV

1.) Municipal leadership requires thick skin, deep respect for constituent perspectives, and courageous behavior.

2.) Always do your homework. Learn as much as you can about the challenge/issue. Again, mine the knowledge base of your constituents.

3.) Become aware of and connected with grassroots leaders. They often have the best ideas.

4.) Be aware of leader loyalties and hidden agendas. These can remain long after the leader has moved on.

5.) Listen, listen, listen, even when it hurts.

6.) Always be prepared to eat crow. You can't know everything, so you are bound to make a few mistakes. Accept it. Admit it. Grow up. Move on.

7.) Just because an idea is right, doesn't mean it's the right time.

Sector V

Social Activism

Catalysts—in the lab and in life—are not consumed by the process. Instead, when a catalyst serves its purpose—creating an alternate path for an accelerated outcome—it is extracted, allowing the process to continue. The reclaimed catalyst is then free to speed significant change in a new undertaking. It's no surprise then that Bost continues to foster multi-sector collaboration—in one endeavor after another—to create sustained and measurable improvement in the lives of the under-resourced.

Chapter 36

Jumping on the Truck

How did this passion for the under-resourced—in my hometown with a large minority community—take seed in my heart? Maybe it came from being raised just one step ahead of poverty, but for His grace.

As early as 13 years old, my dad starts taking me to work. On Saturdays, during the school year and on most days during the summers, I jump on the back of his truck. Then, dad drives a few miles to pick up our day laborers. These are mostly black men from East Winston—in what is now thought of as east of US 52, but primarily in the historic Goler Depot corridor.

As others—one at a time—pile in the truck around me, we are all pretty comfortable. However, sometimes as a fast growing kid, even with a good breakfast behind me, my stomach is growling. This is especially apparent after dad picks up Ladson at the boarding house.

Ladson always hops on the truck with three freshly fried pork chop sandwiches. Once he's settled, he reaches into a "recycled" bread bag to grab the first sandwich. As he takes his first bite, I breathe deeply, trying to inhale all the delicious aroma—the shadow of the reality that he is enjoying.

His sandwich brings back fond memories of my Aunt Ginny. After killing a hog, she always fries up the tenderloin first thing—and that's a real treat. So, I'm always imagining what his sandwich tastes like. Then, one day—he reads my eyes and my drool—he gives me one of his fresh, hot sandwiches.

As I bite through the soft white bread—just like Ladson—the hot and juicy pork chop explodes with flavor as it fills my mouth. Slowly—well maybe not—I devour the rest of the sandwich, even nibbling the final bits of meat from the bone. Then, I pocket that memory for a lifetime.

On the job, dad puts me on the ground pitching bricks with the rest of the day laborers. Sometimes, they feel sorry for me, because my dad is often yelling at me. Better yet, in his eyes, he's teaching me to lead!

So, one day, I ask my dad, "Why are you so hard on me at work?"

A CATALYST FOR CHANGE

He says, "Johnny, I can't fuss at them or they will walk off the job. But I can fuss at you, and they'll hear it, and then they'll keep the brick moving."

His personnel management strategy worked! Incidentally, the men periodically ask my dad to teach them to lay brick. He tells them, "When you get ahead of loading the scaffolding with bricks and mortar, I'll give you a trial." Another management strategy!

This is a big deal, because help—myself only .75—is paid $1.25 for working on the ground and $3.50 for working on the scaffold. (Minimum wage in 1960 is $1.00 per hour.)

When it comes time for Ladson's "internship," he does well. Dad teaches him how to lay brick. So, we all work together—black and white—putting up residential and commercial brick buildings throughout Forsyth County and beyond.

And it's interesting—my dad taught me to honor and value our black community by driving into their neighborhoods, transporting them to work, and working with them side-by-side. My dad would be the first to tell you that—just like Winston-Salem depended on the backbone of black labor—his business did too.

Dad always valued and respected them both personally and professionally, as much as his upbringing afforded him. Let me explain.

Dad's dad integrated him into the black community when he was a teenager. After the farmhouse burned, Grandpa grew turnips, sweet potatoes, and corn, then loaded it all up in a wagon—along with my dad—and hauled it over to "colored town," as it was unfortunately called back then.

These folks didn't always have access to fresh vegetables—and so they were happy to see him coming. Later, when my dad decided to start his own bricklaying business, he understood their culture and they understood his heart. They knew that he would treat them right.

All of these experiences—part of our intergenerational narrative—creates fond memories and a sense of responsibility in my heart. Therefore, in 2002, when an opportunity arises to help restore part of the historic black community—I jump on board.

But first, let's take a quick look at the stories we all tell, our family narrative.

Chapter 37

What's Your Story?

During the Great Depression, my grandfather, Joseph Rowan Bost, lost his farm to the State because he owed $2000 in back taxes. So, he loads his family and belongings into the school bus that my Dad (then 16) drives and relocates to a rented farmhouse in Turnersburg, near Statesville, NC. Tragically, within weeks, that farmhouse burns to the ground.

Though his family escapes, they lose virtually all their earthly belongings, except the school's bus, some odd pieces of furniture, and a few bags of cotton they'd grown on the farm.

Grandpa moves into the city limits of Statesville, walks to work to grind brick molds for JC Steel, and within 20 years, he and his sons buy back a piece of that land that was lost. Then, Grandpa farms the land, while keeping his day job. In a word—recovery.

My father—Ben Ray Bost—faced similar hardships. At one point, he is working two, and sometimes three, jobs to support his wife and four children. For instance, with help from the GI Bill, he earns a diploma from DeVry Technical Institute and takes a day job with Western Electric, and then at night he loads freight at Roadway or Pilot. At a certain point, he realizes that this is not sustainable.

So one day, he takes a risk. He partners with his youngest brother, my Uncle Johnny Crest. JC had also become a brick mason. Both men had learned the trade as boys, but Dad needs to polish his skills.

At first, JC, the most experienced builds the corners, while Dad becomes proficient at laying to a "masonry line." They struggle at first (six kids between them) but soon are off and running with their own company. You can see where my knack for ideation and risk-taking might have evolved.

About the same time, Dad moves our family from a rented house on Tech Blvd. to an unfinished brick house in rural Forsyth County.

A CATALYST FOR CHANGE

A brick house was a big deal to us, so we all pitch in (I'm the oldest boy, at 14) to hang sheet rock, put down hardwood floors, and build a second bathroom which will be upstairs. Together, we make our house a home. I have to laugh now—much of our rough cabinetry comes from a kind shop teacher, Mr. Claude Edwards, who allows Dad and me to use his wood-shop.

That's our family story—our inter-generational narrative.

Does family narrative make a difference? Yes. In *The New York Times* story—The Stories That Bind Us— reporter Bruce Feiler cites the work of Dr. Marshall Duke (a psychologist at Emory University) and researcher Dr. Robyn Fivush.

The story makes two important points. First, "The single most important thing you can do for your family may be the simplest of all: develop a strong family narrative."

Why? "The more children knew about their family's history, *the stronger their sense of control* over their lives, *the higher their self-esteem* and *the more successfully they believed* their families functioned."

Additionally, "Dr. Duke said that children who have the most self-confidence have what he and Dr. Fivush call a strong '*intergenerational self*.' They know they belong to something bigger than themselves."

With this in mind, imagine if this had been my family narrative:

My ancestors were brought to America on slave ships. For generations, they are beaten, dehumanized, and eventually have the same legal rights as a piece of luggage.

Imagine, during the Revolutionary War, my grandfather—six generations back—is promised that if he enlists and fights, he will be freed at the end of the war. He fights valiantly, but finds that like so many other black soldiers—his master does not keep his promise. With no legal recourse, he returns to bitter slavery.

Then, in 1865—by means of the Thirteenth Amendment to the US Constitution—our family is freed from slavery. However, we have no money, no land, and few prospects. So, we remain on the land as sharecroppers.

The landowner lends us some land to use, and provides us with seeds, tools, food, clothing, and a rickety old shack to live in. At harvest time, he takes half the crop right off the top. Then, from our half, extracts the value for everything he's lent us. Some years, we have a small profit. In other years—years of poor harvest—our debt compounds.

However, a big break comes our way with the outbreak of WWII. My grandfather enlists for love of country, and in 1944 learns about the new GI Bill. This Bill promises *all veterans* three important opportunities. 1) Free college tuition. 2) Up to a year of unemployment benefits. 3) A government guaranteed low interest Veteran's loan to purchase a home.

Unfortunately, most black veterans—including my grandfather—are denied these benefits. When grandpa applies to several colleges—he is denied based on segregation. When he applies for his unemployment—the agency finds him a job digging ditches. He can't even support our family with the low wages. But the agency insists he take it or leave it. Either way, he will not receive any benefits.

Eventually, he finds a better job and tries to access the promised Veteran's home loan. He has his eye on a new tract home in the suburbs. However—due to redlining and segregation—my grandpa is excluded from the suburbs.

When he tries to buy a home on the East side of Winston-Salem—with a higher concentration of Blacks—the bank refuses to lend him money. The bank says that these homes lose value and they are not a good risk.

My grandfather is not the exception. A researcher on History.com states, "In 1947, *only 2* of the more than 3,200 VA-guaranteed home loans in 13 Mississippi cities went to black borrowers. "These impediments were not confined to the South," notes historian Ira Katznelson. "In New York and the northern New Jersey suburbs, *fewer than 100 of the 67,000* mortgages insured by the GI bill supported home purchases by non-whites."

A CATALYST FOR CHANGE

In fact, this same researcher says, "There was no greater instrument for widening an already huge racial gap in postwar America than the GI Bill."

Moving forward, my dad struggled before me and now I'm working two jobs—barely providing for my family. Our home, passed on from my dad has little resale value, my children attend underperforming schools, and I'm getting tired of swimming upstream just because I'm black. In my family, we go from one broken promise to another, and no matter what we do, we can't seem to get ahead.

Two very different intergenerational stories—and yet, potentially, people with each narrative live only about a mile apart. I grow up on the south side of Winston-Salem.

Chapter 38

What It's Like to Live in Winston-Salem

Sandi Scannelli lived in three different states before moving to Winston-Salem in 2018. We met shortly after her arrival through a mutual friend—Carolyn Pursel. Look at this amazing city through her fresh eyes.

"This city is rich in history, tradition, and continuity. Families have been rooted in the same place over a long period of time so they all know each other. And this area is blessed with an incredible higher education system—Wake Forest University, University of North Carolina School of the Arts, Winston-Salem State University, Salem College, and Forsyth Technical Community College.

"Then, there's this whole sports enthusiasts infusion in the community that creates a genuine sense of belonging. It's easy to feel wrapped in care and support. There's comfort in being so connected.

"Also, this is one of the richest philanthropic areas for its size of virtually anywhere in the US. The Winston-Salem Foundation is 100 years old—not many communities in the nation can say that. (16th oldest in the US, managing $565 million) There's also the Z. Smith Reynolds Foundation (80 years old, managing $683 million), Kate B. Reynolds Charitable Trust (72 years old, $576 million), just to name a few.

"However, what amazed me most was the neighborhood I moved into—some new loft apartments in Winston-Salem. It's largely one-bedroom units with single people from somewhere else. I think about 30% of the folks are here for residencies—very forward thinkers. And, it's a very diverse building. I can't even imagine how many countries are represented.

"This makes for a very comfortable 'neighborhood.' There is always something new to talk about with someone at the pool, in the fitness room, or in the clubhouse. Because of this, I drew the conclusion that this is a community—a city—that really makes it work. Everybody—people of all colors—live together in peace and harmony. I can live here. I thought the whole city was like my loft neighborhood."

Scannelli is not the only one to see the best of Winston-Salem. *U.S. News and World Report* ranks Winston-Salem #7 in Best Places to Retire and #31 in Best Places to Live in 2020.

In fact, in the past 20 years, Winston-Salem has *transformed itself* from a manufacturing town—heavy on tobacco, textiles, and furniture—to a leader in biotechnology, cancer research, and entrepreneurship.

For instance, Innovation Quarter—a 330-acre business campus, which by the way was once a thriving African-American business district—boasts over 170 high tech companies. One of them—the Institute for Regenerative Medicine—is growing replacement skin, blood vessels, and bladders to reduce the need for donors. It's helping people fight disease right now, and even supplying body part replacements for recent war veterans. Truly amazing!

Or, the new *500 West Fifth*—a recently revamped 18-story glass faced "eagles nest"—for startup entrepreneurs. This "incubator" is a way for Winston-Salem's own Don Flow to say thank you and you are welcome to succeed here in my beloved hometown. Check out a few of the tenants—such as Fly Wheel or Winston Starts which teaches entrepreneurs how to launch, fly, and sustain a new venture.

And then there's Venture Café—the fifth of only 10 in the world—a non-profit whose sole purpose for existing is to grow and support entrepreneurs. David Mounts— named 2018 Power Player of the Year—brought this to town. He's also the CEO of Inmar (a hugely successful and growing high tech company) and the founder of Mounts Robotic Center where students actually build and operate robots.

These are only a few of the new change agents in the city and it's all part of the plan.

Mayor Allen Joines says, "Over 5,300 net new jobs were created last year. Our goal is to be in the top 50 metro areas in the nation."

Interestingly, it's the young professionals—attracted by this transformed ecosystem called Winston-Salem—that are helping to further fit the city for the future. These educated lifelong learners come

WHAT IT'S LIKE TO LIVE IN WINSTON-SALEM

with expectations—for international culinary experiences, upscale retail, arts, plenty of entertainment options, and robust outdoor adventures.

Some of these "expectations" were already in place—10 craft breweries, over 500 restaurants—including Asian, Thai, French, Italian, South American, American, and authentic Southern cuisine—250 years of visual expression captured in the Downtown Art District, Diggs Gallery, Old Salem, Quarry Park, Salem Lake, BB&T Ballpark, and Riverrun International Film Festival. And within about an hour's drive—40 vineyards and the beautiful Blue Ridge Mountains.

Other "expectations" are being constructed and expanded—such as Bailey Power Plant—the entertainment hub of the Innovation Quarter. In fact, Bailey Power Plant—originally a 1947 coal-fired operation epitomizes the entire Winston-Salem transformation concept by smartly overlaying the future on the historic past. Its design allows the best of both eras to be visible to the viewer.

Like other nationally revered historic reinventions—this space engenders a feeling of "intergenerational connectedness." It stands as proof that what we do today really will matter tomorrow. And on that note, it's time to see the other side of Winston-Salem, because that matters too.

It turns out that Winston-Salem—East of US 52 is a very different place:

- Winston-Salem metro area is the 7th worst place to live in the U.S. according to a 2018 Hunger Study by FRAC (Food Research & Action Center) which bases its research on Gallup data. One in five residents (20.2%) struggles with food hardship.
- The overall poverty rate of Winston-Salem is 21%. About 11% of whites live in poverty, 28% of blacks, and 41% of Hispanics. Population in Winston-Salem is 240,000—110,000 white, 82,500 black, 37,500 Latino, 5,370 Asian, 4,630 other. (Latest US Census)
- About 43% of residents in Forsyth County earn income that does not meet their estimated needs. (Forsyth Futures: F.C. Poverty Study)

A CATALYST FOR CHANGE

- "Winston-Salem ranks 20th in the nation for highest child poverty rates. Winston-Salem has higher numbers than places like Chicago, Pittsburgh and Dallas. The report ranks Fayetteville at 39, Greensboro at 50, Charlotte at 88 and Raleigh at 91." (Spectrum News Report 01/16/19)
- In Forsyth County, over 50% of the black population lives in zip codes 27101, 27105, and 27107—known as East Winston. Most live on the *eastside of Highway 52* in what was once the industrial hub of the city. (2018 Study by Black Philanthropy Institute (BFI))
- East Winston-Salem residents have lower income, lower housing, lower education, and greater poverty than in the rest of Forsyth County or the State. The area also has inadequate jobs, poorly performing schools, and only ONE grocery store. (2018 Study by Black Philanthropy Institute (BFI))
- Children born in poverty have a low likelihood of ever escaping poverty. Forsyth County is ranked as one of the worst counties (ranked second from the bottom of 2478 US Counties) for income mobility. (Chetty & Hendren 2015 as cited in 2018 Study by Black Philanthropy Institute (BFI))
- Blacks are now worse off than they were in 2000, suffering a loss in median income in Forsyth County. (2018 Study by Black Philanthropy Institute (BFI))
- In Forsyth County areas of concentrated poverty (at least 40% of residents are living in poverty) are in Winston-Salem, mostly *east of Highway 52* (34 sq. miles) (2018 Study by Black Philanthropy Institute (BFI))
- Black residents are seven times more likely to live in areas of concentrated poverty, compared to whites. (2018 Study by Black Philanthropy Institute (BFI))
- From 2015-2017, property values in Forsyth County appreciated by 6%. In eastern and southern Winston-Salem, property values plummeted by 25%. (2018 Study by Black Philanthropy Institute (BFI))

WHAT IT'S LIKE TO LIVE IN WINSTON-SALEM

Winston-Salem once thrived as a relatively united city. It touted an affluent black middle class and a thriving black business district that complemented the magnificently wealthy whites and their businesses.

Thanks—in large part—to RJ Reynolds Tobacco, blacks and whites both prospered. And for a time, they lived side by side—literally.

In the 1890s—with the advent of the streetcar—wealthy whites move away from the center-city factories to suburbs in south and west Winston-Salem.

At the same time, newcomer, Simon Green Atkins, founds Slater Industrial Academy (later known as Winston-Salem State University, WSSU) and an upscale black suburb—Columbian Heights. Both are a huge success. Columbian Heights becomes *the place* to live for middle and upper class blacks. Doctors, lawyers, grocers, funeral directors, teachers, restaurant owners, ministers, and other professionals become pillars in this prestigious black community which spans 26 city blocks.

Additionally, because segregation prohibits them from attending theatrical or educational events at white venues, blacks host their own cultural events at Slater College. For decades, the black community blossoms—growing deep roots and treasured histories—in Winston-Salem.

However, as more blacks pursue upward mobility, race relations become strained. By 1947—following two strikes at Reynolds Tobacco and a united political push back—the first black alderman since the Jim Crow laws is elected. Alderman Kenneth Williams was an influential minister, educator and then, university president at WSSU.

Tragically and shortly after that, the upward trajectory of black equality turns south and the black community is systematically destroyed. Though Winston-Salem becomes home to 24 black communities—looking at the loss of the Columbian Heights neighborhood will suffice. In a few words, as you will see—it is sliced, diced, and destroyed.

Beginning in the 1950s, US 52 splits Columbia Heights—north to south—putting a noisy highway right in the middle of the *cultural center* of the black community. Several blocks of the neighborhood are destroyed.

A CATALYST FOR CHANGE

Then, in the 1960s, Interstate I-40 cuts the black community –east to west—destroying several more blocks with a massive cloverleaf intersection. Ironically, the final deathblow comes in the 1990s when its own Winston-Salem State University demolishes 75 buildings, which include several blocks of the Columbian Heights neighborhood.

Today, 90% of this neighborhood is gone. Thankfully, Simon Atkins' house is moved and spared. But gone are the roots. Gone are the connections. Gone are the *priceless intergenerational narratives*. Similar demolitions take place in the inner city of Winston-Salem when RJ Reynolds expands from one factory building to 100.

However, most destructive of all is Urban Redevelopment in the 1960s. In the name of urban renewal—it removes some slum houses, but with the same broad broom, it indiscriminately sweeps away the fashionable, historic homes that testify to the existence of a thriving middle and upper class black society.

Those who can afford it, move out of town. However, thousands of displaced blacks are relocated into federal housing or other new dwellings. The new housing may be clean and shiny, but there is a price to pay. Those relocated "never regained their sense of neighborhood—in short, their sense of place and belonging had been forfeited." (See References in Appendix)

I have to admit, I was somewhat grieved after reading these statistics. However—20 years from now—what if we ask that same question again: "What is it like to live in Winston-Salem?" and all join in and say, "*It's remarkable. Winston-Salem is a city that really makes it work. Everybody—people of all colors—live together in peace and harmony. And, we all contribute to its success.*"

Chapter 39

Gain Trust

Shortly after starting Master Counsel, I'm approached by Dr. Seth Lartey.

He asks, "John, can you help Goler with a $1 million capital campaign?"

"Let's talk," I say.

This marks the beginning of my 20-year journey toward social reform. For the first two years, I charge them my standard $1000 a month. After that, I join the board and work as a volunteer.

Oddly, the board had initially rejected me. Unlike Dr. Lartey—who's known me for six years—the board at Goler Memorial A.M.E. (African Methodist Episcopal) Zion Church sees me as an outsider.

I'd met Dr. Lartey in 1992. He'd enrolled his son, Solomon, in the preschool at First Assembly Christian School (now WS Christian). By that time, I am very busy managing two $3 million building projects, so I don't typically spend much time with the parents.

But in this case, someone from the school calls and asks, "Reverend Seth Lartey offered to do the benediction at our Preschool Graduation. I just want to make sure that it's okay?"

I ask, "Why wouldn't it be?"

There is a hesitation, and then she says, "Well, he's an African-American pastor from another church."

I then pause—somewhat confused—because our preschool was launched after Winston-Salem State University's preschool flooded. Everyone knows we are a culturally diverse congregation, but perhaps the cultural shift is more gradual than anticipated.

Either way, I tell her, "Tell him that we'd be honored. And then, set up an appointment. I want to meet him."

Dr. Lartey proves to be a fascinating man. Originally from Liberia, West Africa, he is raised by his grandparents, following the death of his father when he is three years old. Then, when he is 12, his grandfather dies.

He tells me, "I looked around and said, 'God, you will be my father.'"

He applies himself to school and to church and receives a scholarship from the local A.M.E. Zion church to attend college in America. His work ethic and the fact that English is the primary language in Liberia, makes the adjustment easier.

He earns his bachelor's degree at Livingstone College in Salisbury, NC, his master's degree at the School of Divinity at Duke University (NC), and his Doctor of Ministry from Drew University (NJ). In 1992, he is assigned to pastor Goler Memorial AME Zion in Winston-Salem—his fifth assignment.

He tells me, "When I arrive, everything around Goler is decimated. This part of town has eroded so badly, that people are actually coming in on the weekends to illegally dump trash."

This is such a far cry from the once proud and bustling black business community that grew up around the church at 630 N. Patterson Avenue (formerly known as Depot Street). Up until the 1950s—the church was established in 1881—this area had become home to grocery and dry goods stores, cafés, barber and beauty shops, dance halls, tailor, bakery, Chinese laundry, schools, doctors' offices—virtually everything needed by the local black community.

Then, US 52 bulldozes the best of it away. By the time Dr. Lartey talks with me, the only thing left around Goler are some slum apartments, Clark S. Brown & Sons Funeral Home, and some abandoned tobacco buildings. The community is gone.

However, by 1998, he's already been working for a few years to make things better. When he finds out the poor and the homeless are only being fed in the evening, he motivates his congregation to provide a daytime meal within walking distance of the homeless shelters.

The congregation not only supplies food, they offer practical assistance. In the basement of their 11,600 sq. ft. church, they set up help centers manned by agencies such as the Department of Social Services, Goodwill, and Veteran's Administration.

GAIN TRUST

The following year, in 1993, he founds GIDE (Goler Institute for Development and Education, Inc.)—which includes an after school program. His motto: *Our progress in life is less about what's going on outside of us and more about who we are on the inside. Transform the inside to love and respect others and then you will have the tools to transform the outside.*

On the flip side, Dr. Lartey is also learning who I am. He actually joins the board at the Living Waters Family Resource Center (our Smart Start initiative) and later Dr. Lartey, myself, and Paula McCoy will visit Richmond, Virginia to look at a faith-based affordable housing initiative for the Goler community.

Though the word "social capital" has yet to be made popular by Robert Putnam's book *Bowling Alone* (2000), Dr. Lartey recognizes the value of building relationship with someone experienced on the planning board, in building HUD 202s, in starting a preschool for the under-resourced, in running capital campaigns, and dealing with the municipal powers. Plus—and equally important—we both have a vision for restoring the black community. His belief in me, confirms that I made the right move in starting Master Counsel, Inc.

For the record, Putman's definition of social capital: "connections among individuals – social networks and the norms of reciprocity and trustworthiness that arise from them."

In other words, when we know our "neighbors," care about them, and help them—it knits us together and builds trust. Every kindness is like making a deposit in our social bank account. Think: social capital. Then, when we need help, we are comfortable to make a withdrawal—asking for and receiving help. Mostly, we give more than we get, if we truly understand the concept of community!

So, in Dr. Lartey's mind, when he introduces me to his board—it's a no-brainer. However, as I'm presenting my proposal, I see one man push back from the table and move to the corner of the room.

He employs very clear body language to say, "I'm not buying this."

Instead of ignoring it, as soon as I'm done, I ask Dr. Lartey, "Who is this man?"

He says, "Lafayette Jones."

A CATALYST FOR CHANGE

I ask, "Who is Lafayette Jones?"

He says, "He's our land acquisition team."

I say, "You never shared that you have a land acquisitions team. What else do I need to know?"

Then, I begin to look around a little closer and on a nearby foyer wall, I see a fundraising thermometer. Apparently, they've been in the midst of a capital campaign since 1993. This is 1998. That's *not* a successful capital campaign as I understand it.

I immediately ask for a meeting with the Land Acquisition Committee, which by now I understand is meeting every Tuesday night at Lafayette's business, SMSI.

I arrive on time at SMSI and am offered a catered meal. It's actually served by his precious mom, whom I would learn to love.

Shortly into our 6:00 p.m. meeting, Lafayette states plainly, "I'm not working with you."

I ask, "What do you mean?"

He says, "Every time we want to do something for the black community—something our grandchildren can look back upon—a white guy shows up and wants to take all the credit. I'm not working with a white guy."

Dr. Lartey says, "Lafayette, John's not like that. He's already doing work to help people in East Winston. He can help us. *God* wants him here."

Lafayette says boldly, "*We* just don't need him here."

He then adds wryly, "Why he even has a televangelist republican hair style!"

His humor slightly softens his earlier stern accusation. However, I'm a little puzzled.

I say to Lafayette, "First of all, I'm working with your pastor. I'm not working for you. And secondly, we need to have breakfast."

He snaps back, "Meet me at 7:30 in the morning at the Piedmont Club."

The next morning, atop the 19th floor of the BB&T building (now Truist), I meet Lafayette Jones in one of the most elite restaurants in town. He is dressed to the nines—linen napkin on his knee, cuffs out, with an essence of control.

He offers me a seat and motions for coffee, but instead of greeting me with a warm handshake and a smile, he rifles off, "Now, tell me one good reason why I shouldn't fire you!"

I say, "Excuse me. I've already told you, I don't work for you. I work for your pastor. But secondly, you don't know me."

What awkward first words, but I sense a confidence and the need to speak "power to power." It works!

We then settle into a four-hour conversation. I'm the son of a simple brick mason. There's not a privileged bone in my white body. In fact, our family was on the verge of bankruptcy more than once. And, I grew up only 20 minutes away from Goler.

My dad used to drive down Liberty Street, take a right on Patterson Avenue and pick up black workers to lay brick. He paid fair wages and even taught some of them the trade. I told him stories such as the previous, about Ladson, riding in the back of the truck, and the pork chop sandwich.

And, I told him how our family has partnered with the black community for generations. In fact, my first time to really get to know an entire family of African Americans was when we were renting a house on my uncle's dairy farm in Loray, NC. We would see each other daily, never perhaps understanding why we went to different schools.

We got comfortable enough that I could even tell Lafayette the story about my African American "girlfriend" in college. She was from up north as well, very street smart and sharp as a tack. Though I was married at the time, we were very close friends in college.

So, one Monday in our Educational Psychology Class (think 1968-69, in the South), I ask her, "So, how was your weekend?"

She laughs and turns in her desk, "You won't believe this. I was in Fayetteville on Saturday and entered a restaurant drive through. Before I could place my order the clerk says, 'We don't serve n-ggers.'

She arched her head and said, "So, I politely answered back, "Good! Because I don't eat 'em!"

A CATALYST FOR CHANGE

Somewhat between grieved for my friend and amazed at the wit displayed in her sarcasm, I have never forgotten that.

In fact, she had such an impact on me, that during a speech as a visiting Mayor and Keynote speaker at the 2012 Martin Luther King, Jr. Breakfast, I again shared her story. There were about 1000 folk present and they gave me a standing ovation. Proof again, that it's not the color of one's skin that determines their acceptance, but "the content of their character!"

Before we left, Lafayette, an inner city Chicago kid, and myself, a product of tiny Statesville, NC and later the Southside of Winston-Salem—had reached an understanding. We could see a possible way forward toward our common goal.

By the time we left the parking deck, we were laughing with each other. To this day, we are lifelong friends.

Years later Lafayette explains his hard stance at breakfast.

He tells me, "We had to become fighters because white folks kept taking what was ours. For instance, the land around Goler—we may not have had the deed, but we were stewards of the dirt for 100 years so it was ours by history."

"So when you saw me," I ask, "you just saw another white guy coming to take what was yours—be the credit or otherwise?"

"You're #### right!" he says colorfully. "Remember, blacks have to prove to their children that we have value, we can protect what is ours, and what is ours will last for an eternity."

I say, "I get that."

Then he smiles really big and says, "It's our commonalities that have built the bridge to our trust. You repeatedly proved you really wanted to help and you did. And you've earned a place as a friend."

"And you have been a friend too, because real friends tell each other the truth, even when it hurts. And I can always count on you to tell me the truth, Lafayette," I say with a grin.

.

Chapter 40

Build a Machine

Everyone has a reason for being at the table. Dr. Lartey is here to lead the church to serve its community. He's invited me—the man who shares a vision to "reach a city."

Lafayette Jones, though not a religious man, had married Sandra Miller. Her dad—Robert A. Miller—served as a trustee for Goler Memorial for over 40 years. Miller extracted a promise from Lafayette that he will "not let the church go under."

Lastly, Lafayette invites Michael Suggs— in charge of strategic branding at R.J. Reynolds— to the Goler project. Suggs meets Lafayette— an exceptionally talented entrepreneur and marketing specialist—when Lafayette tries to win a contract with Reynolds. The two become friends, and Suggs later joins the church.

Originally, the goal is to rebuild the sanctuary. So, we do the capital campaign—which proves to be more difficult than anticipated. Dr. Lartey believes that the church has 1,000 members—and I'm sure that 1,000 different people have passed through the church periodically. But, in doing an actual analysis—the Church has only 125 "giving units."

Nonetheless, we are able to raise $800,000 over a much shorter time than the original 1993 attempt. The reason for this is that Goler broadens its vision. But more on that later.

Earlier, it seems, when they had gone to pull the building permits, to bring their sanctuary up to ADA compliance per handicap accessibility laws, they discovered that the Church owned only its sanctuary footprint. It doesn't own sufficient setbacks to even accommodate a ramp, let alone the parking they had been using.

Undeterred, their newly formed Capital Campaign Committee takes a field trip to my office. From the 24th floor, we re-imagine what the Goler community can look like. We start with affordable senior housing, because the congregation is aging and this is a real need. Then, we add affordable family housing and imagine the recovery of all the things a community needs—for sure, a bank and perhaps a grocery store.

Next, we have to paint the vision for the congregation—which is currently set on getting a new sanctuary, theirs being only partially repaired after a fire, now decades ago. So, who will paint the vision? By now—after locking horns with Lafayette—we know it can't be the white guy.

So, I bring in Paula McCoy. Paula worked with me on Smart Start and other projects. She is the 13th of 15 children—born to Birden McCoy and Lovie Dalton McCoy. The Daltons are landowners.

Generations back, a white slave owner had a son by a black slave. He gave this son 100 acres in what is now Ogburn Station, east of US 52 in Winston-Salem. Also, one of her grandfathers was an educator. So the family has a solid sense of family pride.

As Paula says, "We were land rich, but money poor."

However, they are *community* rich. The neighbors—black and white—get along, borrow goods, have intact families (biological mom and dad in the home) and when someone has a hog killing—everyone gets a piece.

At school, all of Paula's teachers are black like her. They make her feel loved and motivate her to excel.

At church—their second home—they hear the same message that is preached in their house. Love everyone. Be good. Be content with what you have. Work hard for what you want.

Her first brush with racial tension happens when she is eight. It is then that her family moves to inner city Winston-Salem on 25th Street. For the first year, the neighborhood is integrated. Her best friend happens to be white.

But when they turn nine, her friend tells her, "My mommy says that I can't play with you anymore."

Shortly after that, "white flight" occurs—leaving behind an entirely black neighborhood. There are really no more incidents, until Paula is in high school. Then, on April 4, 1968, Dr. Martin Luther King, Jr. is shot. Riots break out in the streets of Winston-Salem.

Paula's parents tell their children to stay out of it. But, her older brother goes down and actively joins the protest. No harm comes to him, but he brings to the family stories of police brutality and injustice.

BUILDING A MACHINE

Paula keeps focused, graduates from Carver—the historic black high school—and then earns a bachelor's in English and a master's in Administration at North Carolina A & T State University—a historically black college.

It isn't until she travels the world—as the wife of an officer—that she experiences racial prejudice. What she finds is that the people in London, Belgium, and Germany welcome her with open arms. It is only the white Americans that treat her as less of a person.

Once stateside, after Paula begins working in Winston-Salem, she experiences the glass ceiling, the effects of white privilege, and the reality of systemic racial inequity.

So, when she is introduced to the congregation, it's clear that she knows the territory—physically, emotionally, mentally, and spiritually. Besides that, Paula has experience with CDCs—Community Development Corporations.

These are "bottom up" non-profit organizations—often set up by churches or civic groups—to revitalize the surrounding community by building affordable housing, providing job training, and sometimes healthcare.

The beauty of the CDC is three-fold. First, it's led by the very population that it serves. Secondly, it qualifies to receive money from private and public sources. And, perhaps best of all, it empowers the community to create real change by means of *development* versus activism.

However, even with all of this potential—the congregation is not quick to come off its $800,000. It's waited since 1992 to have a new sanctuary. Choice 1: The sanctuary could be a reality now—even if it is in the middle of a social desert.

Choice 2: It can use the money to buy land around the church. At one point, Lafayette Jones takes a green marker and circles 50 acres around Goler. This ultimately ends up being 15 acres, but still—even if the Church buys the land—there is no guarantee that the Goler CDC will find funding. So, if the church is not careful, it could end up land rich and money poor.

In helping the congregation come to grips with this monumental decision, I employ a graph that I put together for Master Counsel. It helps people see the nine P's of change. (See next tool page.)

A CATALYST FOR CHANGE

So, if I'm working with a group for a few months, and the group is not escalating up the chart, then I tell the leader that his or her organization is not ready for change. The people may say they want change, but they don't really mean it. It's premature.

Thankfully, the Goler congregation assumes a positive trajectory and ultimately agrees to sponsor the Goler CDC. Then, the CDC machine begins to pull together. It operates like a machine, because by definition, a machine is: *an apparatus* using or applying mechanical power and *having several parts, each with a definite function and together performing a particular task.* (dictionary.com) Instead of using mechanical power, a CDC uses people power to accomplish its task.

BUILDING A MACHINE

Posturing for Impact—Nine Ps

To determine an individual's or group's readiness for change, measure the shift in energy/enthusiasm at each step. If energy/enthusiasm remains the same or decreases, change is premature. If energy/enthusiasm consistently increases, change is imminent.

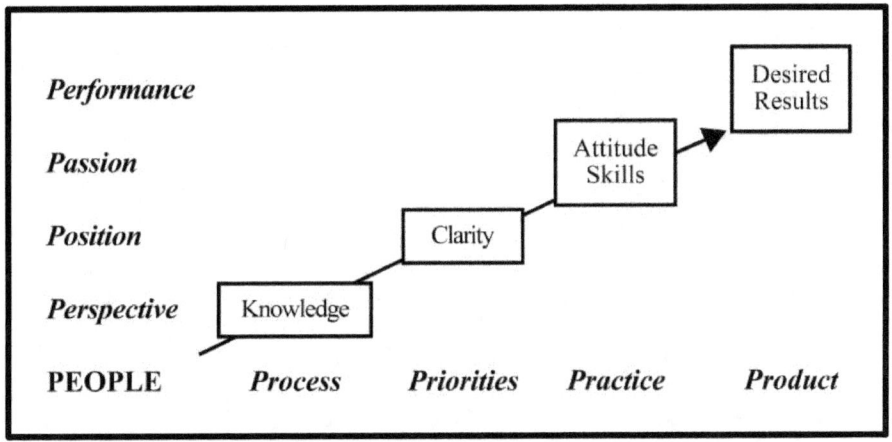

- When the *process* for a particular change is introduced, **people** gain <u>knowledge</u>, and this results a positive shift in their **perspective**.

- When *priorities* are set, the resulting <u>clarity</u> moves people to adopt a **position**.

- As people begin to *practice* the <u>attitudes and skills</u> necessary to accomplish the mission, the **passion** of vision seizes them.

- When the *product*—evidence of the <u>desired results</u> is in hand—people will reach peak **performance**.

For more information visit www.JohntheCatalyst.com

A CATALYST FOR CHANGE

Chapter 41

Money Will Find You

What happens over the next 20 years is perhaps one of the greatest proofs—that it isn't about the money. Frankly, we start out with no money—but we do get started.

As Dr. Seth Lartey explains, "We can't go to the city empty handed. Since we don't have the money, we will put in the time. That will be our sweat equity."

So, every Tuesday night, the four of us—Lartey, Jones, Suggs, and Bost—meet to work on our plan. Sometimes others join us. By the time our first development comes out of the ground seven years later, we've logged 22,000 planning hours.

Eventually we hire our first Executive Director, Larry Weston, a municipal planner whom I had met while on the Planning Board.

While Larry prepares all the paperwork to solidly establish the Goler CDC—incorporated in 1998—Lafayette Jones and Michael Suggs work to gain site control via land acquisition. Dr. Lartey keeps the vision alive with the congregation. And simultaneously with the capital campaign, Paula and I talk to Winston-Salem Foundation about funding. Think: Each part (person) with a definite function and together performing a particular task.

Beginning with land acquisition—we discover that R.J. Reynolds owns six acres around Goler Church. Michael Suggs has a fairly high position at R.J. Reynolds—but probably not high enough to approach the powers to be about buying the land at the best value.

However, in the course of conversation, Lafayette Jones and his wife find out that their neighbor is a Vice President at R.J. Reynolds. When she hears the Goler vision for revitalizing the black community— she supports the team effort.

The three of them approach the company and write a check for $25,000 in good faith money. They are hoping to buy land—worth

A CATALYST FOR CHANGE

hundreds of thousands of dollars. Later, they get a call from R.J. Reynolds refusing their offer, but calling for another meeting.

Long story short, R.J. Reynolds sells six acres for a mere $95,000. It should be noted that Goler Church purchases all the land, and then sells it to the CDC—with the understanding that the CDC will pay it back when the developments are completed.

However, everyone isn't as generous as R.J. Reynolds. Two landowners—who will remain nameless—insist that we pay $700,000 for land valued at $245,000. Why? They know they have us over a barrel. They own the donut hole. So, we overspend—to keep the vision alive.

Then, Lafayette notices the old Brown Williamson Tobacco Building inside the green circle. We talk about it at the board meeting and decide that—at the moment—we can't afford it. Lafayette ignores the board, talks to the owner, and signs an agreement.

I'm livid. You don't go around the board. And, we really don't have the money.

However—completely out of character—Lafayette says, "Where's your faith!"

This is the man that months earlier would say, "Okay, go ahead and go through all your Bible mumbo jumbo, let the preacher pray and let's get on with business."

Lafayette now is one of Dr. Lartey's daily prayer partners!

Surprisingly, Lafayette is right. Because of relationship—he is able to share the Goler vision with the owner. The owner agrees to sell the building for $325,000 on payments, until we find the money to develop the property.

We don't have income stream for payments. Lafayette's idea is to move the Goler Church offices into this building. Then, we can use rental income from the church to carry the property.

Problem: The local planning staff will not allow the church to occupy half the building.

Solution: I know Bucky Frye, the chief inspector who calls the shot on that.

We meet and ask him, "Bucky, can you work with us here? What can we do to make this work? We are doing something really important for the community."

Bucky then tells us how to build a fire retardant "envelope" around the entire lower section to meet the requirements. Think *relationship*.

Meanwhile, Paula and I approach Donna Rader, vice-president of grants and initiatives at the Winston-Salem Foundation. She knows Paula from her previous work with CDCs. And she likes what she hears about the new Goler CDC.

However, the only thing she can tell us is, "I can't talk to you about this right now. But keep talking among yourselves and keep moving forward."

Little do we know that the Winston-Salem Foundation and Wachovia Bank are each in the midst of donating $1 million each to bring in LISC—Local Initiatives Support Corporation.

LISC is a nationally proven program that's all about sustainable community development. It pulls together resident participation, affordable housing, redevelopment of diminished business districts, and creates a sense of community pride. This is a perfect match for the Goler CDC.

LISC comes to town. In 1999, Paula is named Program Officer for LISC, and Goler is one of four local CDCs to receive funding and training. Paula would soon be promoted to Program Director. Think *relationship*, now perhaps at a corporate level.

Once the financial train starts moving—other funders jump on board. This includes $1.2 million from the Millennium Fund (2003) in Winston-Salem—eager to anchor the North side with a mixed-income, multicultural development.

Kate B. Reynolds Foundation—where I have *relationships*—grants us $60,000 for staff salaries. And countless thousands of dollars of tax credits and incentives are claimed by developers now eager to partner with Goler CDC.

However—as expected—finding the first developer is the most challenging. After all—the Goler acreage is literally littered with slum apartments. After being rejected by several traditional developers, I approach Sterling and Nancy Anders.

I've known Nancy—a very successful Realtor—for years. We've worked together on some projects and she has a big heart for the community.

I explain the Goler vision and then ask her, "Would you consider taking some risks? Would you consider building four townhouses knowing that we might not be able to sell them? But also knowing that you could be a catalyst to rebuilding the historic black district in Winston-Salem?"

Nancy and Sterling take the "dare."

However, before the townhouses came out of the ground—in 2005—three major forces shift in Goler's favor. First, through my work at Living Water Family Resource Center—going on simultaneously as my work at Goler—I find out that Wake Forest is building a new Downtown Health Plaza.

In asking clarifying questions, I am told that the front will face US 52. Silently, I realize that the back of the building will be facing the Goler "vision."

Innocently, I ask, "So what is the back of the building going to look like?"

Without missing a beat, the person says, "You know. The usual. Dumpsters and fencing."

At our next Tuesday meeting, I report this to the Goler CDC board. A dumpster view will ruin the value of our development.

Lafayette decides to solve the problem. In a meeting with Wake Forest, he says, "We can work together and you can build your Downtown Health Plaza. But the back of your building—where you put your dumpsters—has to look just like the front of your building."

Of course, Wake Forest—once it understands the vision—is happy to comply.

About this same time, the City releases its New Century Plan. In order to justify the restaurants called for in the plan—the city needs more rooftops. Goler wants to build rooftops. This lays the groundwork for a symbiotic *relationship* between the City and Goler CDC.

Lastly, in this same general timeframe, 180 acres—that adjoins Goler's 15 acres—is optioned for the development of what will come to be known as Innovation Quarter.

Upon this announcement, Lafayette adds a second condition saying, "Some of the money earned on this side of US 52 has to find a way to the other side of 52. If you want to work with us, we will work with you."

Then he adds, with all seriousness, "If you are not willing, we will just call in the Street Team. It won't be pretty."

I suddenly recall my morning breakfast at the Piedmont Club. Folks got to know and appreciate Lafayette early on. Soon, he's appointed to the board of the Downtown Winston-Salem Partnership, an economic development initiative.

The money has now caught up with the vision.

- 2005: four townhouses on Chestnut Street
- 2006: two three-bedroom flats in the historic Craver Building on Chestnut Street
- 2007: 5-story, 79 unit Goler Manor senior housing on Chestnut Street
- 2007: Truliant Federal Credit Union N. Liberty Street (Lafayette was on the board of Victory Credit Union—the oldest black owned credit union in NC. He was instrumental in facilitating the merger of Truliant and Victory and setting up a branch in the historic black business district. This building also houses the Goler CDC headquarters.)
- 2009: The Gallery Lofts 82 upscale historic units in the former Brown & Williamson Tobacco building—25% affordable income. Sold in 2014 for $14.5 million.
- 2013: Mudpies East Child Development Center 7th Street
- 2017: 757 North four story, 115-unit upscale apartments on Chestnut Street

A CATALYST FOR CHANGE

I pretty much bow out in 2007—when I run for Mayor in Clemmons.

As Dr. Seth Lartey later tells me, "You shared your connections and influence with the people who could help us. You taught us how to play ball."

And play ball they did! Goler CDC is still going strong. Under the leadership of Michael Suggs—president of Goler CDC—Goler is now building the workforce with its latest initiative TechCareers 2020.

In an interview with TheHub, Suggs says, "If we're going to be the city that we say we want to be, we have to be interested in what's happening in the entire city. We are just trying to play a role in making sure that more people get a chance to participate in the innovation economy that's coming."

Addressing the elephant in the room: Some people question whether Goler contributed to gentrification—displacing low-income families to make way for middle class living. In reality, few low-income people can afford to live in any of the Goler developments, with the exception of the affordable senior housing—Goler Manor.

However, two factors must be considered. Goler had to partner with developers. Developers study sites for best possible use and highest return on investment. Market studies showed that upscale apartments is what the new Innovation Quarter demanded.

Secondly, Goler made a bold choice—to create a mixed-income, multi-cultural neighborhood that welcomes everyone.

In my opinion—and I'm glad that I could be a small part of it—this really is about "city reaching." What makes Goler's efforts particularly noble is that it is now reaching out to put boots and bootstraps on the under-resourced, so that they can fully participate in the new economy in Winston-Salem.

Chapter 42

Love Out Loud

"This play is nothing more than Christian entertainment," Pastor Mike Rakes objectively points out. He's the newly elected Pastor at First Assembly.

He's talking about the annual *Behold Him* production put on by the Church with a price tag of $100,000. Former Pastor Ron McManus began this Easter drama with good intentions. And, in fact, for the first few years—it's right on target.

Eventually, requiring a crew of 400 people—some paid, some volunteer—a full orchestra, and a partnership with the North Carolina School of the Arts—*Behold Him* proves to be a first rate passion play about the life of Jesus. I know that for me, it's one of the most beautiful and moving dramas I've ever seen.

However, its purpose is to reach the people who don't know the love of Jesus. Its purpose is to present the gospel to people who haven't heard it or who have strayed away from the faith.

To accomplish this goal—and in imitation of Jesus' self-sacrificing love—members of First Assembly seek out the neglected, the homeless, and the disenfranchised.

They search in shelters, in parks, and on the streets. Once found, these "forgotten ones" receive a rose, a delicious bag lunch, and a bus ride to the beautiful Reynold's Auditorium. There, the drama of Jesus' love unfolds like the petals of a beautiful flower.

However, a few years after the play's inception, it has grown to the extent that a new auditorium (Worship Center) has been built that will hold over 2000 people. The primary attenders now are busloads of churchgoers from other counties and even other states who acquire the free tickets during the seven-day season.

It's obvious that the play has become nothing more than Christian entertainment. We're simply preaching to the choir and constantly chasing additional parking acreage for that short overflow season.

A CATALYST FOR CHANGE

So, we take another look at this. We begin to ask the question: What can we do to reach into the very fabric of our city? How can we bring a growing diversity of people, haves and have-nots, more educated (we sit on the boundary of one of the national premier universities) and less educated—really everyone in our city—together.

From a simple conversation between Chuck Spong, Mike Rakes and myself, comes Christmas for the City in 2008. First Assembly uses the $100,000 previous earmarked for the play to launch this city-centered event. And I guess, in hindsight, *Behold Him* proved to be the perfect training for this gigantic undertaking.

Purpose: to give to **people**—everyone's invited—a chance to Love Out Loud and experience the love of God and the love of neighbors.

Process: invite churches, businesses, non-profits, and artists to create an event that puts the good of all ahead of the good of any singular organization or purpose.

Priority: create an "all inclusive" free Christmas event that allows everyone an opportunity to give and to receive love, while sharing a meal (food is mankind's oldest bonding agent) and entertainment—both passive and active—while embracing their "community."

Practice: empower people with the necessary skills and attitudes to feed a crowd, create engaging craft stations, display art, coordinate multiple and simultaneous choral and instrumental programs, maximize social and traditional media, and more.

Product: Let the LOVE that fertilized this idea, be the force that grows the vision, and the spirit that prevails during the unfolding of the event.

Though my partner, Robby Lee, and I help launch this venture—Master Counsel pays to rent the facility—it is Chuck Spong, as associate pastor at First Assembly who leads the charge.

Chuck, formerly a producer for the Willow Creek Church and their Global Leadership conference, is a perfect match. He has an amazing knack for pulling people together, sorting out real needs and skills by means of appreciative inquiry (scores of small group conversations), then matching people to opportunities.

Additionally, First Assembly of God decides to accomplish this mission in a way that could only be deemed as nameless, faceless, and placeless.

Nameless—First Assembly will initiate this event anonymously. Its involvement is disclosed in my book for learning purposes. As a colleague once told me, "A turtle doesn't get on a fence post all by itself." Likewise, Christmas for the City doesn't happen by accident.

At the same time, First Assembly of God in Winston-Salem changes its name to Winston-Salem First. This signifies that the Church is putting the city before its denomination. Also, the purpose of the Church is to serve the people of Winston-Salem.

Faceless—the Church—and every entity involved in Christmas for the City—will leave its brand off this venture, so that people will only see the face of Jesus.

Placeless—this event will be held on "neutral ground" and be nomadic, going where the need is and not tied to any particular building.

Initially, our neutral ground is the Millennium Center. However, within three years, we outgrow it and move the celebration to the Benton Convention Center.

By 2019, over 12,000 people come, eat, and walk in the ways of Jesus. It's a testimony to the potential unity of the city—supported by 67 non-profits, 20 businesses, 72 churches, and over 1200 volunteers. The hope is that if solidarity can happen for one day—maybe it can happen for a week, and then a month, and then a year.

Congrats to Chuck Spong Love Out Loud

Oh, there's another remarkable aspect to the evening. People can choose to serve or to be served. Either way is okay. However, when I see David Mounts—Power Player of the Year—humbly wiping tables, I tell him, "You surely have no idea the social capital you exhibit to and for this city!"

Of course, Venture Café and his many others-oriented investments go far beyond busing tables! Leadership personified!

At the same time—like Irish twins—within 12 months a second non-profit is birthed from Winston-Salem First. Using the same $100,000 *Behold Him* line item budget that launched Christmas in the City, the Church launches Love Out Loud.

In a sentence, Love Out Loud *helps people find their place in the city* of Winston-Salem. It's based on the premise that most people want to give back to their community. The challenge is—they don't know how, where, or when.

Chuck Spong identifies this need while he's working closely with the non-profits and the volunteers in organizing Christmas for the City. He notices that there seems to be an untapped goldmine of resourceful, passionate, skilled volunteers who desire to plug into productive volunteer work.

However, they are challenged by a pervasive lack of optimal alignment—finding the opportunity that stirs the fire in their belly. Because of this, volunteering can be unproductive for both the volunteer and the agency.

Since Chuck clearly sees the problem and the potential solution—he's named executive director for the new Love Out Loud.

In Chuck's words, "We have everything we need—all the people and all the resources—right here in our city to solve all of our challenges."

Imagine if a city really could mobilize thousands of citizens—with tools, resources, and passion—to tackle some of the major challenges—such as hunger, disaster relief, homelessness, opioids, human trafficking, domestic violence, gangs, crime, racism, and under-employment.

That is what Love Out Loud does. It starts with the volunteer—the center of its bullseye—and asks individuals: What do you care about?

Then, it asks: What do you know about this problem that you are passionate about? Would it benefit you to learn more, so you can be most effective in volunteering?

And finally: What are your strengths?

Love Out Loud (LOL) employs a process to groom and grow volunteers. This includes one-on-one coaching with *navigators,* and programs called Pathways (www.loveoutloudws.com), and BASE—all designed to help volunteers find their passion, purpose, and place in Winston-Salem.

At the same time, LOL employs a similar process with the local non-profits. Currently, there are about 500 non-profits in the city, not counting churches. Beginning with 40 non-profits, LOL helps each organization identify its top three needs and what it can do to improve the volunteer experience.

Then, the whole system works a bit like a train station. LOL is the platform. Various non-profit "trains" approach the platform—ready to take "passengers" to specific volunteer opportunities. At the same time, the "passengers" are given "tickets" to board the train that will take them exactly where they want to go.

And, if a volunteer's interest shifts—realizing that all endeavors have a season—the volunteer simply *navigates* again and receives a new "ticket."

LOL is having amazing results locally—having just completed its 10th year of service for the community in 2019. It's also a good neighbor. In 2017, in response to the damage from Hurricane Harvey in Houston, Chuck talked to a conference of historically African-American pastors, Wake Forrest Baptist Medical Center, and volunteers who'd listed Disaster Relief as their passion.

Then a trip to Houston—underwritten by funders—was planned. LOL pulled together 40 passionate volunteers that ranged from a local CFO to a homeless person. The work was so meaningful to that hurting community—and the groomed volunteers—that the Mayor of Houston was compelled to specifically honor the city of Winston-Salem.

A CATALYST FOR CHANGE

Then, the next year—2018—when Hurricane Irma hit eastern North Carolina, Chuck said, "It was like a reunion. The same people responded, plus more."

So whereas the original Goler vision centered on solving a specific community need—*housing* in the historically black neighborhood—these two outreaches focus on the *people*.

Christmas for the City honors and unites the beautiful multicultural people of Winston-Salem by immersing them in love.

Love Out Loud mentors, mobilizes, and connects passion-driven volunteers to the opportunities where they can make a significant impact.

Sometimes, however, a "perfect" volunteer opportunity finds you. That happens in 2014, shortly after I lose the election to serve a fourth term as Mayor of Clemmons.

Chapter 43

Clemmons Community Foundation

The phone rings and a voice on the other end says, "John, we'd like for you to serve on the board of the Clemmons Community Foundation."

It's Joanna Lyall, always direct and to the point.

Before letting her continue, I interject, "You do understand that I just lost the election, Joanna? I'm the last guy in Clemmons that you want going around asking for money."

Joanna laughs and says, "We all know that, but we really do want you. In fact, we want you to fill the seat of Chuck Alexander (an attorney and board member who had recently passed) for the remainder of his term. Then, we'd like you to serve as President."

I sense possibilities for the community, so I accept.

"I'll fill Chuck's seat," I say guardedly, "and we'll see how that goes. Then, you guys can make a decision about me being President."

Apparently, the Foundation has thought of me for several reasons. I'm a Paul Harris Fellow and former Rotary member—the Clemmons Rotary had founded the Clemmons Community Foundation.

Also, as a former Mayor, I know the vision of our community via "The Compass." Additionally, my experience in non-profit work and my Master's degree in fund development might prove valuable.

However, my chief reason for accepting the position is that I'd like to see it become a true community foundation. And as I learned deeply—while serving as Mayor—change is challenging for Clemmons, even Clemmons Rotarians.

Here's a brief history: For years, Clemmons Rotary Club donates to the International Club. Like every other Rotary Club across the US, it then has to vie to get that money back.

Brainstorm: In 2004—to keep their gifts local and tax-deductible —Clemmons Rotary establishes the Clemmons Rotary Foundation.

A CATALYST FOR CHANGE

This upstart entity would be initially funded through the sale of a house donated by Wayne Shore and his wife, Bradley.

The home would soon to be rehabbed by a core of local Rotarians armed with hammers and saws, then flipped, netting approximately $160,000. Other monies, from local founders, led by Rotarian Tony Golding, adds to the sum. The board—as rightfully expected—is composed entirely of Rotarians.

Sometime later, two sisters—who wish to remain anonymous—donate $500,000 each. Then, about the time I come on board, local business owners—Thad and Mary Bingham—donate another $1 million.

Although the Clemmons Rotary Foundation officially changes its name to the more inclusive Clemmons Community Foundation (CCF) in 2011— it still functions like an extension of Rotary. One cup of coffee at a time—Ken Burkel, then President, and I spend countless hours with key board members and founders examining what we're doing right, versus what we'd like to do differently, our history, our motives, and our possibilities.

True to my nature—a Reformer—I soon find myself on a team, guided by legal counsel from the Council on Foundations, charged with transforming CCF into a legitimate Community Foundation. We then hire Frank Samuelson, a former president and community leader to research and create a policy manual so we can get our house in order.

Things get really exciting when we find out that we have $9 million incoming from the Wayne A. Shore Estate. We then hire Kevin Bokeno—formerly on staff at the Wake Forest Foundation—to do a listening tour of our community. His recommendation would be to hold community wide interviews of key individuals during which we poll the community, ascertain the true needs and wishes of the people at large, repopulate the board, and then together create a vision and mission.

Again, much would be drawn from "The Compass", the Village of Clemmons' comprehensive plan. This of course serves the greater good of the donor and directs the investment of our majority donor-advised funds.

Expectations soar and now, more than ever, it's important that we hire the right leader. We launch a nationwide search.

It's in this time frame that my church friend—Carolyn Pursel—introduces me to Sandi Scannelli from Florida.

I ask Sandi, "So, what do you do?"

She says, "I work with community foundations."

No lie!

I say, "We need to talk."

In talking with Sandi, I'm not so transfixed by what she's done—she has a stellar resume—but more by who she is. Sandi loves people and understands community, as you read earlier. That's the value add—the rare find—that we are looking for.

I encourage Sandi to go online to apply for the position of CEO/President. In my eyes, she is the missing gear—with the best motive and the technical skills to match—to take Clemmons Community Foundation to the next level. Thankfully, the board sees the same potential, and though we have three excellent final candidates—Sandi Scannelli is hired.

Under her leadership—when the board is inclined to have the new president create the vision and mission—she gently pushes back and explains that this is their job. She references the former work of Kevin Bokeno and now insists that as many citizens as possible be included and take ownership.

When it comes time to review the existing grants—she brings fresh eyes and encourages the committee to ask the hard questions.

One long-time grant recipient—a bit perplexed by the new level of accountability—says, "Well, we're a legacy grant. You've been funding us for years."

Sandi gently says, "Whoops. We don't have any legacy grants."

One of the committee members agrees with Sandi and says, "That's good, because I just noticed that this organization had a loss of over $90,000 last year."

The rep requesting the grant says, "I didn't notice that."

Sandi then says boldly to the committee, "We are doing a terrible disservice to an organization when we don't hold them accountable and ask the hard questions. They will soon be out of business. So, if we are looking to build capacity and bridge pathways—we have to be asking the right questions and looking for accountability."

It's Sandi's gentle, yet inclusive leadership, holding everyone accountable—the grant committee and the grant applicants—that I admire. With her guidance, we launch Leadership Lewisville Clemmons. This serves two purposes. First—designed after Leadership Winston-Salem—we are growing new leaders.

Secondly, we are uniting our communities. For whatever reason, Lewisville, a more wealthy rural community, and its nearest neighbor, Clemmons—a business and bedroom district— are each content to keep to themselves. But the truth is: We share boundaries, values, and history.

In reality, Clemmons Community Foundation needs to reach even farther than Lewisville. Our $10 million (by the time stock was transferred and liquidated) from the Shore family originates in Yadkin County. That's where Wayne Shore grew up and is buried.

So, in addition to funding grants in Clemmons for needs such as Cancer Services, Clemmons Food Pantry, and West Forsyth High School—the Wayne Shore Endowment also funds 16 scholarships in Yadkin County.

For the Clemmons Community Foundation to reach its potential, we need to be broadly inclusive. This can be like walking the razor's edge. On the one hand, most of the surrounding counties have their own Foundations—Yadkin, Forsyth, and Davie. So, we don't want to compete; we want to collaborate. And Sandi Scannelli is just the person for this job.

One key to growing our base is that we let donors know that they can keep their funds under their current investment advisor. In that way, if a donor directs money toward the Clemmons Community Foundation, their advisor doesn't lose the management fee.

Lastly, most of our funds are donor advised. That means that while the Foundation may run ideas past the donor, in the end, the donor decides. It seems that as the population ages, more people have a sense of where they'd like to make a difference. So, more donors are leaning toward the donor advised option.

However, many donor advisors are open to new ideas. For instance, Karen Shore Hopper and Debrah Shore Blase—the two daughters of Wayne and Bradley Shore—are delighted when I introduce them to Chuck Spong. Again, think: *Relationship*.

Chuck listens to the family story. He learns how Wayne Shore made his millions in South America (with British American Tobacco)—but always made it back to his family's homeplace for the holidays. Constructed in 1895, his Yadkin County home served as a gathering place—for friends and family—a center of Southern hospitality.

When Chuck suggests restoring the home and repurposing it as a Gathering Place for Yadkin County and the launch pad for Yadkin County Love Out Loud—the sisters love the idea. So, they gift the farm house, 13 acres, and designated funding from the Clemmons Community Foundation in order for Love Out Loud to make that happen.

As Karen shares, "Dad's property was gifted with hopes that it could be used in a way to honor Dad and his life...*to bring together people* in Yadkin County and surrounding areas."

BAM! This is a perfect match for the family, the Foundation, Love Out Loud, and the greater community.

I have to laugh now. It wasn't that long ago when Sandi Scannelli told me that I almost scared her off.

She said, "Right after I was hired, you said to me, 'We need to have a debriefing.' Of course, I have no context—I'm not from Clemmons or North Carolina. I'm brand new. And you do a three-hour brain dump—shooting off 30 years of every notable name in the community and how things came about."

She laughed and continued, "You thought you were comforting me and fortifying me for my new role. In reality, you scared me half to death. But you made up for it. You shared your contacts, pointed out the landmines, and supported my goals without trying to take charge. It's really a gift to be able to do that."

A CATALYST FOR CHANGE

She also revealed my secret for getting people involved.

Sandi said, "You don't push people and you don't pull people. Instead, you look inside, find their hot button, and push that button for them. That—their own hot button—pulls them into whatever it is that moves them. And their reaction is: Wow! John showed me the most wonderful opportunity. I call that stealth leadership."

Chapter 44

Salt Box

In the summer of 2017, the Clemmons Community Foundation sends me to the inaugural ESHIP (**E**ntrepreneur**ship**) Summit hosted by the Kauffman Foundation (KF). For three days I find myself surrounded by change-agents from 48 states and 10 countries—450 people in all. Our mission: To develop entrepreneurial ecosystems.

Why? Entrepreneurial ecosystems are the key to the *new economy* and the best way to *eradicate poverty*. Our duty is to bring our best practices, share our ideas, and *discover* the principles of ESHIP. Amazingly, the process is successful.

So when I come back to Clemmons, I share with the board the basic ideas of entrepreneurial (starting businesses) ecosystem (interconnected support network) building. (See next page.)

Then I suggest that the Foundation give back to the greater Forsyth County in the most profound way—push some money under US 52 to help the under-resourced build an ESHIP ecosystem.

While the board sees the value—they also see that what I'm proposing will take an ongoing commitment of time and funding. After much discussion, the board decides that for now—as a very young Foundation—it will decline to participate. Instead, it will focus on programs and projects that have a direct impact in Clemmons and Yadkin County—the main source of its funding.

Undeterred, I start sniffing around East Winston for a prime location—area of high need—to plant the seeds of ESHIP.

At the same time, a former youth pastor—Andrew Viator—is looking for an inexpensive location to house his budding metal and wood fabrication business. I'd met Andrew at First Assembly and unfortunately—though he loved helping youth—he was turned off by the bickering and office politics that can be common in large churches.

Thankfully, he comes under the mentorship of my friends, Kevin and Beth Frack. They know of his construction background and ask

A CATALYST FOR CHANGE

Entrepreneur**ship**
(ESHIP)

Creating and operating a new business—with all its associated risks—in hopes of making a profit. It is believed that entrepreneurial ecosystems (inner-connected support networks) are the key to the new economy and the best way to eradicate poverty.

The Seven Principles of ESHIP

1) Entrepreneurs need an ecosystem—a community of support & resources
2) Entrepreneurship is the new model of *economic* development
3) Collaboration is key—investing in other peoples' success
4) Diversity is an *economic* asset—most innovations come out of diversity
5) Break Down Barriers—help open doors, make introductions
6) Focus on the whole community—we all work together to create the future
7) Future generations depend on this model—it's larger than our lifetime

Kauffman Foundation (KF) ESHIP
Entrepreneurship Summits ('17, '18, '19)
Https://www.kauffman.org/ecosystem-playbook-draft-3/

For more information visit www.JohntheCatalyst.com

him to remodel their home. This allows him to keep bread on his table—while sorting out his next move.

As expected, Kevin urges Andrew to take his skills and Christian values to the marketplace. Think: Original Moravians.

Andrew soon learns that he can purchase 24,000 square feet of space in East Winston for the same cost as only 12,000 square feet in a more marketable area.

Andrew takes a chance and opens Viator Design and Construction, Inc. at 1650 Ivy Avenue near 17th. Zip code 27105—is one of the three zip codes in Winston-Salem known for high poverty and high crime.

Despite the location, Andrew's business takes off like a proton in a particle accelerator. He constructs one-of-a-kind wood and metal staircases, furniture, and art. If you draw it, he can make it. And, his workspace is housed on the lower level of this abandoned convenience store.

So, I go see Andrew and ask him, "What are you going to do with the 12,000 square feet up top?"

He says, "That's my retirement. I'm going to lease it out."

I ask, "What would happen if a band of true Christ followers were involved in the abandoned parts of Winston-Salem? What if we could make the community East of 52 as *livable* as the community West of 52?"

Then, I explain how an entrepreneurial ecosystem—planted right in the middle of this neighborhood—could transform the community over time. That would make it better for everyone.

Andrew is genuinely intrigued. He gives me a tour of the building. He shows me some office spaces he's built upstairs, but he has no takers on leasing it. This is partly due to the location and partly due to the fact that this space needs a bathroom.

I suggest, "Why don't you let LaDonna and me sublease the upstairs? We'll pay the first two years for the lease and I'll bring in sector leaders who can establish the ecosystem. After that, we'll index the rent upward until it reaches market rate for this area."

Andrew agrees. Then, I ask him, "How much will it cost to put a Class-A bathroom on this end of the building?"

A CATALYST FOR CHANGE

He says, "Twelve thousand dollars."

I say, "LaDonna and I will write you a check for $12,000 for our first year's lease, and you can use that to put in your bathroom."

LaDonna and I name our new space the Salt Box, because salt is a *preservative*. We don't want to push East Winston residents out by purchasing inexpensive property and then building new housing that they can't afford. Gentrification.

Instead, we want to stabilize and *preserve* this neighborhood. We want to collaborate to build an economic engine—an entrepreneurial ecosystem. Then, we can build affordable workforce housing and connect the East Winston residents to the Innovation Quarter. In this way, everyone can share in the growth and prosperity of Winston-Salem.

In search of my first transplant—a tree of a tenant to firmly root the ecosystem—Paula McCoy comes to mind. She's now executive director for Neighbors for Better Neighborhoods (NBN). NBN is all about community development for the under-resourced. It actually uses the ABCD (**A**sset **B**ased **C**ommunity **D**evelopment) model.

This means that her team goes door-to-door surveying the neighborhoods assets—individual skills, resources, spaces, and organizations. Next, these assets are plotted on a literal map.

Then, development of each community is based on its assets—its inherent strengths—and not its deficits. The idea is to grow the positive and change the neighborhood from the inside out.

My challenge is that NBN is currently planted in the pleasant comforts of the Augsburg Lutheran Church—on West Fifth Street near Summit. Aside from safety—they also enjoy very low rent.

When I share my vision with Paula—for creating this entrepreneurial engine and ecosystem in East Winston—she's excited. This is something her team would love to do. However, they would prefer to do their work from their current, comfortable location.

In fact, while Paula is cautious about making a move, her board outright refuses. They point to the high level of sex offenders in the area, blatant drug dealing, and open prostitution. In short, they feel that their personal safety will be at risk.

SALT BOX

Let the conversation begin. NBN is all about transforming communities from the inside out. What greater proof of commitment could NBN offer, than to plop itself right into the middle of the very community that it is seeking to help?

This makes sense to Paula. However, it will take another 11 months of talks, tours, and appreciative inquiry to reassure the board. In the end, I guarantee NBN the same low rent that it is currently paying—for two years—if it will be our anchor tenant in our Salt Box.

During that year, Wise Man Brewing approaches Andrew to lease half the space—6000 square feet upstairs. I give Andrew the nod, because it is proving more challenging to build this ecosystem than anticipated. And, 6,000 square feet will be plenty of space for our venture.

Next, I talk with my friend, Chuck Spong—executive director for Love Out Loud (LOL). He sees the advantage of moving into the Salt Box right away. Chuck knows that Mayor Joines' Poverty Thought Force has recently published 56 recommendations to address inner city poverty. So, what better place for Chuck to be than in the very area that needs the LOVE.

He tells me excitedly, "NBN is laser focused on *residents*. We are laser focused on *volunteers*. Just think what could happen if we are rubbing shoulders together on a daily basis!"

LOL brings a score of white, black, and brown leaders to the Salt Box, including Terrance Hawkins. To me, Hawkins embodies the vision and articulation of Martin Luther King, Jr. He's partnered with LOL and Dr.Clay Cooke to direct the School of Love.

School of Love educates the community on "radical discipleship"—looking at leaders as diverse as Romero, Martin Luther King, Jr., Perpetua and Felicitas, Hamer, Augustine, Day, Thurman, Sojourner Truth, and Deitrich Bonhoeffer. Look them up.

Bonhoeffer is a favorite of mine because he really gets the concept of being others-oriented. We are only free when we genuinely care about others and they genuinely care about us.

In part, Bonhoeffer says, "Freedom is not something man has for himself, but something he has for the others…It is not a possession, a presence, or an object...but a *relationship* and nothing else. In truth, freedom is a *relationship* between two persons. Being free means 'being free for the other,' because the other has bound me to him. Only in *relationship* with the other am I free."

Imagine a city that reforms itself from the inside out, by attending class at the School of Love to learn the history, the language, and the power of freedom, justice, and liberty for all.

All of this dovetails perfectly with what was said by Dr. Cornel West—a Professor Emeritus at Princeton University—"Justice is what love looks like in public."

Incidentally, NBN hosts additional educational programs presented by the Racial Equity Institute. These programs help change agents understand the historic and system nature of racial inequity, while searching for solutions.

While we have all of these conversations going on, NBN invites the North Winston Neighborhood Association to the table. They will represent the residents who live around the Salt Box. They, too, have a space at the Salt Box. We have "family meetings"—the Neighborhood Association and all the tree-like tenants—every Monday at 1:30.

The goal of the Salt Box is not to ride in on a white horse to save the neighborhood. Far from it, our aim is to come to know the residents, so we can leverage resources to grow *their ideas* into sustainable entrepreneurial ventures.

Creating this ESHIP ecosystem is a little trickier than it might seem. For instance, we had Fay Horwitt, CEO of HUSTLE Winston-Salem, join us at the Salt Box. She mirrors our mission—creating a new economy by accelerating underrepresented entrepreneurs—mainly women of all colors. However, she is so talented, that Forward Cities—a grantee of Kauffman Foundation's ESHIP Communities—hires her away. She is now serving as their President.

Then, Paula McCoy—executive director of NBN—is called to serve as the interim director of the Mayor's new initiative Partnership for Prosperity. This is good—by having worked with so many agencies and programs, Paula has the expertise. And part of her job will be to better integrate existing programs for the people in low-resource (poverty) neighborhoods—like the neighborhood surrounding the Salt Box.

At the same time, she'll be advocating for better housing, better bus routes between the neighborhoods and available jobs, and a living wage for workers. Currently minimum wage in North Carolina is $7.25. The City of Winston-Salem adopted a living wage of $15 for full-time *City employees only* beginning in 2021.

She'll also be advocating for better healthcare, universal Preschool, an ease of the benefits cliff (Health care and housing subsidies drop off suddenly—rather than gradually—as income rises), and a greater awareness and accessibility to community resources.

So, though we lose Paula—as an everyday presence in the Salt Box— she won't forget about us. And, NBN remains. Paula's move allows Kenneth Holly—program director—to step up and take the lead as interim. Kenneth has been organizing communities since he was boy—literally.

He used to go door-to-door offering to take people's garbage cans out to the road for a nickel a can. From there, he progressed to community-based youth projects, the Veteran's Homeless Project, and countless ministries including Whole Man Ministry.

Little by little, via the "family meetings," everyone unites to build a vision for the neighborhood. This is a process. Though I'd like change to happen at the speed of light, it's going to take a few years.

In the next step, we mobilize assets. This is already happening in a small way—through Time Banking. Paula McCoy actually introduced this concept—and it's working. Residents and members of the greater community can bank time on the NBN website. For instance, 10 hours of volunteer work at Big Brothers and Big Sisters equals 10 Time credits.

These credits can be "cashed in" for various services such as auto mechanic work, chiropractor visits, or discounts at retail stores. Or, people can make a trade. One person might exchange a delicious homemade cake for another person to mow his or her lawn.

As Kenneth notes, "Time banking levels the playing field by allowing people to use their time and gifts to help others (volunteering) and then to receive the help that they need, but cannot financially afford."

In the not too distant future, resources will be leveraged to launch accelerated entrepreneurial ventures and to build better affordable housing. As programs and projects spin off, lessons will be learned, adjustments will be made, and the cycle will continue—just like a rainforest ecosystem. In this way, the neighborhood will experience an upward spiral—changing from the inside out—and uplifting itself.

It's exciting to see the vision take root. There are undeniable signs that the ecosystem is sprouting—with the grassroots of residents, and undergrowth of LOL and NBN, and some tall tropical trees of major Foundations. However—like in any ecosystem—we have to be aware of opportunists.

And in saying that, though the Salt Box just turned two years old in January 2020, I'm counting on it to bring East Winston into its rightful place in the larger Winston-Salem ecosystem. Because that's the kind of world I want for my grandchildren.

In fact, I expressed my hope—which Kauffman Foundation caught on film during my two years with ESHIP—when I said, "They (my grands) need a future they can live into and it won't be the past that I lived out of."

Moving that back a generation, one of my heroes, Dietrich Bonhoeffer once said, "The ultimate test of a moral society is the kind of world that it leaves to its children."

As I write this, the Corona Virus scare is rampant, with our world seemingly on the brink of disaster; not only with its health care, politics, and economics, but also the press with its alarmist tendencies. It seems the time is right for all five sectors of our society, education, religion, municipal governance, marketplace, and its plethora of nonprofits to rewrite our script—to work together to solve the problems that threaten us.

SALT BOX

Learnings from Sector V

1.) Learn to spell "community"—COMMON UNITY.

2.) Treat every person you meet as a gateway to community.

3.) If you really appreciate life and abundance, then you have a responsibility to share your life with others.

4.) Don't underestimate the power of family narrative. What's yours? What's the narrative of the person with whom you are hoping to connect and collaborate?

5.) Relational Capital—relationships built on mutual trust and respect—is the most precious asset you will ever own.

6.) When you get your time on stage, remember you are responsible to set up the next act.

7.) Collaboration is the foundation to true community.

8.) If I have anything to offer—it's being others-oriented. Acknowledge other people and you will impact their lives.

SECTION VI

A Call to Action

In his most far-reaching undertaking to date, Bost calls to all communities— in Any Town, U.S.A. or even around the world—to seize the moment.

The world is calling out for social equity. Now is the time for each community to assess its individual challenges, engage in more fierce conversations, identify its catalysts, and locally unite the five sectors. Optimal outcomes will require courage, an others-oriented posture, and an abandonment of traditional sector motivations—to do what is best for all the people.

In this final section—you will experience a shift in Bost's style—as he is no longer recounting history. Instead, he is using history to shed light on the preferred future.

The following pages—which by necessity zooms in on the very real community of Winston-Salem, NC—is designed to inspire all communities to collaborate with the intention of creating an ecosystem that is genuinely inclusive.

Now is the time.

Chapter 45

Rewriting Our Script

On Friday, February 8, 2019, a standing room only crowd gathers at the Stevens Center in downtown Winston-Salem. As I look around, I see people of every color and from all five sectors—Business, Education, Religion, Municipal Governance, and Social Activism—abuzz with excitement. We are here for one purpose—to *watch* the new musical *Union* today so that we can *talk* about how to heal our city tomorrow.

Union—based on the 1968 sanitation workers' strike in Memphis, Tennessee and the subsequent assassination of Dr. Martin Luther King, Jr.—portrays the black and white perspective of racial inequity.

Employing music—both choral and rap—step dancing, and excellent scripting, this high-energy performance brings to life the panoramic view of racism in a most touching and thought-provoking way.

For instance, the white Mayor feels *entitled* to a privileged life because he's always been told by his daddy that his grandfathers worked hard to build the city. At the same time, the blacks have always been told that the city was built on their backs and so—at the very least—they are *entitled* to humane working conditions and a living wage.

The play powerfully parallels the story of Winston-Salem. As corporate sponsors, Don and Robbin Flow, note in the playbill, "…it (Winston-Salem) also has *a tragic dimension*, primarily around *race and the inequities*…In essence, we have co-existed, on occasion even co-operated, but we have only rarely collaborated, and thus *we have never been a single community.*"

Interwoven in the play is the powerful chant, "We the people, we the people, got something to say, got something to say."

It creates a natural segue to the planned public forum, because the purpose of this musical is not to entertain us. It is to ignite a

A CATALYST FOR CHANGE

conversation—with the singular goal of forging a "more perfect union," by understanding how our local past has impacted the present, so that we can create our preferred future.

Amazingly, over 600 people—of all colors and backgrounds— pour into Union Baptist Church at 9 o'clock the next morning to discuss racial inequity, economic justice, and police violence. Emotions are running high.

Moderator Terrance Hawkins lights the torch when he says, "The conversation we are embarking on today is dangerous. It's jarring, it's painful, it's messy, it's hard, but it's absolutely necessary."(Appendix)

He is right. I can feel the tension in the room and a few people are so uncomfortable that they leave. But the majority stay and participate in the tough conversation. Much of the panel discussion spotlights the tragic statistics highlighted in my earlier chapter, *What is it like to live in Winston-Salem?* The main plea—at the conclusion of the four-hour forum—is for the community to keep the conversation alive.

The next day, Wake Forest President Nathan Hatch writes in a published letter to the *Winston-Salem Journal* that this is "a catalyzing moment in the life of our city." (Appendix)

I would add that it's a dangerous moment.

In all sincerity—some of my black friends have said in essence, "Something's got to give or we're going to take this to the streets."

And, I've had white friends answer, "Bring it on! I'm locked and loaded."

Now while these viewpoints are extreme—and not held by the majority of residents black or white—they do make the point that talk is cheap. Talk and time—alone—will never solve the problem.

At the same time, true reformation is not going to come from fear—fear of danger if we don't change. We need to reach a little higher.

The truth is: Winston-Salem has outgrown the once common, "acceptable," and flagrant practice of racism. Systemic racism no longer suits us—as a transformed city—any more than lead pipes suited the Romans. It's poisoning us.

Additionally, we can't have it both ways. The national press has come to our door and shined the spotlight on our beautiful Innovation

Quarter (IQ). We are ahead of the curve in science, technology, and building the new economy. This brings us great community pride.

However, we are stuck in the past—in the horse and buggy days—when it comes to racial inequities. Having the "profoundly tragic" neglect, stagnation, and deterioration in East Winston on the front pages of national news is embarrassing. But, it's also a good thing, because we are finally compelled to address it.

So, in these final chapters of my book— and my life—I'm suggesting that we rewrite our script and this time, that we will follow through with the *actions* to make it a reality.

<u>Old Script</u>		<u>New Script</u>
Winston-Salem only cares about *whites*.	→	Winston-Salem cares about *everyone*.
Winston-Salem is *racially divided*.	→	Winston-Salem is an *inclusive* city.
Winston-Salem *neglects* the under-resourced.	→	Winston-Salem *fosters* upward mobility.

We no longer need to be "sick and tired of being sick and tired" as my friend, Nigel Alston often says, when referencing the ongoing leadership narrative, full of promises, yet short of any real change. Below are some observations, learnings, and hindsight that might contribute to the healing of the divide in Winston-Salem.

1) ***Script a new vision.***

Mention racial inequities and a thousand different pictures pop into people's minds—along with the story-lines to support it. We could spend our lifetimes comparing the stories and documenting them. Or, we can create a vision that makes sense to everyone and proceed with the healing.

Integration of Natural Science and Research—such as research at the Kaufman Foundation—now identifies communities as *ecosystems*.

A CATALYST FOR CHANGE

Like a Rain Forest, in contrast to weeded gardens with straight rows, in a dense Rain Forest, one never knows where the next species might be found that holds biological secrets to human ailments.

In a simple analogy—whether looking at rain forests or the human body—as an ecosystem, Winston-Salem has one hand that is strong, well-nourished, and healthy. However, it's other "hand" (East Winston) has been strangled, malnourished, and is continually "crying out" in pain.

As expected—in its current state—East Winston is not seen as able to contribute much to the body, if you're looking for straight rows!

So what are our choices? Without getting tangled up in the past or the blame, we can evaluate our current condition. One choice is to simply ignore the symptoms until the situation becomes gangrenous. But that's the old script.

Instead, thinking about it quite literally, Winston-Salem has some of the world's best healthcare and economic experts. So, we are not going to heal our economics without healing our greatest resource—our people.

In making the better choice, we are going to embrace our "hurting hand" as a full-fledged member of our body. We are going to unite all of our resources. And we aren't going to stop, until the whole body is healthy.

What will that mean? We don't know yet. Think of the possibilities of having two hands working together. What contributions—beyond our wildest imaginations—might the "healed hand" have to offer? We must move beyond the bias as a privileged majority with a tendency to offer underfunded moral mandates that never fully materialize.

When human capital is lost, we *all* lose the failed opportunities for true community. Might a new vision that is fully inclusive take Winston-Salem to the next level? After all, Wake Forest University—which began as a small transplant to this manufacturing giant called Winston-Salem—later grew into the virtual heart of the city.

One thing we know for sure: Whenever we do what is right—what is fair for everyone—providence will come around to find us. And so will the national news, eager to document our amazing story.

2) **Learn the language.**

Our ecosystem is comprised of as many as 5 sectors—Marketplace; Religion; Non-profits to include Healthcare; Municipal Governance; and perhaps most meaningful to the next generation, Education. After having spent 20 years—sometimes concurrently—in each of the five sectors, it is apparent that no single sector of the community can create lasting social reform. It's going to take collaboration—with all five sectors playing a role—to bring about true healing.

The challenge is that each sector speaks its own language. Unfortunately, we don't yet have a Google translate option—where CEO speech is translated into Pastor lingo. Or, where Mayor rhetoric is translated into Principal language. However—when that software is developed, it will be priceless!

Currently, when each market sector attempts to see the racial equity challenge through its own lens and language—each sector misses the target. However, if each sector can learn to see through each other's lens—placing five crosshairs on the target—together we can hit the bullseye.

This sounds complex, but Peter Block, in his book *Flawless Consulting* identifies a process that actually works. A small group—two people from different sectors—sit face-to-face with their knees nine inches away (no table or obstacle between them). Then they explain to each other the what, when, why, where, and how of their lives and their businesses—appreciative inquiry. They also describe their risk factor—the thing they must protect to survive.

Oversimplifying this, imagine a racially diversified group of 20 leaders—four from each sector. Ten members sit in an outer circle arms-length apart. The remaining 10 members sit in an inner circle, knee to knee with the outer circle. Then, the one-on-one conversations begin. Discussions may last hours or perhaps several sessions. They continue until each person can see life through the eyes of his or her pairing.

Then, the inner circle shifts one chair to the right and the process continues. Even when leaders of the same sector are paired—they share.

One of the most important ideas to share is regarding the various filters through which each sector understands its *risk factor*.

Risk for the Marketplace (business)

The marketplace is in the business of making money. It converts time, effort, and ideas into an exchangeable asset. It drives our economy. It creates wealth.

Therefore, the *risk factor* that the marketplace must protect is ROI (Return on Investment). If a venture is not profitable, it will be difficult to obtain marketplace buy in.

Risk for Religion (organized church; places of worship)

Our Houses of Worship are the places—the bricks and mortar—where many people learn values—such as treating others with integrity, honesty, and justice. However, it seems when the church veers too far toward equity and social justice (the word itself a lightning rod for some), it can begin to lose followers. Fewer followers mean less money to maintain the building and pay the staff. So for the church—it *risks* nickels and noses if it strays too far from what the congregation wants to hear. Like its marketplace sister, she battles her own "Bottom Line"

Risk for Non-profits (foundations and other 501(c)(3)s...to include Healthcare)

Boys & Girls Clubs, Goodwill, Habitat for Humanity, Experiment in Self Reliance, Winston-Salem Rescue Mission, Salvation Army Boys Club, Children's Home, Second Harvest Food Bank, and United Way—491 in all—and yes our healthcare institutions, along with our foundations—provide priceless social outreach in my hometown of Winston-Salem.

Each of these organizations embraces a mission. However, each can only stay in business if it finds funding. In reaching out to help a "current cause" a non-profit might *risk* straying from its *mission* to follow the funding. Following the funding is a short-term fix for finances. However, once a non-profit veers into unknown territory—it is no longer effective in moving the needle in alignment with its stated mission. Hence, it *risks* losing its primary funders.

Risk for Municipal Governance (local elected officials)

Elected officials are responsible in part to grow and protect the community—representing the interests of their voter base. Officials are provided guidance as well as constraints by mandates such as the aforementioned comprehensive plans.

Though it might seem that the Mayor or the City Council could mandate sweeping changes—that's not the case. If leading officials try to push the *lever of change* faster than the public is able to absorb the adjustment—the "offending" officials will simply lose in the next election. Then, regardless of the historical knowledge and personal passion they might otherwise bring to the table, some of the best intended of society forfeit the power to make lasting change in the community. Although elected officials can and must lead progress—they are rarely willing to *risk* re-election to do this. And, indeed, until *collective action* and *political will* reaches a tipping point—any sustainable change is highly unlikely.

Risk for Education (Public Schools)

Public education is designed to give students the most basic *skills* for immediate workforce or college entry. Unfortunately, if employment needs drive the curriculum, then often *the student's natural bent* takes the back seat. At the same time, the jobs that most students must be prepared for do not even exist yet! Additionally, schools depend on test scores for funding. So, even if individual schools come up with innovative ways that result in considerable student *growth* (measuring a student's *personal gains* in proficiency over the course of a year)—if those schools then fail to meet often rigid State or Federal *proficiency* standards (comparing a student to the grade level expectations) schools *risk* lower funding or even a State takeover.

3) ***Do it for the right reason.***

Once the 5-sector group becomes a true ecosystem—with a free flowing network of honest communication and trust, it can examine its motives. Members can be mirrors for each other and resolve conflicting intentions. To be effective, the motive for healing our communities can't be profit, personal prominence, fear, guilt, power, or anything else, except—it is the right thing to do. In a nutshell, it's not about me, it's about we. This is an *others-oriented* endeavor. It's about making our communities—North, South, East, or West—truly livable for everyone.

4) ***Expect compromise and concessions.***

Each of the five sectors can often be territorial—protecting the *risk factor* necessary for its survival. However—for this mission of reforming inequities—each sector will be called upon to make sacrifices, even to put at risk the very thing that it treasures most. And yet, *when everyone takes a risk simultaneously—that is the safest risk of all.* It is only possible to arrive at this step—collaborate, cooperate, contribute—when the previous three steps have built sufficient trust.

5) ***Collaborate.***

After the 5-sector "team" is clear about who they are (a united group of change-agents who promise to put the good of all residents ahead of their personal or professional interests) and what they do (seek equitable solutions to the racial/social and economic disparities), then they can collaborate across what had heretofore been impenetrable barriers. In my hometown, we know that as "Crossing 52!"—the racial divide in our city.

In a true spirit of being *others-oriented*, the team will have, at least figuratively, those one-on-one, nine-inch conversations until they come to *genuinely care* about all people, and in an orchestrated way, begin to address their real needs. Once trust and understanding is built—the 5-sector team and the local residents will imagine, design, and implement solutions to rectify the economic, social and racial disparities.

Chapter 46

One Step at a Time

Creating a "more perfect union" in "Any Town, USA" is a monumental task. In our case, Winston-Salem and the greater Forsyth County, has undergone numerous economic shifts as corporate headquarters rotated in and out of the community.

The Innovation Quarter (IQ), the latest and most fascinating revitalization stands as proof that the nearly impossible can happen. It's taken 20 years of engagement across multiple sectors to pull IQ out of the ground. It may take another 20 years to truly reform and heal Winston-Salem. But it's time to get started. With the desire, commitment, vision, and a new script—it will materialize.

These aforementioned steps toward collaboration are not designed to oversimplify the process. In fact, it's just the opposite. It should be obvious that were it that easy, the brilliant leadership that drives each of those five sectors would have already arrived at the solutions.

So, just to demonstrate the complexity of the problem and the solutions, I'd like to walk through some of the challenges facing public education alone. Why use education as a focus here? Many people believe that education is the key to lifting people out of poverty. The tendency is to lay all the responsibility on the schools, a convenient whipping post.

That is not my objective. Sadly, in November 2019, the North Carolina Department of Instruction released a list of eight schools in Winston-Salem that are at risk for State takeover. Six of the eight schools are in East Winston (zip codes 27101, 27105, 27107). Of those six in East Winston, five of them have a white population of 5% or less. One has a white population of 16%.

Most people would agree that the racial segregation and the failure of East Winston schools are unacceptable. And yet, a solution is much more difficult than expected. So, I will use this—the education dilemma—to illustrate the complexity of just one aspect of the racial inequity so often discussed in communities.

Brief History: In the 1970s, the Winston-Salem Forsyth County Schools (WSFCS) were court ordered to desegregate. The district began busing elementary students out of the city and into the suburbs and busing middle school students out of the suburbs and into the city. Mission accomplished! The schools achieved racial and economic diversity and the achievement gap (between blacks and whites and/or higher income and lower income students) was significantly closed.

However, there was an unforeseen consequence. Higher income white families spawned an academic "white flight" by flocking to newly created private schools. This was tantamount to kicking the pillars out of the public education system.

Public schools depend on "parent advocates"—with money, time, energy, ideas, volunteer-spirit and corporate backing—to flesh out and bring to life the skeletal public education structure. Middle income parents—predominately white—were the primary "parent advocates."

This unanticipated loss moved schools to begin measuring its student base just like a business measures market share. So the question was raised: What is the market share of all the students in Forsyth County who attend grades K-12? (This is before Charter schools.)

According to Dr. Don Martin, former WSFCS Superintendent (1994-2013) and current Vice-Chairman Forsyth County Commissioners (2014-current), "When we started measuring market share of students in 1995, Guilford County had the highest (89%), followed by Wake County, Charlotte, Winston-Salem (85%), and Durham.

Fast forward, the last time this was calculated was 2015. Guess what? The largest market share is now held by Winston-Salem Forsyth County. We only dropped a half of a percent over the past 25 years."

Why? What happened? To stem the loss of middle class white students, the mainly white school board voted to redraw the school lines to create "neighborhood schools." The new lines—mirroring the neighborhoods—reflect the existing racial and economic segregation.

These racially segregated neighborhoods, of course, trace their roots to real estate *redlining* that occurred decades earlier. (See earlier chapter *What's Your Story)*.

To offset the resulting racial segregation, the neighborhood school plan includes "controlled choice." Controlled choice allows (still in effect in 2020) parents to *choose optional schools* for their children, if they are unhappy with their home-base neighborhood school.

However, the parent's choice of schools is "controlled" by the district. Even though parents are promised to be awarded one of their top three choices—what are those choices?

Students are guaranteed a seat in their "home" school or residential school. For a non-residential choice, school capacity determines which school is selected.

So if the first non-residential school is overcrowded, then the second choice is considered. If all of the non-residential choices are overcrowded, then the student will be assigned to the least overcrowded school.

The district also grants sibling preference so that a younger sibling can attend a school where the sibling already attends regardless of capacity. In practice, too many East Winston students stay stuck in the failing East Winston schools.

Twenty-five years later, we ask: Are neighborhood schools with "controlled choice" working? Well, from aspect of market share and slowed white flight—it's a huge success.

But from the original Civil Rights mission to integrate the schools for educational equity—it is an abysmal failure. In fact, in October 2019, *New York Times* award winning journalist, Nikole Hannah-Jones, reported, "This (WSFCS) is one of the most segregated districts in the state."

Money is Not the Answer: According to former Superintendent Dr. Don Martin, "For about 15 years, the schools in poorer neighborhoods received extra funding—called Equity Plus. Later, after the recession, this became Title I funding. These schools receive extra funding because we know that to achieve equity; they will need smaller class sizes, which mean more teachers. Also, when we upgraded technology—the technology went into the poor schools first."

However, more money and computers didn't bring about educational equity in these poor and highly segregated neighborhood schools. In fact, as earlier noted, these failing schools are now at risk for State takeover.

Additionally, cultural attitudes—unrelated to funding—have a huge impact on student outcome. Middle class parents tend to tell their children that education is the ticket to a good life—thereby fostering a desire to excel in school attendance, homework assignments, and academic competition.

However, negative peer pressure—the pressure to "not be too smart"—clips the wings of many talented students in failing schools. These are wings that might take the students and the community to new heights if these students were—instead—surrounded by peer groups that support academic achievement.

Usually, it is *relationships*—not money—that change our belief system.

The Education Solution: The purpose of this exercise is not to arrive at a solution. It's the community's job to rewrite the script. But hopefully, it demonstrates the complexity of the problem.

In brainstorming, perhaps we can look at other counties—such as Wake County, NC. When busing was banned based on *race*, Wake bused students based on their *economic diversity*. In the process—it created racial diversity.

According to a *Winston-Salem Journal* story titled, "Forsyth County Schools Resegregated," reporter Travis Fain stated, "Black students in Wake County test better on average in reading, for example, than their Forsyth counterparts." While Wake is now doing less income-based busing, its evidence of impact remains.

We can even look at other countries—such as Finland. Here, a child is cared for from prenatal to graduation. Regardless of parents' economic standing—each child receives a "Baby Box" that serves as a first crib and includes a mattress, sleeping bag, gender neutral clothing, and about 50 high quality items. What it says to parents is: The whole community loves my baby.

Finland is also peppered with Family cafés. Supported by non-profits and plopped into the middle of neighborhoods—these meeting centers offer a place to share a coffee, make friends with other parents, engage in group activities with children, and participate in parenting and problem solving sessions.

Also, parents receive 164 days of paid parental leave when a child is born—mother AND father—with an additional 158 days of partial paid leave. Unpaid leave is available for up to three years. Finland appreciates the value of the *relationship* between a child and both parents.

According to the February 22, 2020 CNBC report titled, "It's Almost Free," Finland is consistently ranked #1 on the World Happiness Report."

What does this have to do with education? The Finns get it. It's all about *ecosystem* and *relationships*. Education is not a problem when the ecosystem is healthy. In fact, students in Finland consistently score at the top of the PISA (Programme for International Student Assessment)—a worldwide program measuring students' performance in math, reading, and science.

So, this provides another clue as to what "Any Town, USA" needs. It needs inclusion, healthy relationships, and compassionate healing as part of our community ecosystems.

A CATALYST FOR CHANGE

Chapter 47

Possibility Thinking—5 Sectors Strong

What if the five sectors could—in collaboration with the residents—build the kinds of *relationships* that open up opportunities to work, play, learn, and contribute for *everyone* in the community? As you read these possibilities, jot down your own ideas. There is no bad idea when we are brainstorming.

- What if the <u>marketplace</u> creates entry level jobs—located right in under-resourced neighborhoods—with built in ladders for advancement via on-the-job education or apprenticeship? What if these jobs are subsidized to provide a living wage as workers advance in skills and experience? What if support is also brought in for fledging entrepreneurs? Might the resulting *healthy relationships* and *mutual enrichment* contribute to a new sense of hope, economic growth, and community pride?

- What if under-resourced <u>schools</u> (identify the under-performing schools in your area) publish a wish list? This list can include study-buddies, lunch buddies, listeners for young readers, classroom helpers, homework helpers, playground partners, scientist and business owners to share their careers, and mentors. The schools might list things like playground equipment, science and math equipment, free books, a school vegetable garden, sports equipment, and field trip funds. And what if the community responded to this wish list—coming to the schools by the hundreds to prove that every child matters. Also, the schools can ask for partnerships, with universities, core businesses or the local version of the Innovation Quarter—to bring classrooms of students on site for an afternoon of shared learning. Conversely, those same entities can send interns into the classroom to share personal stories. *Think relationships.* Additionally, what if under-resourced schools open their doors for free multigenerational learning—so students and adults can learn afterschool and on weekends?

- What if the <u>churches</u> unleash their people power to become surrogate "parent advocates"—showing up at underserved schools for the sole purpose of doing right by every child and *building relationships* with students of all colors. And what if these "advocates" help raise money so that *all students* can take the kind of field trips and share the kinds of educational experiences that middle class students regularly enjoy. How might it change a child's life—to see that he or she is genuinely cared about by the greater community?

- What if <u>non-profits</u> establish and maintain *free* before school and after school sports and academic programs—with three healthy meals a day—right in the under-resourced neighborhoods. Instead of being left to roam the streets or the Internet—students can be building *healthy relationships*, study skills, and community service experiences. And what if the non-profits set up *free* Family cafés, preschools, and day cares right in the neighborhoods. What if non-profits work *one-on-one with families* to remove stigmas and obstacles—real or perceived—that might keep the people from fully benefiting from these programs?

- What if the <u>municipal government</u> helps landlords bring slum housing up to livable standards. And, what if the planning and zoning board starts mandating diversified neighborhoods—with blended housing? What if government agencies—Social Services, the Health Department, and even doctors and dentists—dispense services right at the school? What if public transportation reaches right into under-resourced neighborhoods so that residents can readily access the jobs, relationships, and opportunities in their greater community? How might this improve the residents' *relationship* with its city?

Realistic Expectations:

If the 5-sectors—with community support—implement all of these suggestions, the new script might still fail. Why? We have to meet the under-resourced community where it is. Right now, it has limited strength, health, flexibility, and resources. So, even if we put all of these opportunities right at the doorstep (identify any areas of gross disparities which likely exist in your town), residents might not access them. Why?

Of course, the initial feeling might be—we tried, they didn't want it. It's the old "why don't they pull themselves up by their boot straps" conversation. *But what we can miss is that intermediary step of helping the under-resourced community acquire their proverbial boots and the means to use them.*

Going back to the ecosystem of the body, if we had been bedridden for months and someone delivered food, crutches, medicines, books, and tools—10 feet away from our bed—we could not access those resources on our own. We would need someone—a compassionate nurse or a caring volunteer—to bring those things to us and maybe even spoon-feed us, until we gradually gain enough strength to access the resources on our own.

There's no shame in being bedridden—in need of compassionate care. And it is no insult to the caregiver, to give more remedial care to a bedridden patient than to a more mobile patient. The only shame comes from failing to distinguish the needs and then to meet them.

So, of course, the under-resourced population will not—cannot—respond to an "equal" opportunity in the same way that the middle class community responds. It will require patient, compassionate, resourceful commitment—over an extended period of time—to fully heal our land. Only then will we attain a "more perfect union."

My Wish for My Community and YOURS:

Twenty years from now—at age 92, when I'm an "old man"—I want to pick up the *Winston-Salem Journal* (for you this will be your local newspaper), *the New York Times, U.S. News and World Report, and Yomiuri Shimbun* (the most widely circulated newspaper in the world) to read about the amazing social transformation in my community.

The stories will tell how the under-resourced side of town—once poverty stricken and neglected—is now a thriving community, fully integrated into the city. None of the public schools are segregated because everyone knows that segregation short changes everyone.

Indeed, our town (your town) discovers what a huge intellectual, innovative, and artistic treasure await them when residents of all colors are allowed to unpack who they are. And, when both hands begin to work together—our community soars to claim a top award for successful and significant metro areas in the U.S.

And as I lean back in my porch swing (and you in yours), we'll tell our grandchildren, "Your mimi and I were a small part of that. Now, it's your turn to take the stage."

Epilogue

Landing the Plane

Visionaries spend most of their time at the 30,000-foot view. However, as with air travel, there comes a time to land the plane.

"Ladies and gentlemen, this is your captain speaking. We are now entering our descent. Please take your seats and fasten your seat belts."

Take a moment. Catch your breath. Look out the window. Our plane is breaking through the clouds. Can you see the city? Don't be surprised by the cranking noise. Our landing gear is coming down—that's a good thing! Hold tight, our rubber tires are kissing the asphalt.

Please remain seated until the seatbelt light goes off. Okay, now it's time to disembark.

But while I have you standing in the aisle with carry-ons in hand, here are a few takeaways. Oh, and thank you for flying Bost Airways.

Learn to listen to your 3 brains. They are real, look it up! Your *gut* physically is an ecosystem, amazingly connected with your *heart* and *brain* by way of a complex nerve aligned infrastructure.

Strive to be more self-aware (not self-absorbed). *Your life is much more than your earnings or your stockpile of knowledge from others.* Know yourself and your personal universe. That will add value to others as you mutually unpack your reason for being. There will never be another John Bost. (I heard your sigh laden, "Thank God!") One is truly enough, if he does his job. Nor will there ever be another you. Uniqueness of calling is my point here.

Explore your personality strengths and work on your weaknesses. Lifelong learning is not only for the purpose of adaptation for multiple careers, though now a reality in the workplace. *The joy of life itself is dependent upon testing your strengths and yes, failing...but failing forward.* We learn by stretching ourselves, and you have not stretched until you have failed in your most passionate of moments.

Above all, nurture your spiritual being. *Find your calling.* If I duck out on this one, I have almost abandoned who I am. The "I Am" has fashioned you from your mother's womb for a tremendous journey of delight and favor. You—like the story of the man who found a great treasure hidden in a field—must find it. Then, like this man, "with great joy, he goes and sells all that he has, and buys that field."

Guard your relationships—your relational capital. My 72 years of blessing was not built upon some silver spoon, unless that spoon was the strong work ethic modeled by my Dad. Since my days as a child, I've been discovering new friends, studying their strengths, and along the way with God's help, shedding their weaknesses. It is a life-learned trade secret! Being closely aligned with others, yes, *others-oriented, as you have heard repeatedly throughout the book, has been the secret sauce of my life!* With integrity as one's base, guarding, protecting, recovering those relationships at all cost is key to success and constructive collaboration.

Always be on the lookout for moments to bring justice and equity to your greater community. While social justice has become a word tainted—and at times a lightning rod—it does not remove us from *responsibility to our fellow man*, even globally! That's bottom line stuff! I don't want to get all preachy, as you may have sensed, but:

> "He has shown you, O man, what *is* good;
> And what does the Lord require of you
> But to do justly,
> To love mercy,
> And to walk humbly with your God?
> Micah 6:8 NKJV

Give generously as money finds you. And, if you live by these parting reminders, money will find you. However, your goal for living is not about the money...need I say that again? *Your reason for living is to bring value to others, something capitalists may have lost along the way.* A strong work ethic in a free market, by a person who understands and loves others, will naturally foster generosity. Generosity is the by-product of great joy in living!

Dream and live fearlessly as you follow your dreams. Explore the risk factors—the thought processes of key leadership—within multiple sectors. Know that engaging each sector is key to collaboration, a necessity for sustainable community. *The better you know yourself—while respecting others—the better you can live into your dreams and add value to their dreams,* thus discovering the place of impact that daily restores your soul!

Now, let life happen through you and those with whom you are called to live.

Oh, before you exit the plane, I'd like you to meet my wife, LaDonna.

Before publishing my manuscript, I ask her, "Honey, do you mind proofing my book? After all, you've lived through it with me, and you used to be an English teacher."

With her typical guarded caution, she says, "What if I don't approve?"

I tell her, "It's your decision. If you don't approve, then we don't publish. But if it passes muster, then Nigel has agreed to write the forward."

Three days later, she announces, "Everything in here is true. I know the people and I know the challenges. I'm glad you stayed positive!"

She knows me like a book!

"As to the self-awareness you profess," she says playfully, "I'm not sure I get all the Enneagram and ENFJ stuff. But I do know that you are a unique person, with a unique calling. Just give God the glory."

Then, she says more seriously, "You know, John, I've been supportive of your dreams for our entire marriage. However, at some point you've got to hand over the reins. Perhaps your grandkids should be your focus now?"

Brutal honesty is another of LaDonna's gifts!

Then she asks, "Does Patty Jo know that you are currently involved in three other communities!"

A CATALYST FOR CHANGE

She senses that I have not yet thrown in the towel! Ironically, my devotions the next morning are in Isaiah Chapter 38, as Hezekiah pleads to the heavens for a life extension of 15 years! Isaiah 38:15-29.

I'll take that!   Now I can let you off the plane. It's been a good flight. However, it's time to get to work!

About the Author

John R. Bost

John Bost fondly refers to himself as a blind hog in a field of acorns. In other words, life is so full of opportunities to do what is best for everyone, that it doesn't take extraordinary skills. It takes heart.

He learned to be "others-oriented" from his father and grandfather—blue-collar workers who respected all people long before it was politically correct.

Standing on this core value—genuinely caring about the other person—Bost has built relationships that have lasted a lifetime.

In fact, he claims, "Relational capital is the most precious asset that I own. And I will protect my relationships at all cost."

It's these hard-earned relationships; with people in all five sectors, that consistently allow Bost to be the catalyst—the trusted connector—to achieve results only possible with cross-sector collaboration.

His record stands for itself—50 years in five sectors moving the needle—Public Education (Associate Superintendent), Religion (Executive Pastor), Business (Owner), Politics (Mayor), and Social Reform (Activist).

While most of his learning came from living and giving, he did earn his Bachelor of Science in Biology, Master's in Community Development, and subsequently an Ed.S. in Leadership and Administration from Appalachian State University.

In 2018, Appalachian State University inducted John Bost into the *Rhododendron Society*, in honor of his significant impact as a teacher and a humanitarian. Like the rhododendron flower, Bost continues to bloom.

Bost lives with his wife and soulmate, LaDonna Setzer Bost, in Clemmons, North Carolina.

Contact John R. Bost
mastercounsel@gmail.com
www.JohntheCatalyst.com

About the Co-Author

"I've always wanted to know how the 'real world' works. John Bost to the rescue! He pulls back the curtains—exposing the inner-workings of all five sectors.

As a result, I've adopted new approaches to old problems—resulting in better outcomes.

John's gems are unconventional, authentic, and highly relevant."

—Patty Jo Sawvel

Patty Jo Sawvel

Award-winning writer, Patty Jo Sawvel, learned the art of storytelling on her father's knee. Bypassing the traditional route of college, Sawvel jumped into the newspaper business.

In her first year, the North Carolina Press Association awarded her work First Place for investigative reporting. Within two years, she'd collected a second award.

Next, Sawvel honed her skills as a journalist by writing cover stories on her favorite subjects—people and their awe-inspiring lives. It was then that Sawvel found her true fascination—writing and publishing biographies.

Her trademark—capturing the voice of her client, while connecting the reader to the story in a most personal way. Three of her authored/co-authored works have received global recognition*, including her own story, *Under the Influence: The Town That Listened to its Kids*.

Clients often ask me, "What's my book going to be like?"

I tell them, "I have no idea. My job is to collect all the mud and then let the book reveal itself."

This truth doesn't bring much comfort to clients—but it is the reality. Book writing is a trust—a trust between the author and co-author, a trust between the authors and the audience, and a trust in the process.

And then, it's a tremendous amount of work, and yet, one of the most satisfying occupations imaginable.

Do you have a story to tell? Sawvel's services include interviewing, framing, writing, co-writing, editing, layout, design, and publishing.

Recent Co-Authored Titles

- *Lynched by the Law**　　　with Anthony L. Parker
- *The Man from Peru*　　　with Fermin Bocanegra
- *Both Sides of the Bars*　　　with Anthony Bryant
- *Sharecropper's Wisdom**　with General J.R. Gorham
- *Bored to Death*　　　　　with Henry Flowers

*Global Ebooks Award

Contact Patty Jo Sawvel
pjsawvel@gmail.com
www.ClassicWritingPR.com
Phone: (336) 906-7238

Appendix

Chapter 2

In 2014, a record 200,000 people attended the Lexington Barbecue Festival. It has been named one of the "Top Ten Food Festivals in America," by *Travel & Leisure Magazine*. Sadly, my friend, Kay Saintsing passed away unexpectedly in 2002, but the Festival and the community pride lives on. The Lexington Barbecue Festival is always celebrated on one of the last two Saturdays in October. For more information visit www.barbecuefestival.com

Chapter 6

Robert Katz, Key essentials in selecting a team.
https://hbr.org/1974/09/skills-of-an-effectiveadministrator

Chapter 20

https://www.Moravian.org
https://www.greatsite.com/timeline-english-bible-history/john-hus.html

Chapter 21

Regarding my Enneagram: With an even balance, at times the nine personality shows out more so than the one, a personality type referred to as the negotiator. They are hardworking, creative, and friendly in their behavior. They are generally more idealistic and serious than other nines.

Reformers' greatest fear: Getting it so wrong or being so bad that they are completely unworthy of love and acceptance.

Lastly, the Enneagram details how to best work with Reformers. Parents, spouses, bosses, or peers of Reformers can model admitting and accepting their own mistakes, assuring the Reformers that they are loved even when they make mistakes, focusing on the positive and minimizing the negative, and encouraging the Reformers to regularly schedule wholesome pleasurable activities. When Reformers learn to accept themselves and others as they are they can experience peace of mind.

My attention is predictably focused on what is right, what is wrong, and how to fix it. And, I'm constantly getting out the yardstick to see if I'm measuring up. Therefore, my principle preoccupation is "getting it right." The good news is people with a "type one wing nine" personality tend to be judicial and rational in their behavior, but are generally more calm and balanced than other type ones.

As I tackle my self-improvement, I am equally interested in how to bring out the best in the other eight personality types. Without going into such detail with the remaining types—free information and testing is readily available on the Internet—what I found is that one type has the *need* to create conflict while another type has the *need* to avoid conflict at all costs. Additionally, one type feels the *need* to be self-serving, while another type has a *need* to be self-sacrificing.

You are not one single type; you are complex and multifaceted; you are interconnected. This is a vital paradigm shift. When you consider having access to all nine numbers simultaneously, you increase and expand your capacity for thriving. (*Jerome D. Lubbe, Whole-Identity: A Brain-Based Enneagram Model for (W)holistic Human Thriving (Thrive Neuro: 2019), 30-31. Artwork by Aimee Strickland; used with permission.*)

Considering what you know of the Enneagram so far, in what numbers do you experience ease, or in Lubbe's language, sense "efficiency"? Where do you feel less efficient?

See https://www.amazon.com/Brain-Based-Enneagram-Jerome-Lubbe/dp/173329452X/.

Ibid., 32. Dr. Lubbe's upcoming book, which will be available

https://enneagramexplained.com/enneagram-core-motivations/

DISC   https://www.crystalknows.com

As well, during this writing, I came upon one leadership tool that I had not yet discovered, The Five Voices Assessment: *My Foundational and Secondary Voices are **Connector & Creative;***

The latter (3-5) areas for growth
1. Connector *You are a champion of relationships and strategic partnerships!*
2. Creative *You are a champion of innovation!*
3. Pioneer *You are a champion of results and progress!*
4. Nurturer *You are a champion of people!*
5. Guardian *You are a champion of responsibility and stewardship!*
You might want to explore further: https://5voices.com/assessment/

All of this is easily accessed through self-reporting instruments. Once again the idea is that, the better we know ourselves, the easier we can work with other people.   All leading to healthier relationships.

Chapter 24

Our initiative proves to have long-lasting benefits in Winston-Salem. According to a 2016 story in the *Winston-Salem Journal*—Operators Use New Methods to Extend Landfill's Life—trash is now being *compacted* at the Hanes Mill Road Landfill.

Additionally, the original 110-acre site which was active when I lived on Murray Road, closed in 2005. That same year, the landfill opened a newly purchased 90-acre site adjoining the old. This site reaches Murray Road.

Chapter 36

1993 Architectural & Planning Report: Winston-Salem's African-American Resources, *Winston-Salem's African-American Neighborhoods: 1870-1950*.

Black Philanthropy Institute, Rethinking *Philanthropy: An Exploration of Black Communities,* 2018.

Chapter 45

https://faithandleadership.com/creators-new-musical-pursue-healing-and-reconciliation

https://www.wfdd.org/story/carolina-curious-why-are-winston-salemforsyth-county-schools-still-segregated

https://www.journalnow.com/news/local/forsyth-county-schools-resegregated-but-opinions-differ-on-whetherthat/article_9c6d9c7e-a68b-5347-904a-7c16f0bb2060.html

https://triad-city-beat.com/icyminikole-hannah-jones/

https://www.nytimes.com/2020/02/06/world/europe/finland-parental-leave-equality.html

https://qz.com/1755299/how-finlands-family-cafes-teach-lonely-new-parents-to-raise-kids/

https://www.theguardian.com/lifeandstyle/2017/dec/04/finland-only-country-world-dad-more-time-kids-moms

https://www.cnbc.com/2020/02/21/why-finland-is-the-best-place-to-give-birth-childbirth-costs-compared.html

Courtesy of Walker Armstrong   www.walker@pmba.org

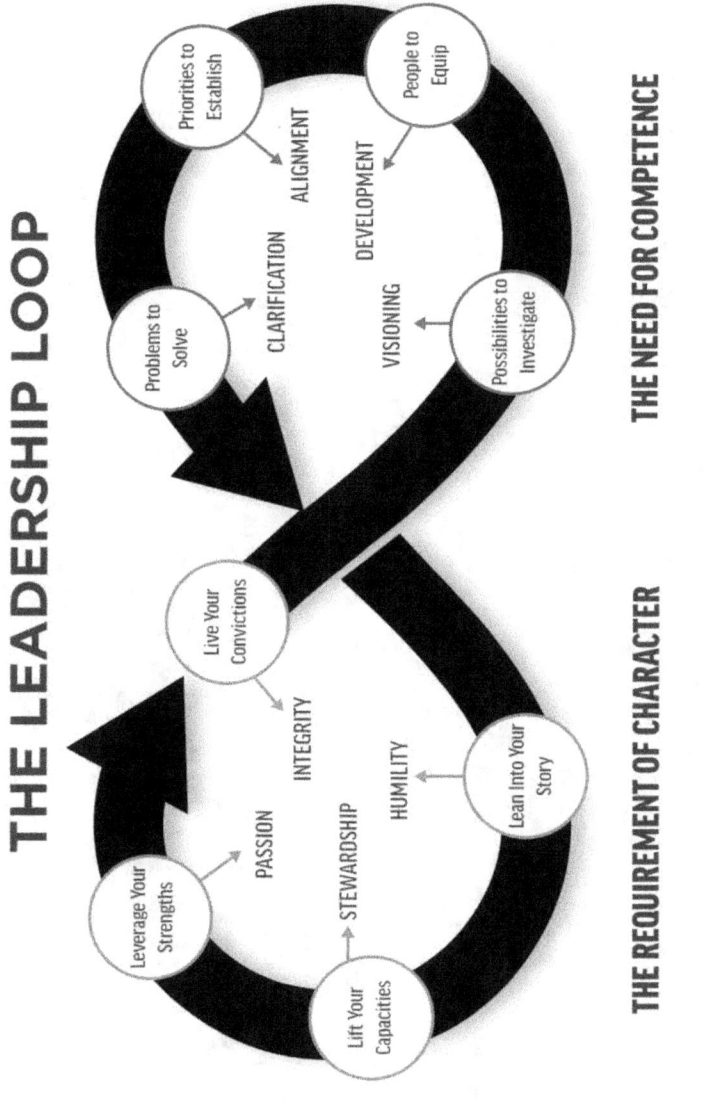

Graphic by www.tandemcreative.net

Notes

www.ingramcontent.com/pod-product-compliance
Lightning Source LLC
Chambersburg PA
CBHW052342220526
45465CB00003BA/923